'An essential text for every educational psy
must-read for all those working with the 16–
A highly recommended bc

Dr Juliet Whitehead, Chair of the Division ⌐. ....⌐..⌐..⌐ a.⌐
Child Psychology, British Psychological Society

'The editors describe this volume as an "introductory foray". In my view,
it goes much further. The editors and contributors should be congratulated
for combining research and theory with practical strategies and case
studies, while always keeping young people at the heart of the matter.'

Liz Robinson, Principal Educational Psychologist,
Portsmouth City Council

'Applied psychology with young adults has long been a comparatively
neglected field. This book provides a valuable resource for anyone wishing
to gain greater understanding of the contributions that educational
psychologists can make to work in this area.'

Julian Elliott, Professor of Educational Psychology, Durham University

Applied Educational Psychology with 16–25 Year Olds

Applied Educational Psychology with 16–25 Year Olds

New frameworks and perspectives for working with young people

Edited by Brian Apter, Christopher Arnold and Julia Hardy

UCL
IOE Press

First published in 2018 by the UCL Institute of Education Press, University College London, 20 Bedford Way, London WC1H 0AL

www.ucl-ioe-press.com

British Library Cataloguing in Publication Data:
A catalogue record for this publication is available from the British Library

ISBNs
978-1-78277-270-5 (paperback)
978-1-78277-271-2 (PDF eBook)
978-1-78277-272-9 (ePub eBook)
978-1-78277-273-6 (Kindle eBook)

Typeset by Quadrant Infotech (India) Pvt Ltd
Printed and bound by CPI Group (UK) Ltd, Croydon, CR0 4YY
Cover image © Katarzyna Bialasiewicz/Alamy Stock Photo

Contents

About the contributors

Dr Brian Apter was the chair of the Division of Educational and Child Psychology in 2017, and is its current vice-chair. Brian sits on the editorial board of the journal of the Association of Educational Psychologists (AEP), *Educational Psychology in Practice*, and has published a wide range of articles in different publications. He works as a clinical supervisor for both educational psychologists and counselling psychologists in Wolverhampton and is an associate lecturer/researcher conducting post-doctoral social-psychology research at the University of Wolverhampton.

Dr Christopher Arnold worked in local authority services for nearly 30 years before establishing Psychologicalservices.gb ltd. His publications range from reducing drop-out rates in Europe to numeracy assessment and working with teaching assistants.

Dr Cathy Atkinson is Curriculum Director of the University of Manchester's Doctorate in Educational and Child Psychology programme and also works at an alternative provision in Liverpool as the school's educational psychologist. Her research interests include motivational interviewing, the role of the educational psychologist in supporting mental health, children's right to play, and working with young people aged 16–25.

Dr Louise Bason is a senior practitioner educational psychologist with Liverpool's Child and Educational Psychology Service. Louise has carried out research in transition planning to post-16 opportunities for young people with special educational needs and contributed to local authority working groups. She has recently set up PsyCATS, private psychological consultation, assessment and training services.

Dr Caroline Bond works as practice placement director for the Doctorate in Educational Psychology programme at the University of Manchester and as a partner educational psychologist at Catalyst Psychology,

Manchester. Her research interests include developmental differences, professional supervision, safeguarding and programme implementation.

Dr Tim Cockerill works as a senior educational psychologist for Babcock Learning and Development Partnership with Devon County Council. He has particular interests in the 16–25 age group and in supporting the progress and well-being of children in care.

Baruti Damali is an independent educational psychologist and has worked for a number of educational psychology services in London and across the United Kingdom. Baruti's interests include race, culture and spirituality in educational assessment and digital solutions to issues in educational psychology.

Enomwoyi Damali has worked as an educational psychologist for 28 years in two local authorities and also as a child mental health specialist in a multi-agency Tier 2 child and adolescent mental health services (CAMHS) team. She is currently employed as a senior educational psychologist in Lewisham, south London. Her particular interests are in mindfulness and narrative approaches.

Dr Brian Davis has extensive experience as a principal educational psychologist and in senior leadership roles in local authorities. He is the director for the Essex University-accredited Educational Psychology training courses at the Tavistock and Portman Clinic, London, and is the founding director of PEACHES Psychology Ltd. Particular interests include promoting the impact of psychology in systems and communities, emotional well-being and mental health.

Dr Rai Fayette works as an educational psychologist at One Education in Manchester. His areas of interest include autism in education, selective mutism, acquired brain injury and mediated learning experiences.

Dr Julia Hardy works as an associate educational psychologist for Oxfordshire Educational Psychology Service and for other organizations, through Psychologicalservices.gb ltd, with interests in consultation, qualitative research, deafness, cognitive behavioural therapy (CBT) and leadership skills.

Dr Charmian Hobbs worked as an educational psychologist in local authorities and at Newcastle University for nearly 30 years and is committed to developing narrative therapy as a trainer and practitioner.

Dr Rebekah Hyde works as an educational psychologist with Cornwall's Educational Psychology Service. She has a particular interest in working with the 16–25 age range and in furthering the potential of children in care.

Dr Michael Hymans works in private practice as an expert witness in the family and criminal courts, as well as in special educational needs and disability tribunals. He is an associate of a number of legal organizations and is also commissioned by parents and schools.

Dr Gay Keegan has worked for local authority educational psychology services for more than 30 years and is currently senior educational psychologist in Hampshire and Isle of Wight Educational Psychology. Her current interests and experience include developing the role of educational psychology in the 16–25 age range, and promoting successful and meaningful equality and inclusion through person-centred approaches.

Dr Catherine Kelly works as Assistant Director for Service User and Social Diversity for the Doctorate in Educational and Child Psychology programme at the University of Manchester and as a senior educational psychologist at Bury Educational Psychology Service, Greater Manchester. Her research interests include resilience, belonging, working within cultural and linguistic diversity, video interaction guidance and programme implementation.

Dr Jayne Manning works as an educational psychologist for Doncaster Educational Psychology Service. Prior to completing doctoral training at Sheffield University she worked in pastoral roles in secondary schools and a further education college. Further interests include consultation and supporting whole-school development.

Dr Dorota Martin is an educational and child psychologist working for Kirklees Educational Psychology Service, West Yorkshire. Previously Dorota was a doctoral student at the University of Manchester. Her research interests include child and adolescent mental health, therapeutic interventions, mindfulness and person-centred approaches.

Dr Rebecca Murphy is senior educational psychologist for Hampshire County Council, working in the south team of Hampshire and Isle of Wight Educational Psychology, with special responsibility for the Isle of Wight. She is also a field tutor for the Educational Psychology doctorate course at Southampton University. Her interests are post-16 work, autism and language and literacy difficulties.

Dr Jane Park works as an educational psychologist for Telford and Wrekin Educational Psychology Service. Since joining the service in 2016 Jane has furthered her interest in working with the 16–25 age range, alongside consultation-based systemic work and establishing the Emotional Literacy Support Assistant initiative locally.

Dr Gabrielle Pelter works as an educational psychologist in a project-based multi-agency team, supporting vulnerable young people and their families. Her areas of interest include promoting social, emotional and mental health, therapeutic approaches, children's experiences of hospital and hospital education, consultation and anti-oppressive practice.

Dr Sarah Relton works as an educational psychologist for Wandsworth Schools and Community Psychology Service. Areas of interest include metacognition and reading comprehension, therapeutic approaches and family systems.

Dr Amy Selfe has worked in local authority services and as a highly specialist psychologist in the NHS. Her areas of interest include paediatric neuropsychology, neurodisability, supporting young people aged 16–25, CBT and therapeutic approaches.

Dr Garry Squires is an experienced educational psychologist, previously working in Staffordshire. He is now a senior lecturer in special educational needs and educational psychology at the University of Manchester and continues to work in private practice with adults in a variety of settings. He has a wide range of publications and engages in research and academic consultation. See www.manchester.ac.uk/research/garry.squires.

Introduction: The context of new legislation

Brian Apter, Christopher Arnold and Julia Hardy

The special educational needs and disabilities (SEND) reforms nominally heralded in England with the Children and Families Act 2014 were regarded by educational psychologists as a necessary development but also a curate's egg with 'excellent parts'.[1] A significant element of the Act was to extend SEND legislation in England as it applied to children and young people (CYP), from 0 years up to 25 years.[2] This meant that local authorities, the National Health Service (NHS) and subsidiary professional agencies that had statutory responsibility and involvement with CYP with special educational needs under previous legislation up to a young person's 19th birthday were compelled to extend their local offer and their graduated statutory response to the SEND of CYP up to 25 years, when adult services are required to take over.

The context from the time of implementation of the legislation in 2014 became much more pressurized over the next few years. Educational psychologists working within statutory timescales and an overarching SEND reform deadline of March 2018 became concerned with rapidly expanding workloads. They have struggled to meet the requirement to convert a backlog of existing but redundant Statements of Special Educational Needs into Education, Health and Care Plans (EHCPs) while simultaneously working with newly emergent casework and new projects bought in by schools. It also began to become apparent that local authority educational psychology services for a range of reasons were carrying more unfilled educational psychology posts than had previously been experienced.[3]

The arguments for and against the safety net of a protected statutory role for educational psychologists and attendant statutory responsibilities within the revised *Special Educational Needs and Disability Code of Practice* are now being debated again within the profession, just as they were debated previously, in the wake of Warnock and the 1981 Education Act when the assessments of educational psychologists were written into the legislation as a legally required 'gate-keeping' task for the first time. For a fuller account of this see *British Educational Psychology: The first*

100 years produced by the Division of Educational and Child Psychology (DECP) in 2013.

By 2014 an increasing number of local authority educational psychology services were already necessarily branching out into 'trading' (direct selling) their wares to schools and sometimes to parents and health agencies in order to partially offset their staffing and running costs. Governmentally imposed 'austerity' (so-called) strictures scythed-off significant proportions of local authority budgets ensuring that there was less to be shared out between competing budgetary divisions such as social care and education; children's services and adult services; family work, youth work, youth offending and early years provision; housing, refuse collection, sewage and highway maintenance.

The requirement for educational psychologists to respond simultaneously to the 'mental health' agenda as it took shape in schools, in the community and in the minds of policymakers at that time by offering therapeutic services to schools and families was also burgeoning and tempting in equal measure. Like everybody else, health trusts had been subjected to 'austerity'-driven budgetary reductions. Child and adolescent mental health services (CAMHS) had found their staffing budgets significantly reduced. This worked indirectly to increase pressure on local authority social care and education services and particularly upon educational psychologists to service the mental health agenda[4] – it was a 'perfect storm',[5] as they say, of competing demands. At the same time that the hot breath and teeth of this perfect storm were being felt on the back of their necks by educational psychologists, they were presented with an additional new client group of young adults requiring new age-related solutions.

While professional responsibilities were significantly stretched by the new requirement to include young adults up to the age of 25 years, there was also much optimism: we educational psychologists are extremely good at focusing upon, developing and enacting solutions.

This book is an initial introductory foray – the beginning of a 'work in progress' – by applied psychologists for applied psychologists. The book aims to provide educational psychologists with advice, practical ideas and technical support to aid and assist them as they newly extend their professional arms to embrace the needs of young adults, 16–25 years old.

While the statutory context might rapidly evolve and change, applied psychology and its overarching theoretical models is slower to respond. Established applied psychology does not change significantly in the way its principles, practices and ethical constraints are applied as the client group grows older, but the changing legislation and issues of child development require new professional perspectives, reflections, sensitivities and accommodations. This book, chapter by chapter, attempts to illuminate some of these in valuable and practical ways.

Part 1 of the book concerns settings, opportunities and ethical issues. Gay Keegan and Rebecca Murphy in Chapter 1 provide an optimistic vision of new horizons for the work of educational psychologists in colleges of further education and 'sixth forms'.

In Chapter 2 Louise Bason looks at how Education, Health and Care Plans can be adapted and utilized to empower students in training placements, apprenticeships and further and higher education settings; and in Chapter 3 Garry Squires looks at ways in which educational psychologists can work with students with SEND to support them and enable them to overcome obstacles to their admission to university. In Chapter 4 the issue of informed consent is explored by Brian Davis and in Chapter 5 Brian describes 'mental capacity assessments' and how educational psychologists can contribute.

In Chapter 6 Cathy Atkinson and Dorota Martin explore the use of psychological therapy with young adults, and a range of issues including ethical considerations, informed involvement in therapy and factors that an educational psychologist should consider when evaluating efficacy.

Part 2 of the book concerns casework and psychological interventions. In Chapter 7 Jayne Manning uses interpretative phenomenological analysis to focus down onto the lived detail of transitions between school and further education in case studies; and how the agency, self-determination and enablement of autonomy of students can be enhanced by educational psychologists at individual and systemic levels.

Jane Park in Chapter 8 uses a psychoanalytically derived Grid Elaboration Method (GEM) to explore the lived-experience phenomena of young adults diagnosed with an autism spectrum disorder (ASD). Rai Fayette and Caroline Bond in Chapter 9 take as their subject group young adults with an ASD diagnosis, and examine their experience of their transition to adulthood using a single case-study design.

Michael Hymans in Chapter 10 describes the use of George Kelly's personal construct psychology in two case studies: of a young woman, A and a young man, M. Michael shows how a range of Kelly's techniques can be used with young adults in an effective and supportive way; and Charmian Hobbs in Chapter 11 provides a guide to adapting narrative therapy to the needs of young adults.

Part 3 of the book concerns systemic responses to the extended young adult client group.

In Chapter 12 Tim Cockerill and Christopher Arnold look at the identification of risks and vulnerabilities associated with young people becoming 'NEET' (not in employment, education or training).

In Chapter 13 Cathy Atkinson, Rebekah Hyde and Catherine Kelly develop a new structure – the SDT (self-determination theory) interdependence model – that an educational psychologist is able to follow in order to support young adult care leavers in their journey to independence and autonomy. Enomwoyi Damali and Baruti Damali in Chapter 14 describe a potential systemic adaptation of an educational psychology service's local offer designed to improve outcomes for young adults.

In Chapter 15 Amy Selfe, Gabrielle Pelter and Sarah Relton consider how an educational psychologist can work with and harness the resources of a multi-agency partnership when working with young adults. They look at possible obstacles and inherent pitfalls in multi-agency collaborations, whereby 'multi-agency confusion' can be the unintended result.

We very much hope you enjoy this book and find it of practical use in applying your psychology in this new and exciting extended 0 to 25 years context. Every word of the content has been written by applied psychologists like yourself who are currently working with young adults in this field. We hope this provides a guarantee that this book is very much of its time and a valuable resource for you. Please note that all names of subjects have been changed to ensure confidentiality.

Notes

[1] Cartoon in *Punch* by George du Maurier, 1895, entitled: 'True humility', and captioned: Bishop: 'I'm afraid you've got a bad egg, Mr Jones'; Curate: 'Oh, no, my Lord, I assure you that parts of it are excellent!'
[2] Reforms in Wales and Northern Ireland have led to a similar statutory extension from 0 to 25 years. Scottish legislation continues to apply up to the age of 18 years, at the time of writing.
[3] Association of Educational Psychologists: www.tes.com/news/lack-educational-psychologists-will-delay-send-reforms-new-survey-suggests
[4] British Association for Child and Adolescent Public Health: www.bacaph.org.uk/blog/48-blog-item1-8
[5] *The Perfect Storm* (fictitious disaster movie, 2000; a fishing boat sinks when it takes a short cut back to harbour through a storm and there are no survivors).

Part One

Settings, opportunities and
ethical issues

1

New horizons: Extending educational psychology involvement into further education colleges and 'sixth forms'

Gay Keegan and Rebecca Murphy

Introduction

Since 2015, following the enactment of the Children and Families Act in 2014 and the revision of the *Special Educational Needs and Disability Code of Practice* (Department of Education (DfE) and Department of Health (DoH), 2015) to include young people up to the age of 25 years, educational psychology services in England and Wales have at last been given the official opportunity to become involved more comprehensively with the post-16 population. This extension of the role of the educational psychologist (EP) has been called 'one of the most significant developments the profession has ever experienced' (Atkinson *et al.*, 2015). The potential benefits of EPs working with young adults and their educational providers had been noted as early as 1956 in a survey of school psychological services in ten European countries reported in the Wall Report (quoted in MacKay, 2009); however, opportunities have been limited and often dependent on the local specialist interests of educational psychologists themselves and the local authority's priorities. In recent years in the United Kingdom, it is mainly educational psychology services in Scotland that have been proactive in moving the post-16 agenda forward. MacKay (2006) evaluated post-school psychological services across 12 education authorities in Scotland, and his work demonstrated the impact being made. Hayton (2009: 65), after reviewing MacKay's research, proposed that 'by helping to develop a positive sense of identity, to promote a positive career orientation and to raise aspirations, educational psychologists can assist in addressing the particular issues faced by young people'.

The current legislative change is now requiring all educational psychology services in England and Wales to recognize the need for involvement with this population, at the very least in terms of giving statutory psychological advice to the local authority. This chapter goes beyond this limited role and describes how a steering group of EPs in Hampshire and Isle of Wight Educational Psychology was set up to develop working practices, in both traded and statutory work, to meet the psychological and learning needs of post-16 young people. It will describe the rationale, process and journey undertaken by the steering group, including research into college staff's views, the production of a traded offer and the identification of future opportunities for service development.

Although historically EPs in Hampshire had worked with this age group, this had primarily been in out-of-county placements and in special schools with post-16 provision, at the specific request of the local authority. The introduction of the new legislation in 2015 and a renewed desire to support students of this age group led to the creation of a steering group of EPs in our service to move this work forward. We were excited by the opportunities offered by working with an older age group and wanted to ensure we had the appropriate knowledge and skills to begin to apply and develop our experience with these young people in their educational and community settings. We recognized the need to explore what existing knowledge we had that might need extending to cover this age group and what new knowledge and process skills we required (Atkinson *et al.*, 2015).

Finding out what colleges need

One of the service needs the group identified from the start was to understand and explore the experiences and views of staff working in further education (FE) colleges, to inform the development of our practice and our service delivery to this phase of education. We wanted to explore what FE colleges were thinking about meeting the needs of their students with special educational needs and disabilities (SEND) as they implemented the changes included in the new legislation and began their journey along a potentially rocky road. The revised *Special Educational Needs and Disability Code of Practice* (DfE and DoH, 2015: 25) states that: 'Early years providers, schools and colleges should know precisely where children and young people with SEN are in their learning and development.' They should:

- ensure that decisions are informed by the insights of the children and young people, and their parents
- have high ambitions and set stretching targets for them

- track their progress towards these goals
- review the provision that is made for them, that is 'additional to or different from' that provided for all students
- promote positive outcomes in the areas of personal and social development
- ensure that the approaches used are based on the best possible evidence and are having the required impact on progress.

The 16–25 steering group was particularly interested in gaining FE college staff's views and experiences in meeting the needs of young people (post-16 years) with SEND, with a view to producing a potential traded offer proposal, as well as developing appropriate EP assessment and consultation capacity across the service for statutory work. At that time each community EP team had an attached assistant psychologist and, as part of the process, assistant psychologists were asked to conduct interviews to this end with college staff.

To prepare for this, the steering group asked the assistant psychologists to pull out relevant information from the revised *Special Educational Needs and Disability Code of Practice* (DfE and DoH, 2015) and the Ofsted regulations (as they existed following an update in August 2014) and create a summary document, which was subsequently used to help formulate the interview questions. This document was also sent to the colleges prior to their visit in the hope of focusing staff thinking and helping them to feel more prepared. We wanted to stress that it was a new journey for all of us and the summary document would help us to structure the conversation.

The steering group devised an introductory script for the assistant psychologists to explain to the college why they were there, emphasizing that they were only gathering information at this stage. A recording pro-forma was also created, to ensure that the assistant psychologists summarized key pieces of information needed by the working group and to encourage a consistent approach to the questioning and write-up across the county.

Two assistant psychologists, accompanied by an EP, ran a pilot interview in one of the colleges that allowed the questions to be refined, to encourage more open sharing and less defensive responses. Then, over the course of a month, the assistant psychologists carried out the interviews in pairs at various other colleges around Hampshire, using the semi-structured questionnaire (see Appendix to this chapter), gathering information relating to the opportunities and challenges posed by the changes to the SEND legislation for FE college staff.

Carrying out the thematic analysis

The response rate was favourable with 9 out of 16 FE colleges agreeing to participate in the interviews. Many of the colleges appeared extremely enthusiastic about the prospect of working with an EP service. All of the responses were summarized by the assistant psychologists and a sub-group of three educational psychologists then undertook a thematic analysis on the responses received, using the approach outlined by Braun and Clarke (2006).

All the responses gave valuable insight into the current experiences of FE staff in meeting needs and implementing the changes brought about by the revised *Special Educational Needs and Disability Code of Practice* (DfE and DoH, 2015) and also highlighted the challenges and opportunities faced by FE staff. See Figure 1.1 for a summary overview of the thematic analysis.

THEMATIC ANALYSIS RESULTS
What are the experiences and views of staff from FE colleges
in meeting the needs of young people with SEND?

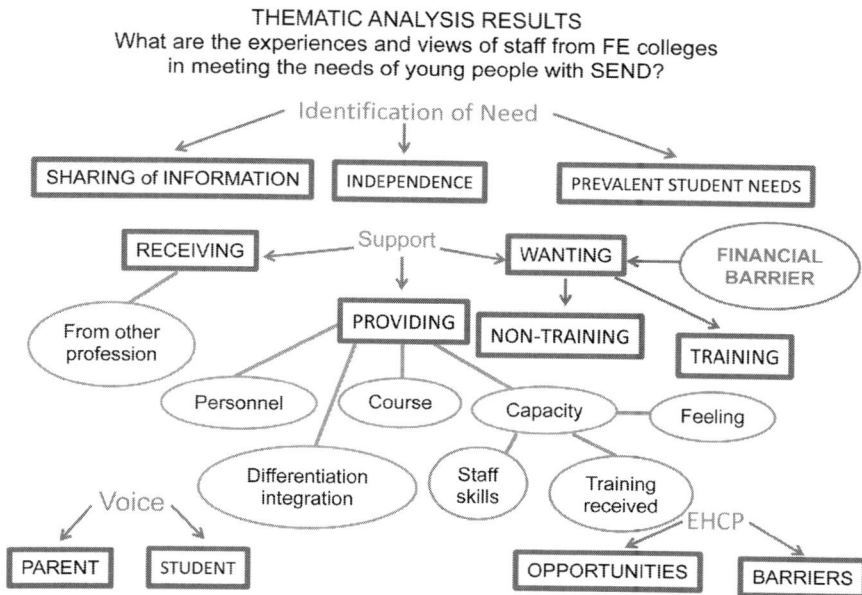

Figure 1.1: Summary overview of the thematic analysis

There were four overarching themes: 'Identification of Need', 'Support', 'Voice' and 'Education, Health and Care Plan' (EHCP).

In the first theme, 'Identification of Need', FE staff described the ways in which they currently identified special educational needs, the needs they felt were the most prevalent at the current time and the importance of independence. These sub-themes can be seen in Figure 1.2.

Identification of need

SHARING of INFORMATION

INDEPENDENCE

PREVALENT STUDENT NEEDS

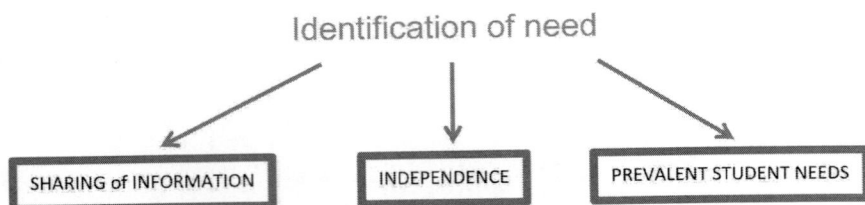

Figure 1.2: Theme: Identification of Need

The sharing of information between schools and colleges was seen as the primary method for identifying students' needs and the sharing of accurate information relating to individual students was considered as essential by most respondents. Some college staff felt that they had a good relationship with schools and that quality information was passed on to support the college in meeting the young person's needs. In particular they spoke of the value in attending Year 9 annual reviews. Other respondents were more critical of the information they received from schools, citing it as 'sparse' or even not forthcoming at all. All college staff spoke about the importance of fostering independence in young adults. However, the data showed that this was achieved primarily through allocating to students the responsibility of seeking support if they needed it. When asked how independence skills were taught, one respondent commented, 'When an LSA [learning support assistant] is off sick, we see how the student copes.' The final sub-theme of this overarching subject of 'Identification of Need' concerned the needs that FE staff viewed as currently prevalent. The most frequently reported of these were mental health needs including anxiety (especially exam anxiety), depression and self-harm. Other prevalent needs reported included literacy difficulties, social communication difficulties and behaviour (with some respondents commenting on the difficulty that students face in adapting to the freedom of college).

Figure 1.3 shows the second overarching theme that reflected the support college staff reported that they already received, the support college staff already provided and the support college staff felt they were likely to need in the future.

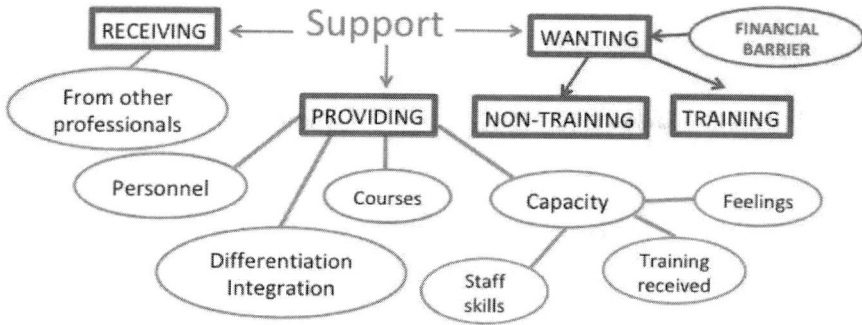

Figure 1.3: Theme: Support

Respondents commented on the external support they were already receiving prior to the changes to SEND legislation. This support came from a wide range of external services including child and adolescent mental health services (CAMHS), charities (e.g. Barnardo's), specialist teacher advisers, police, occupational therapists and physiotherapists. There was a frequent reference in the responses to these services being financially free to the colleges.

In the responses FE colleges described the support they provided for their students with SEND. The importance of the role of the personal tutor was frequently emphasized and referred to as the main source of support. 'Counsellors' and 'LSAs' were also presented by most respondents in a positive manner as providing significant support. 'Capacity' was included as a theme within the sub-theme of 'Support' as it was mentioned frequently by respondents. Some referred to excellent staff knowledge but 'pockets of poor practice' were also reported. A wide range of training was identified as having been received by staff although this was mainly specialist training relating to a specific need of an individual student, for example training on the autistic spectrum continuum, rather than general systemic training. The overall feeling about meeting the needs of young people with SEND was one of 'we do our best' but 'we are only equipped to meet certain needs'. Only two of the colleges mentioned offering specific courses to students with SEND (although a review of prospectuses showed that all the colleges offered these courses). Specific skills courses that were reported included social skills training, functional literacy and numeracy skills, and general life skills. Differentiation was viewed by all respondents as very important in meeting the needs of students with SEND but the capacity to be able to do so appeared to be mixed from the responses given. Central to the methods of differentiation reported was the use of equipment such as laptops and also specific examination access arrangements.

The support that respondents reported as 'wanting' included training: particularly on mental health needs, social communication difficulties, difficulties in managing sexualized behaviour and gaining the views of non-verbal students. The analysis also showed an interest in joining up with other colleges to share experiences and the possibility of an educational psychology telephone helpline. The main barrier cited to accessing support was financial.

The third overarching theme from the analysis was 'Voice' as seen in Figure 1.4.

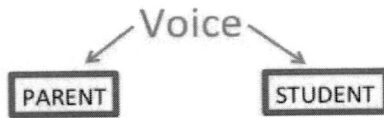

Figure 1.4: Theme: Voice

Gaining the views of the parents to determine support for students with SEND at FE colleges was not reported as commonplace, but, some college staff commented on inviting parents to annual reviews. Gaining the voice of the student was viewed as much more important and was referred to by all respondents. Many mentioned 'person-centred planning' although few offered concrete examples of what this actually involved. Student surveys (using information technology) were mentioned frequently as were the liaisons between students and personal tutors. The responses showed an overall reliance on students being willing and able to give their own views about the support they receive.

The final overarching theme prevalent throughout the interview data was the EHCP. It was clear from the responses that college staff were in a process of 'getting to grips' with the introduction of the EHCP. The respondents emphasized the difficulties in working with different local education authorities and the inconsistencies in processes and paperwork that this brought about. They also highlighted feeling under pressure due to short deadlines, the overwhelming amount of paperwork involved, and also the legal obligations involved. On a positive note, the FE college staff reported that the EHCP was effective in highlighting emotional needs, and also provided an opportunity for increased funding to buy in external specialists.

Overall, the thematic analysis provided valuable information relating to the experiences and views of FE college staff as they implemented the changes to the *Special Educational Needs and Disability Code of Practice* (DfE and DoH, 2015), showing some positive indicators that FE staff had a good understanding of the changes and their responsibilities in meeting the needs of students with SEND. The changes were creating some challenges for FE staff, particularly in the completion of the EHCP documentation and in gaining the views of young people, but were also providing opportunities for shared working between educational psychologists and FE colleges.

The implications of the findings of this thematic analysis for educational psychology services were significant. There appeared to be a financial barrier to be overcome to provide traded services to this sector; however, there was also a clear pathway for providing training and systemic work to meet the needs of college students with SEND. For example, support could be provided to FE staff to understand the increasing issue of mental health difficulties experienced by young people. In addition, as EPs, we felt ourselves to be in a good position to support and guide colleges on person-centred planning. It was felt that FE colleges were at the start of their SEND Code of Practice journey but that the rich experiences gained by EPs already in supporting secondary schools make a similar journey and could only make the pathway less bumpy.

Devising the traded offer

Having carried out the thematic analysis and received the feedback in our 16–25 steering group (and shared it with the whole service by way of an update), we began to develop our traded offer. We decided that our costings would be in line with our current charges to schools, and we would aim to cover actual costs, in terms of EP time, to both develop and deliver the work.

We wanted to start small by offering things we could already do, which would take minimal adaptation to fit into the college setting and meet the needs of post-16 students. This would help us to keep the costs down and give us a secure base as a starting point, as we gradually built our experience of working in colleges and with this age group. We already had some training initiatives that college staff might join (e.g. Emotional Literacy Support Assistant training and supervision; Framework for Enhanced Individual Pastoral Support (FEIPS); we had some training that could easily be rewritten for an older age group; and we had a couple of things newly developed, such as our 'Planning for the future: Writing and reviewing achievable outcomes' training (based on guidance from Preparing for Adulthood, 2015). We anticipate that, as we become more familiar with the settings and the psychological needs of both staff and students, we can develop further new initiatives over time as required.

We decided to promote a contact EP model, and that person would devise a bespoke package through conversation and discussion with their college contacts. The college would buy in an amount of educational psychology time, then decide with their contact how they would use this time.

When we had drafted our traded offer document, we showed it to a few of the colleges we had interviewed, and received unanimous, positive feedback: 'sounds like it would meet all the issues we are faced with regularly and would get a good uptake'; 'it looks really good ... definitely things that are really relevant to us and our students'.

Delivery so far

The Service Level Agreement (SLA) offer from Hampshire and Isle of Wight Educational Psychology (HIEP) was launched in January 2017, initially through direct emailings to colleges. In February 2017 the authors visited the Wessex colleges' network Learning Difficulties and Disabilities (LDD) group meeting to talk about what our psychologists were able to offer and to answer direct questions. This meeting proved to be a catalyst for action, and requests to take out agreements with us started to arrive. Seven colleges to date have purchased some time for our involvement. The rationales for these agreements have been variable and have included a range of requests for work at the various levels of student support, staff support and professional development opportunities.

Student support

At the current time, colleges have been keen to request support from HIEP to work in partnership with college staff to support students with additional needs. With regard to individual student support we have so far been primarily involved with student-centred problem-solving consultations recommended for individual educational plans by the *Special Educational Needs and Disability Code of Practice* (DfE and DoH, 2015). Some of the problem-solving consultations have utilized the 'Circle of Adults' framework (Wilson and Newton, 2006) with groups of college staff who have an interest in facilitating change for a young person. There has also been an interest in post-statutory support for individual students to facilitate the implementation of their EHCP, which have also taken the form of person-centred consultations, usually with the young person there to present their thoughts and opinions. We have found that being an advocate for the voice of the student has been particularly well valued, and also provides us with the satisfaction that we have helped to explore the situation and possible solutions through the eyes and voice of the student. The presented problems have thus far included a wide range of issues such as anxiety and selective mutism acting as a barrier to accessing the most appropriate (and most desired by the student) college courses and working with students who have experienced trauma and loss. EPs are noted to be well equipped to explore an individual's or group's understanding of their own social, emotional and mental health needs, through their consultation skills (involving 'curiously questioning'), and use of positive, person-centred psychological techniques, etc. (Devereux, 2017).

Staff support

In addition to the individual student support, college managers have also requested work with college staff over a period of time to help them develop role-specific knowledge, skills, confidence and resilience and to enhance their personal growth. This has taken the format of group supervision sessions and work discussion groups. The group supervision sessions have taken place half-termly over a period of two hours at college. They have included a 'check-in' to explore the emotional impact of the attendees' work with students with additional needs, leading to identification of a 'problem' to collaboratively discuss and for which to explore possible solutions. The frameworks used for developing a shared consideration of the context of a piece of work and exploring positive possibilities and new understandings have been 'solution circles' (O'Brien *et al.*, 1996). Problems discussed so far have included managing challenging behaviour, differentiation of teaching approaches and work–life balance (stress management). Following a series of these group supervision sessions, one college has now additionally requested some individual coaching for five members of staff from the contact EP, based on the approaches of Rogers (2016).

The work discussion groups that have taken place have been based on a model practised by practitioners at the Tavistock Clinic over the past 50 years (Jackson, 2008). These have been regular meetings outside the pressures of the study setting, to which homogeneous groups of college staff (e.g. support staff; managers; personal tutors) have brought concerns, issues and difficulties relating to a range of issues including their work with individual students or study groups. The group thinks about the situation together and, as an outcome, group members feel less self-critical and anxious, are open to seeing and thinking differently and feel supported in their work.

Other systemic support has included consideration of issues such as working with a college leadership team to develop their provision for students with social, emotional and mental health needs, using the Making an Action Plan (MAP) process (O'Brien *et al.*, 2010), facilitated and drawn up by two EPs.

Professional development opportunities

Following the launch of the traded offer with HIEP, there has been some interest from colleges in commissioning training designed to lead to better outcomes for young people through developing the skills of college staff. An example of a training course that has been delivered is 'Motivating Reluctant Learners', identified as a need by college staff who were increasingly challenged by demotivated students retaking maths and English GCSEs. The training aims to promote the attainment and well-being of demotivated students by giving them more constructive ways of viewing the world. Evaluations of the training delivered showed that staff felt that the training had developed their understanding, knowledge and skills, and increased their use of strategies to change their students' beliefs and expectations, thereby increasing the students' motivation to engage in learning. Another training being commissioned is that of 'Mediating Learning' for learning support assistants. In addition, we have extended our Emotional Literacy Support Assistants training and supervision programme into several college settings.

Where next?

After more than three years of operation, the 16–25 steering group decided to take a step back and examine what had been achieved so far, and what yet needs to be done. At the start of 2018 we held a MAP session for ourselves (O'Brien *et al.*, 2010). This is a person-centred approach that involves a 'group process for clarifying gifts, identifying meaningful contributions, specifying the necessary conditions for contribution and making agreements that will develop opportunities for contribution' (O'Brien *et al.*, 2010: 16).

The MAP highlighted several areas where the group wished to further develop the contribution of our EPs when working with this population. First, we agreed that we needed to establish closer working relationships with adult services to enhance our knowledge of the provision available, and also to support their work with young adults with whom we may have been involved. In addition, we intend to empower all EPs within our service to feel confident to work with this population. We have decided that we will investigate the current views of EPs in the service in this regard, asking them which areas of FE work they already feel confident with and where they feel they need more experience or training. We also wish to keep the rest of the service up to date on our developments in this fast-growing area by producing a regular newsletter to which all EPs in the service can contribute.

The 16–25 steering group has currently co-ordinated the production of a pilot video for young people that has been created and edited by a 16 year old (son of one of the EPs). The intention of the video is to explain to young people what an EP is and what one may do if they are asked to become involved with a young person. The video prototype has been completed and is currently being piloted with the aid of a semi-structured questionnaire designed for completion by the young people who view it. We intend for the video to be accompanied by a leaflet explaining the role of the EP and therefore enhancing and more confidently gaining truly 'informed' consent from the young people for our involvement.

A further consideration of the group for the future is our wish to emphasize person-centred work with young adults in colleges and sixth forms. Along with a desire to be involved in further research within this area, the possibility of using young people for action research projects is being discussed.

Finally, there is a drive within the group to measure the impact of our work with young adults at all its various levels, and consideration and development of how this is to be achieved will be a significant part of our work for the future.

We will be revisiting the Wessex colleges' network LDD group meeting to give an update on what we have achieved with the colleges we have worked with over the last year and to continue to raise our profile and explore and build on the range of possibilities for our continuing work together, for the benefit of the young people and their families in Hampshire and Isle of Wight.

Acknowledgements

The authors would like to acknowledge the contribution of the other members of the 16–25 steering group in this work. They are Laura Giles, Lisa McSpadden, Caoimhe Weekes and Alex Wood. In addition, we would like to thank the assistant and trainee educational psychologists who have contributed.

References

Atkinson, C., Dunsmuir, S., Lang, J. and Wright, S. (2015) 'Developing a competency framework for the initial training of educational psychologists working with young people aged 16–25'. *Educational Psychology in Practice*, 31 (2), 159–73.

Braun, V. and Clarke, V. (2006) 'Using thematic analysis in psychology'. *Qualitative Research in Psychology*, 3 (2), 77–101.

Devereux, S. (2017) 'How Do Staff in a Post-16 College Co-Construct Social, Emotional and Mental Health (SEMH) Needs in Their Setting? A discourse analysis'. Unpublished doctoral thesis, Tavistock and Portman NHS Foundation Trust and University of Essex.

DfE (Department for Education) and DoH (Department of Health) (2015) *Special Educational Needs and Disability Code of Practice: 0 to 25 years: Statutory guidance for organisations which work with and support children and young people who have special educational needs or disabilities*. London: Department for Education. Online. https://assets.publishing.service.gov.uk/government/uploads/system/uploads/attachment_data/file/398815/SEND_Code_of_Practice_January_2015.pdf (accessed 23 August 2018).

Hayton, R. (2009) 'Young people growing up in rural communities: Opportunities for educational psychologists to work with emerging adults'. *Educational and Child Psychology*, 26 (1), 60–6.

Jackson, E. (2008) 'The development of work discussion groups in educational settings'. *Journal of Child Psychotherapy*, 34 (1), 62–82.

MacKay, T. (2006) *The Evaluation of Post-School Psychological Services Pathfinders in Scotland (2004–2006)*. Edinburgh: Scottish Executive.

MacKay, T. (2009) 'Post-school educational psychology services: International perspectives on a distinctive Scottish development'. *Educational and Child Psychology*, 26 (1), 8–21.

O'Brien, J., Forest, M. and Pearpoint, J. (1996) *Solution Circle: Getting unstuck: A creative problem solving tool*. Toronto: Inclusion Press.

O'Brien, J., Pearpoint, J. and Kahn, L. (2010) *The PATH and MAPS Handbook: Person-centered ways to build community*. Toronto: Inclusion Press.

Ofsted (2014) 'Inspecting further education and skills: Inspector's handbook'. Online. www.ofsted.gov.uk/resources/handbook-for-inspection-of-further-education-and-skills-september-2012 (accessed 25 August 2018).

Preparing for Adulthood (2015) 'Writing Outcomes and Developing Study Programmes'. Workshop presented by members of the Preparing for Adulthood team, Queen Elizabeth II Court, Hampshire, 18 December.

Rogers, J. (2016) *Coaching Skills: The definitive guide to being a coach*. 4th ed. Maidenhead: Open University Press.

Wilson, D. and Newton, C. (2006) *Circles of Adults: A team approach to problem solving around challenging behaviour and emotional needs*. Nottingham: Inclusive Solutions.

Appendix: Semi-structured questionnaire

1. In light of the requirements included in the Revised Code of Practice (2014), what do you see as the main opportunities and challenges for your college?

    Prompts (if they don't specifically address these areas in their response to Question 1)

    - And what about the opportunities and challenges in relation to EHCP planning and review processes?
    - When are the times you find it most challenging to identify individual additional needs?
    - What about providing appropriate support (to meet these individual additional needs), and evaluating their progress?
    - With regard to gathering the views of the young people, and enabling them to be involved in decision-making about their learning, when are the occasions that you find this challenging?
    - Are there any opportunities and/or challenges you foresee in stretching and challenging young people with additional needs?
    - How about in providing care and support for pupils outside of lessons?

2. One section of the *Special Educational Needs and Disability Code of Practice* states that the governing body must ensure college staff know who to go to if they need help in identifying a student's SEND, if they are concerned about a student's progress or need further advice. Can you tell me a bit about how this currently works within your college?

    - Do you have access to specialist support services such as educational psychologists? If so, who are you currently working with/have you worked with in the past?
    - Have you considered buying in an EP to seek advice from?
    - Do you currently access support from external services in meeting the continuing professional development (CPD) needs of your staff? If so, who?
    - Would you consider buying in CPD from the EP service and, if so, what sort of training would you be interested in? (For example, social communication difficulties, attachment, motivation, etc.)

Education, Health and Care Plans for students with special educational needs in post-16 educational settings

Louise Bason

Introduction

The advent of the Children and Families Act 2014 and the Special Educational Needs and Disability Code of Practice (2014) brought about the replacement of a Statement of Special Educational Needs with an Education, Health and Care Plan (EHCP) for pupils who are deemed to require a high level of support to meet their needs. With the changes in legislation and the age range for an EHCP extended to young people with special educational needs and disabilities (SEND) up to age 25, there were not only changes in local authority policies and responsibilities but also implications for various professional roles, including educational psychologists (EPs).

The implementation of the new SEND system meant that EPs were likely to be one of the professionals involved in the assessment of the needs of young people beyond school age. For those psychologists, who like me also had a background in supporting young adults with learning difficulties in a range of mainstream community settings and having worked as a lead psychologist for a multi-disciplinary team within a specialist post-16 college, this indicated the formalization of another major transition point, that from secondary education to post-secondary opportunities. Furthermore, it meant that EPs were to be involved in EHCP requests for students who were leaving secondary school and who were about to embark on further education (FE), as well as those who were already attending post-16 settings.

The field of post-16 education and training can be varied; it includes FE colleges, sixth forms within mainstream schools and post-16 classes within special schools, independent special post-16 colleges and 16–19 academies. There are also voluntary and private organizations that offer education and training at post-16. All these settings may operate in diverse ways and the nature and form of SEND support young people receive will be organized differently from in schools. Most FE colleges will not have a special educational needs co-ordinator (SENCo) but there should be a named person with a clear role to ensure that students with SEND will get the help they require to make progress.

Funding streams have facilitated increased provision for young people with SEND in FE. The Education Funding Agency (EFA) provides funding for students between the ages of 16 and 19 years and the Skills Funding Agency (SFA) funds colleges and training providers for students aged 19 and over (Stevens *et al.*, 2017), which is referred to as Learning Support. For students with an EHCP the funding comes from both the local authority and the EFA up to the age of 25.

This chapter will seek to provide the reader with the context relevant to EHCPs in FE. While respecting the heterogeneity of pupils with SEND, this chapter will aim to outline the key aims of an EHCP at post-16 and explore the areas of need and related objectives that ought to typically characterize the content of an EHCP for students with SEND within colleges and sixth form settings. However, there is also ample need to discuss social and political ramifications related to post-16 FE opportunities for students with SEND and there is a need to reflect on the nature and purpose of post-16 education. This chapter also intends to identify the key areas that EPs need to focus on when they assess young people with SEND, and implications for educational psychology practice in FE are also discussed.

Contextual factors relevant to transition into post-16 FE settings

The transition from secondary school brings about several changes for young people with SEND, some not always immediately clear or anticipated. From a developmental psychology perspective, the experience of moving on from secondary school is perhaps the first task associated with the notion of becoming an adult, the quality and outcome of which will have an impact on the achievement of future adult identities and roles (Bason, 2012). Young people with SEND are a heterogeneous group of students with diverse strengths, difficulties and needs, who go through different experiences in terms of transition to post-16 planning. Political discourse about increasing young people's participation in FE and training has inevitably led to appreciable focus on those young people who are NEET (not in employment, education or training). Several researchers have highlighted the variable social and economic factors that can result in unequal opportunities to continuing educational pathways and links to NEET status. Sociological research such as that by Yates *et al.* (2011) revealed that young people from low socio-economic backgrounds with uncertain or misaligned occupational aspirations and educational expectations were associated with increased likelihood of becoming NEET. Although their research was not specifically about students with SEND, Yates *et al.* (2011) identified an individualized responsibility for negotiating one's pathway from school to adulthood, so that for those young people who are vulnerable and unable to make good decisions about a complex range of post-16 options, it was more likely they would experience poor outcomes in transition. It transpires that the onus is placed more on the individual young person and their individual agency (Heinz, 2009) and ability to be flexible about their plans, than on policy aiming to change the social and organizational structures shaping the labour market. From this perspective there will be various implications for young people with SEND.

The percentage of all young people in the United Kingdom who are NEET was 11.1 per cent in the third quarter of 2017 and having a SEND increases the likelihood of becoming NEET (Powell, 2018). Statistics just published at the time of writing (Department for Education (DfE), 2018), focused on a cohort of young people who were 18 at the start of the 2013/14 academic year, sought to identify the characteristics of young people who were NEET for a year, three years after completing Key Stage 4. This showed that looked-after children, young people who attended a pupil referral unit or experienced alternative provision at some point in their education, young people who had been permanently excluded during secondary school and pupils who had a Statement of Special Educational Needs at age 15 accounted for the highest proportion of those NEET (DfE, 2018). Arnold and Baker (2012) have also identified these possible NEET risk factors, arguing for preventative work, since about half of children at risk can be identified at least three years before they become NEET.

Changes in national policy in the last decade reflected the government's target to reduce the number of youths that were NEET by supporting the drive for young people to continue in compulsory education or training when they leave secondary school (e.g. raising the participation in education or training until at least one's 18th birthday). However, the move into college as a post-16 destination for young people with SEND has been historically perceived to be a default destination (Abbott and Heslop, 2009; Kaehne and Beyer, 2008), one that is smoother to organize strategically than other possibilities (Kaehne and Beyer, 2009), with employment often not a choice presented to young people with SEND as a post-secondary option (Bason,

2012; Grove and Giraud-Saunders, 2003; Kaehne and Beyer, 2008). There has also been a lot said about young people's lack of qualifications and poor job knowledge and skills. This led to new qualification routes and more young people extending their educational journeys, including pupils with SEND. Viewed from this perspective, post-16 education becomes the first of a series of transitions that marks the start of adulthood.

Another political factor that emerges as important is the service transitions often taking place within the transition to adulthood. This includes the transfer from children's social services to adult social care and from paediatric health services (e.g. child and adolescent mental health services) to adult health services. Longitudinal studies that followed up pupils after leaving secondary school were characterized by considerable attrition, where pupils were consequently unknown or lost to services (Caton and Kagan, 2006; Thomson and Ward, 1995). Previous research suggested that there are pupils who 'slip through the net', particularly if they lacked a specific diagnosis that could make them more identifiable. This may be attributed to the predominant medical categorization of conditions adopted by adult health and social care to enable access to services. Research carried out just before the onset of EHCPs (e.g. Bason, 2012) found that careers advisers (previously known as Connexions personal advisers) highlighted the lack of support available out of education, thus providing more of a real-world reason for supporting college entry, because education is perceived to adopt a more inclusive approach than other strata in society. Other research (e.g. Sloper *et al.*, 2010; Ward *et al.*, 2003) highlighted poor availability of information about adult services and they identified a mismatch between what young people's parents think is helpful to them and their child, and what they seem to get.

In view of the complex contextual factors described, the principal feature of the EHCP aimed to go beyond what the Statement of Special Educational Needs had previously achieved, to include specific consideration of the young person's health and care needs and to qualify the support the young person will require to meet these needs.

The Education, Health and Care Plan: The assessment process and the document

The EHCP aims to bring together the young person's educational, health and social care needs into one legal document, although the young person being assessed will not necessarily have high-level needs in all three areas. The main purpose of the new EHCP has been to devise specific, measurable, achievable, realistic and time-bound (SMART) short-term and long-term outcomes and to be clear about how these outcomes are linked to a young person's needs and future aspirations. The definition of an outcome is outlined in the *Special Educational Needs and Disability Code of Practice* (DfE and DoH, 2015, para. 9.66) 'as the benefit or difference made to an individual as a result of an intervention'. The EHCP also identifies the kind of provision that should be available for a young person to achieve these outcomes.

The EHCP endorses a person-centred approach to identifying the needs of young people by maintaining the individual young person and his or her family at the centre of the planning process. The support for more personalized approaches has been advocated by adult social and health services from the turn of the century and it took centre stage in the Valuing People agenda (DoH, 2001) and then in Valuing People Now (DoH, 2009), with a vision of services working in partnership to develop and support a young person's person-centred plan. It is likely that local authorities have sought different ways of implementing a person-centred approach, the nature and extent of the person-centeredness possibly debatable. However, the emphasis of prioritizing the views, aspirations and preferences of young people and their families has led local authorities to utilize some form of person-centred tools to achieve this. According to Michaels and Ferrara (2006), person-centred planning should be characterized by a collaborative process among the various stakeholders maintaining focus on both process and outcomes. Research relevant to person-centred planning carried out prior to the advent of EHCPs has highlighted both positive outcomes for young people as well as inequalities in both access to and the efficacy of person-centre planning (Robertson *et al.*, 2005, 2007). In terms of specific transition planning to post-16, Bason (2012) focused on both special and mainstream schools in one North West local authority and case study data showed that person-centred reviews held in special schools were more effective in involving external services, particularly social care, than regular annual reviews in mainstream schools. However, the delivery of a person-centred format did not guarantee a specific transition plan and any actions identified were not linked to explicit outcomes or necessarily followed up. The nature of person-centred planning and how this affects the quality of EHCP assessments and the achievement of EHCP outcomes is an area for enquiry. Some local authorities have sought to carry out a person-centred meeting with a young person and their family once professionals have completed their assessments to discuss the draft plan and the outcomes. What should follow now is real-world research about the impact of these processes.

The change in the legislation meant that those young people who had a Statement of Special Educational Needs had to have their Statement transferred to an EHCP. Both this transfer process as well as the EHCP as an initial assessment have had several implications on local authorities and professionals involved, particularly at a time when resource cuts to local authority services were happening simultaneously. The implications for professionals will be considered in further detail when the role of the EP is discussed. However, at this point it is relevant to identify a core change in the assessment of a young person with SEND at post-secondary transition and those who were already in FE. Students with SEND in colleges have also often been referred to as young people with learning difficulties and/ or disabilities due to having had a Learning Difficulty Assessment. Prior to the Code of Practice (2014) the Connexions personal adviser from the Connexions service had the role of offering careers advice for pupils with a Statement of Special Educational Needs, overseeing their transition plan from Year 9. Since April 2008, when funding for Connexions passed from Connexions Partnerships to local authorities, personal advisers carried out Section 139a or Learning Difficulty Assessments (LDAs) (Learning and Skills Council (LSC), 2009). This process was then replaced in September 2014 with schools and colleges being informed that they still had the statutory duty to provide independent career service provision for students with SEND, but there is still uncertainty about who should be providing this careers advice, the skills that are required by the advisers providing this (Robinson *et al.*, 2018) and the point at which access to careers advice is provided within college to inform career opportunities post-FE. If the person providing the careers advice is a college member of staff, their impartiality is inevitably questionable. The role of careers advice in the EHCP process itself is likely to be inconsistent.

The focus of most local authorities, as well as recent research, has predominantly been on the process of the EHCP assessment and the quality of plans produced. It has required the involvement of several professionals from different ideological and service backgrounds providing advice to inform a single plan of how the needs of young people with SEND will be met. A recent research report produced by DfE (Adams *et al.*, 2017) focused on the EHCP process of a sample of pupils who had an assessment carried out in 2015 and one of the aspects they investigated was the extent to which children, young people and families were satisfied with the process and with the EHCP itself. The authors reported that just under two-thirds (62 per cent) agreed that the help/support described in the EHCP will achieve the agreed outcomes for the child/young person and the difficulty in getting this support was cited most in cases where the EHCP was for a young person aged 16–25 years in contrast to when the EHCP was for a child aged 15 or younger (17 per cent versus 12 per cent).

A tool published by DfE to aid the development of EHCPs for children and young people with SEND is the Preparing for Adulthood outcomes document (Preparing for Adulthood, 2017). It presents a framework that is particularly useful to the post-16 cohort, outlining the four areas relevant to adult life as employment, independent living, community inclusion and health. These areas should therefore inform both the assessment process and the suggested outcomes for young people with SEND.

Aims of EHCPs for students with SEND at post-secondary education

The 'Preparing for Adulthood' (Preparing for Adulthood, 2017) framework presents a useful framework for outcomes but it is limited in terms of operationalizing the specific skills that require development to achieve the outcomes. The EHCP should therefore be effective in outlining not only the post-16 provision suitable for a young person with SEND, but it should also specify the skills that the provision should seek to help the young person develop in order to be able to achieve those outcomes. Research has yet to focus on providing evidence of how EHCPs are affecting the quality of young people's educational experiences at post-16 FE. In the research report about the experiences of EHCPs mentioned earlier, Adams *et al.* (2017) found that the families of young people aged 16–25 years were less positive about the achievement of long-term outcomes related to community participation, independent living and the young person's chances of getting paid or unpaid work. Another small-scale qualitative study by Skipp and Hopwood (2016), which tried to map user experiences of the EHCP process, omitted post-16 provision from the sample, hence there was no opportunity to consider adulthood-related outcomes.

Through non-participant observation, Bason (2012) found that annual reviews in the final two years of school, including those adopting structured person-centred formats, showed limited focus on teaching and learning towards skill building. If the perceived post-secondary outcome for the pupil was moving on to college, the action would merely focus on helping parents to visit colleges, but there was limited discussion about which courses will help the young person develop named skills and what were the long-term aspirations following college attendance. Although this case study work was carried out prior to the advent of the EHCP, the previous Statement of Special Educational Needs still declared a statutory duty for transition planning and the research outlined gaps in the transition practices of both mainstream schools and post-16 provision in special schools. This has key implications for those professionals involved in developing quality EHCPs for young people both within secondary school and college settings. It warrants the need for a thorough consideration of the skills that the young person would need to learn to achieve specific outcomes and a consideration of how the content of college courses will address this. The concern that emerges from the new EHCP process is that there is still no clarity related to who will be accountable for the achievement (or failure) of outcomes.

In considering the skills that a young person should be supported to develop, the concepts of adaptive behaviour skills and self-determination skills are extremely relevant. Adaptive behaviour includes behaviours that enable a person to live independently and to deal with the demands of daily life (Bason, 2012) and it involves several coping skills that facilitate community integration (Nihira *et al.*, 1993). Self-determination is a key focus in North American SEND literature and it encompasses personal and interpersonal competencies such as autonomous behaviour, self-management, understanding one's difficulties and goal-setting (Getzel and Thoma, 2008). Adaptive behaviour and self-determination skills have been associated with positive transition to adulthood outcomes (e.g. Alwell and Cobb, 2009; Madaus *et al.*, 2008) and Table 2.1 outlines the main component domains of adaptive and self-determined behaviour (Bason, 2012).

Table 2.1: Component domains of adaptive and self-determined behaviour

Adaptive behaviour	Self-determined behaviour
■ Communication skills (e.g. language and non-verbal skills)	■ Making choices
■ Personal independence (e.g. self-help skills)	■ Decision-making skills
■ Domestic activities (e.g. cooking)	■ Problem-solving skills
■ Community living skills (e.g. money recognition and handling, health and safety awareness)	■ Self-awareness
■ Vocational activity (e.g. job-related skills)	■ Goal-setting and attainment
■ Social skills (e.g. co-operation, conflict resolution)	■ Self-instruction skills
■ Economic activity (e.g. basic numeracy skills and time concepts)	■ Independent living, risk-taking and safety skills
	■ Self-advocacy, leadership and team skills
	■ Understanding one's difficulties

Source: Bason (2012)

The importance of developing adaptive behaviour and self-determination skills in post-secondary education should inform professional reports as well as the identification of specific outcomes in EHCPs.

The centrality of employment as a key outcome in adult life cannot be dissociated from political influence, linked to what is valued within the labour market. It is important to mention that the notion of employment in government agendas is viewed as some form of paid work. The Valuing People Now (DoH, 2009) made wider suggestions than the previous Valuing People agenda (DoH, 2001) by identifying planning for employment as a central objective in person-centred planning. The notion of employment as a desirable outcome has been challenged by some researchers such as Thomson and Ward (1995) based on data that showed employment to be an unrealistic outcome particularly for people with severe learning difficulties. This criticism was expressed more recently by Robinson *et al.* (2018), who also supported a wider view of career and work. The 'SEND Pathfinder Programme' for the provision for older young people aged 19–25 (Thom and Agur, 2014) identified further challenges, such as limited supported employment opportunities and travel costs to sustain employment of young people with SEND.

Reflecting on the emphasis of positive mental health in the real world and given that the new Code of Practice (2014) has explicitly resulted in the inclusion of a section that focuses on a young person's social, emotional and mental health in an EHCP, whether this has or will, in effect, have an impact on support within a college setting and the curriculum offered at post-16 education remains to be seen. More specifically, will there be a focus on the development of social skills and emotional literacy within college courses outside the narrow perception of social skills relevant to gaining employment?

Provision for students with SEND who have EHCPs in colleges of FE

Under the Equality Act 2010, colleges and training providers must make reasonable adjustments for young people with SEND. This means that they are expected to provide support and make changes to help a young person learn. This has extensive implications for colleges, at the organizational level, the curricular level and the level of the individual. Having focused on curricular aspects in the previous section, it is important to look at the way in which features relevant to the organization can have an impact on the provision for individual students. Whole-college ethos and policy about SEND and inclusion, and the creation of specialist roles such as the 'inclusion manager' or the 'learning support manager' and their position within the senior management team, will have an impact on the nature of provision for all students with SEND. The inclusion manager should have the role of ensuring that tutors have key student information achieved from secondary schools, including information about strategies that help students learn.

When a student has an EHCP the college should ensure that all staff members involved with the young person are familiar with the content of the EHCP. Furthermore, there needs to be consideration of how the support to achieve specific outcomes is translated to day-to-day practice. Research focused on the college experiences of young people with an autistic spectrum disorder (ASD) highlighted that support tends to be designed around learning and curricular access rather than non-academic support, such as how to manage the social demands of college settings and aspects that may reduce the experience of social anxiety (Bell *et al.*, 2017). Adreon and Durocher (2007) state that colleges should focus on goals and adaptations that address communication and social skills, sensory and organizational needs. This links to the need for FE settings to focus on the development of self-determination skills described earlier.

Exploring whether an EHCP brings about difference or additional support to meeting the needs of young people with SEND within an FE setting is an area for future research. Information acquired from one learning support manager of a North West college indicated that EHCPs can provide valuable information about possible progression routes for a student and they can help in the decision-making process of enrolling onto a suitable programme. However, an EHCP was not necessarily viewed as a key document that would contribute to course choice or level. Anecdotal experience of working in mainstream college settings tends to indicate that EHCPs have brought about increased focus on meeting administration requirements, namely the human resources and time required to organize annual reviews of the EHCP. Colleges are also likely to seek input from external services to try to meet the social and emotional needs of students who have specific conditions such as ASD.

A recent development for students with an EHCP (aged 16–24 years), linked to the focus on work preparation, has been access to supported internships or traineeships. In a supported internship an employer provides a work placement for a year, including unpaid work for six months. The experience aims to develop young people's skills and it is characterized by the support of a job coach to help the young person to learn about a job role. All FE colleges, sixth forms and independent specialist providers in England can offer supported internships as part of their learning programme for students with SEND (Stevens *et al.*, 2017). Traineeships include similar focus on work preparation and work experience to help a person move into a job or apprenticeship and their duration is six weeks to six months. Traineeships could lead to a job interview if a role becomes available.

The role of educational psychologists in EHCPs with students at post-16 FE

The *Special Educational Needs and Disability Code of Practice* (DfE and DoH, 2015) has served to lay out further work for the profession of educational psychology. Although this may be narrowly viewed in terms of the statutory EHCP process, it is hoped that EPs are able to extend their application of psychology to a variety of post-16 settings.

The 'SEND Pathfinder Programme' for the provision for older young people aged 19–25 (Thom and Agur, 2014) expressed concerns about the extension of skills of professionals who worked predominantly with children and about the training required for EHCP co-ordinators (e.g. SEND officers). This document proclaimed the expertise of the EP, but it noted that there would be difficulties in terms of capacity to deliver additional services and that most EPs would require additional training to work with young people with SEND aged 16–25 years. This 'additional training' has been interpreted differently across various educational psychology services (EPSs) and several services have sought to invest in training within continuing professional development initiatives, whereas others went a step further to create senior practitioner roles to develop this area within their EPS.

An issue that has emerged for EPs has been the nature of the assessment work that should be carried out when asked to be involved with a student in FE. The process of assessment may or may not need to involve the typical literacy or cognitive psychometric tests. The profession has several transferable skills, such as those involved in consultation, motivational interviewing and personal construct psychology, which can easily be applied to working with the young people with SEND in post-16 FE. A standard approach to inform assessment is always exploring the reason why an EHCP has been requested and carrying out activities that will achieve information about the student's strengths, difficulties and needs.

There are several theoretical frameworks that can inform assessment. A framework that relates well to the Preparing for Adulthood framework (Preparing for Adulthood, 2017), and which is linked to the development of person-centred philosophy, is O'Brien's (1987) five accomplishments identifying the aspects that people with disabilities should be helped to achieve: community presence and participation in meaningful activities, choice, respect, experience of valuable relationships, and competence to learn new skills. Together these accomplishments constitute quality experiences in adult life and should also inform post-16 curricula for pupils with SEND.

There are also further implications on EP practice that often feature in supervision sessions and wider forums such as conferences, the main one being related to the art of report writing. With the emphasis on devising specific objectives for the young person and the need to operationalize outcomes relevant to the transition to adulthood, there have been requirements for the various professionals involved, including EPs, to reflect on the quality of their writing skills in reports. The ability to draw up age-appropriate and SMART outcomes depends on the assessment work carried out. Theoretical frameworks can help professionals, including EPs, to develop their own questions to inform consultation sessions in post-16 settings. Ultimately the key question that should inform the work of EPs is, *which skills does the young person need to develop at post-16 to help achieve the outcomes identified as important for them?* If the development of self-determination and adaptive behaviour skills are linked to positive outcomes, the inclusion of an adaptive behaviour skills assessment is encouraged (Bason, 2012) and it should lead to the identification of goals relevant to a young person's skill building.

Student involvement in the EHCP process and achieving insight into their future aspirations has become a core aspect of person-centred planning. Mainstream transition literature cites a lack of research that explores the link between NEET status and young people's aspirations for future occupations and educational expectations (Yates *et al.*, 2011). As already mentioned, personal agency and motivation have been identified as having the potential to determine whether young people with SEND will gain some form of employment. A qualitative study by Andrews and Rose (2010) used visual communication aids to help explore motivation with ten adults with some learning disabilities who attended supported learning courses at an FE college in England. They found three factors related to employment motivation: monetary gain, social contact and perceived competence. Research by Hensel *et al.* (2007) also found motivation to be an important psychological factor not just in gaining but also in maintaining employment. This generates reflections on the nature of EP involvement when working with college students and eliciting their views.

With concern expressed about the lack of career professionals with specialist training in SEND (e.g. Abbott and Heslop, 2009; Robinson *et al.*, 2018) and the need for reliable assessments of students' skills and needs to inform the identification of goals having transition-to-adulthood relevance

(Bason, 2012), the prime role that EPs must play in both assessment and training within multi-professional spheres is clear. EPs should be involved in liaison meetings with careers advisers and college staff to ensure that young people with SEND receive high-quality teaching and appropriate careers guidance.

Following the Children and Families Act 2014 and the *Special Educational Needs and Disability Code of Practice* (DfE and DoH, 2015), opportunities for professional services to develop partnerships with colleges and other post-16 settings have gained importance. EPs are key professionals who should be involved in supporting positive post-secondary transitions both while young people are in the process of leaving school and in the first few months of college attendance. Although this chapter is concerned with EHCPs, in the changing world of educational psychology services, it has become important to view these opportunities beyond the EHCP framework. EPs should also seek proactive ways of working in FE settings and multi-agency community services that do not restrict them to EHCP involvement.

Do EHCPs fulfil their intended purpose? Discussion point

Such a question could form the basis for several research projects in the years to come. This chapter has tried to explore EHCPs within the field of post-16 education by focusing on those areas that an EHCP in post-16 should seek to address and how these areas link to skills associated with transition to adulthood. It has also been important to discuss the social and political context of transition to post-16 education and the transition to adulthood. This is important for students with SEND and for those who are NEET to take part in FE and raise the age of educational participation. The extent to which educational objectives within an EHCP are achieved will inevitably be an important research question for the future and the use of EHCPs in post-16 FE settings is a work in progress.

As mentioned earlier, alongside this issue there is the question of whether EHCPs are ultimately useful because they can have an impact on post-16 curricula and practices to produce better outcomes for students with SEND, rather than becoming another paper document that merely determines access to specific pathways. From this perspective, this would require joint working between college senior management teams and local authority professionals to investigate the way in which course content is able to address young people's needs as cited in EHCPs. Ultimately this is also likely to require investigation of FE courses to ensure that these are effectively addressing the development of skills required to increase the independence, employment opportunities and quality of life of young people with SEND.

The use of EHCPs for college students has implications on the quality of EHCPs developed for students with SEND both in mainstream and special secondary schools, and the extent to which they are effective in developing and delivering a curriculum that focuses on transition-to-adulthood objectives besides the academic focus driven by league tables. For young people with SEND, leaving secondary school has been described as a challenging period. Researchers in the field of transition have described it as a complex issue for pupils with SEND (Beresford, 2004; Grove and Giraud-Saunders, 2003; Hudson, 2006), with many young people leaving school without any transition planning (Bason, 2012; Polat *et al.*, 2001; Ward *et al.*, 2003). Schools are often falling short of providing pupils with SEND opportunities to finish schooling, pursue FE, experience social inclusion and meaningful employment (Rusch *et al.*, 2009). Carter *et al.* (2009) argue that literature on inclusive practice in secondary schools suggests a combination of obstacles may combine in ways that limit consideration of a range of career development experiences for young people with SEND. Flexible timetables, the availability of resources within schools, accessible curricula and poor teacher attitudes towards inclusion are factors that play a role in this. This argues for early involvement from EPs, preferably from Year 9 or even before.

From a psycho-educational perspective, schools have a major role in developing a pupil's personal competency and social adaptive functioning. If an EP is involved in writing psychological advice for an EHCP assessment of a pupil in Year 9 or Year 10 in a mainstream school, educational objectives need to have transition-relevance and look beyond academic achievement. If an EHCP application is left to Year 11, educational psychology involvement may involve a more active role in supporting the transition process itself.

My experience as an EP with a special interest in transition to post-16 has often revealed there is a lot to be done in terms of quality assessments and informed choice in relation to college courses rather than mere college placement, and in the process of guiding a student to decide which college course to pursue. It has been noted that some recent college Ofsted reports have linked poor planning and insufficient information about courses to later drop-outs. This could therefore be a risk factor to NEET status. It transpires that an EP is therefore well placed to carry out a thorough assessment of a young person with SEND and in suggesting the areas that FE needs to focus on.

The scope of the EHCP to bring together educational, health and care needs does not necessarily imply that young people will experience service transitions smoothly, and legislation and policies never guarantee change and progress in practice. Poor integrated working between child/adolescent mental health services and adult mental health services and between child/ adolescent mental health services and social care has not met the various needs of young people with SEND (Kaehne, 2011). Media coverage also continues to identify the gaps for mental health services for young adults with autistic spectrum disorder and those with attention deficit hyperactivity disorder. It is now hoped that the new Green Paper *Transforming Children and Young People's Mental Health Provision* (DoH and DfE, 2017) will yield consultation that will be able to reflect the various needs of the SEND population, and not solely those who qualify for EHCPs. In terms of the EHCP assessment and document, anecdotal evidence suggests it is hard to determine the extent to which health and social care professionals have been able to contribute SMART outcomes and whether there could potentially be a mismatch between outcomes suggested and the reality of service operations. These aspects are possibly key areas for future research.

Ultimately there is an important question that will need to be answered – will EHCPs help to have an impact on the nature and quality of FE curricula for young people with SEND? The purpose of this chapter is not merely to describe the current provision for students with SEND who have EHCPs. There is the need to go one step further and highlight the need for FE settings to include a transition-focused education that endorses an explicit personal and social development (PSD) module that incorporates the development of emotional literacy and emotional well-being. The latter should be an entity that is developed within a proactive FE curriculum and not merely by the provision of a counselling service that only works with students from a reactive capacity. In effect, what is required is not solely a whole-college approach to mental health, but a whole-college commitment to teach students core skills relevant to their social and emotional well-being. The same applies to secondary schools if change is to have a long-term impact. Pupils with SEND are often experiencing gaps in educational provision, such as reduced academic timetables and lesson exemptions. If there is a national, governmental policy that prescribes a PSD curriculum to run alongside academic learning, with pastoral teachers trained to develop and implement it from a small group, 'circle time' delivery framework, then this could be the medium that could potentially fulfil the achievement of social, emotional and positive mental health outcomes for pupils. Similarly, with colleges often only engaging students for three days a week, it leaves ample time for the implementation of a PSD curriculum and would, in effect, be a first-step commitment towards having a transition-to-adult focus within the FE curriculum.

This chapter has sought to focus on the use of EHCPs for students with SEND in post-16 settings. Such a topic cannot be considered in a vacuum and bringing together the educational, health and care needs of a student inevitably has implications on the systems within which the young person operates. Ultimately there is no point in changing legislation if these changes do not provide transformations and modifications in these organizational systems. It is hoped that the educational psychology profession will continue to aspire to be a leader in the organizational and strategic changes that should follow in the next few years.

References

Abbott, D. and Heslop, P. (2009) 'Out of sight, out of mind? Transition for young people with learning difficulties in out-of-area residential special schools and colleges'. *British Journal of Special Education*, 36 (1), 45–54.

Adams, L., Tindle, A., Basran, S., Dobie, S., Thomson, D., Robinson, D. and Shepherd, C. (2017) *Experiences of Education, Health and Care Plans: A survey of parents and young people*. London: Department for Education.

Adreon, D. and Durocher, J.S. (2007) 'Evaluating the college transition needs of individuals with high-functioning autism spectrum disorders'. *Intervention in School and Clinic*, 42 (5), 271–9.

Alwell, M. and Cobb, B. (2009) 'Functional life skills curricular interventions for youth with disabilities: A systematic review'. *Career Development for Exceptional Individuals*, 32 (2), 82–93.

Andrews, A. and Rose, J.L. (2010) 'A preliminary investigation of factors affecting employment motivation in people with intellectual disabilities'. *Journal of Policy and Practice in Intellectual Disabilities*, 7 (4), 239–44.

Arnold, C. and Baker, T. (2012) 'Transitions from school to work: Applying psychology to "NEET"'. *Educational and Child Psychology*, 29 (3), 67–80.

Bason, M.L. (2012) 'The Planning and Implementation of Post-School Transitions for Young People with Special Educational Needs'. Unpublished doctoral thesis, University of Manchester.

Bell, S., Devecchi, C., Mc Guckin, C. and Shevlin, M. (2017) 'Making the transition to post-secondary education: Opportunities and challenges experienced by students with ASD in the Republic of Ireland'. *European Journal of Special Needs Education*, 32 (1), 54–70.

Beresford, B. (2004) 'On the road to nowhere? Young disabled people and transition'. *Child: Care, Health and Development*, 30 (6), 581–7.

Carter, E.W., Trainor, A.A., Cakiroglu, O., Cole, O., Swedeen, B., Ditchman, N. and Owens, L. (2009) 'Exploring school–employer partnerships to expand career development and early work experiences for youth with disabilities'. *Career Development for Exceptional Individuals*, 32 (3), 145–59.

Caton, S. and Kagan, C. (2006) 'Tracking post-school destinations of young people with mild intellectual disabilities: The problem of attrition'. *Journal of Applied Research in Intellectual Disabilities*, 19 (2), 143–52.

DfE (Department for Education) (2018) *Characteristics of Young People Who are Long-Term NEET*. London: Department for Education. Online. https://assets. publishing.service.gov.uk/government/uploads/system/uploads/attachment_data/ file/679535/Characteristics_of_young_people_who_are_long_term_NEET.pdf (accessed 23 August 2018).

DfE (Department for Education) and DoH (Department of Health) (2015) *Special Educational Needs and Disability Code of Practice: 0 to 25 years: Statutory guidance for organisations which work with and support children and young people who have special educational needs or disabilities*. London: Department for Education. Online. https://assets.publishing.service.gov.uk/government/ uploads/system/uploads/attachment_data/file/398815/SEND_Code_of_Practice_ January_2015.pdf (accessed 23 August 2018).

DoH (Department of Health) (2001) *Valuing People: A new strategy for learning disability for the 21st century: A white paper*. London: The Stationery Office.

DoH (Department of Health) (2009) *Valuing People Now: A new three-year strategy for people with learning disabilities*. London: Department of Health.

DoH (Department of Health) and DfE (Department for Education) (2017) *Transforming Children and Young People's Mental Health Provision: A Green Paper*. London: Department of Health. Online. www.gov.uk/government/ uploads/system/uploads/attachment_data/file/664855/Transforming_children_ and_young_people_s_mental_health_provision.pdf (accessed 25 August 2018).

Getzel, E.E. and Thoma, C.A. (2008) 'Experiences of college students with disabilities and the importance of self-determination in higher education settings'. *Career Development for Exceptional Individuals*, 31 (2), 77–84.

Grove, B. and Giraud-Saunders, A. (2003) 'Connecting with Connexions: The role of the personal adviser with young people with special educational and support needs'. *Support for Learning*, 18 (1), 12–17.

Heinz, W.R. (2009) 'Structure and agency in transition research'. *Journal of Education and Work*, 22 (5), 391–404.

Hensel, E., Stenfert Kroese, B. and Rose, J. (2007) 'Psychological factors associated with obtaining employment'. *Journal of Applied Research in Intellectual Disabilities*, 20 (2), 175–81.

Hudson, B. (2006) 'Making and missing connections: Learning disability services and the transition from adolescence to adulthood'. *Disability and Society*, 21 (1), 47–60.

Kaehne, A. (2011) 'Transition from children and adolescent to adult mental health services for young people with intellectual disabilities: A scoping study of service organisation problems'. *Advances in Mental Health and Intellectual Disabilities*, 5 (1), 9–16.

Kaehne, A. and Beyer, S. (2008) 'Carer perspectives on the transition of young people with learning disabilities to employment'. *Journal on Developmental Disabilities*, 14 (1), 95–104.

Kaehne, A. and Beyer, S. (2009) 'Views of professionals on aims and outcomes of transition for young people with learning disabilities'. *British Journal of Learning Disabilities*, 37 (2), 138–44.

LSC (Learning and Skills Council) (2009) *Learning for Living and Work Framework: Guidance notes.* Coventry: Learning and Skills Council.

Madaus, J.W., Gerber, P.J. and Price, L.A. (2008) 'Adults with learning disabilities in the workforce: Lessons for secondary transition programs'. *Learning Disabilities Research and Practice*, 23 (3), 148–53.

Michaels, C.A. and Ferrara, D.L. (2006) 'Promoting post-school success for all: The role of collaboration in person-centered transition planning'. *Journal of Educational and Psychological Consultation*, 16 (4), 287–313.

Nihira, K., Leland, H. and Lambert, N. (1993) *Adaptive Behavior Scale – Residential and community.* 2nd ed. Austin, TX: Pro-Ed.

O'Brien, J. (1987) 'A guide to life-style planning: Using The Activities Catalog to integrate services and natural support systems'. In Wilcox, B. and Bellamy, G.T. (eds) *A Comprehensive Guide to The Activities Catalog: An alternative curriculum for youth and adults with severe disabilities.* Baltimore: Paul H. Brookes, 175–89.

Polat, F., Kalambouka, A., Boyle, W.F. and Nelson, N. (2001) *Post-16 Transitions of Pupils with Special Educational Needs* (Research Report 315). London: Department for Education and Skills.

Powell, A. (2018) *NEET: Young people not in education, employment or training* (Briefing Paper SN 06705). London: House of Commons Library.

Preparing for Adulthood (2017) *PfA Outcomes across the Age Ranges for Children and Young People with SEND.* Rev. ed. Bath: Preparing for Adulthood. Online. www.preparingforadulthood.org.uk/SiteAssets/Downloads/yeded5wb636481748062535810.pdf (accessed 23 August 2018).

Robertson, J., Emerson, E., Hatton, C., Elliott, J., McIntosh, B., Swift, P., Krijnen-Kemp, E., Towers, C., Romeo, R., Knapp, M., Sanderson, H., Routledge, M., Oakes, P. and Joyce, T. (2005) *The Impact of Person Centred Planning.* Lancaster: Institute for Health Research.

Robertson, J., Emerson, E., Hatton, C., Elliott, J., McIntosh, B., Swift, P., Krinjen-Kemp, E., Towers, C., Romeo, R., Knapp, M., Sanderson, H., Routledge, M., Oakes, P. and Joyce, T. (2007) 'Person-centred planning: Factors associated with successful outcomes for people with intellectual disabilities'. *Journal of Intellectual Disability Research*, 51 (3), 232–43.

Robinson, D., Moore, N. and Hooley, T. (2018) 'Ensuring an independent future for young people with special educational needs and disabilities (SEND): A critical examination of the impact of education, health and care plans in England'. *British Journal of Guidance and Counselling*, 1–13. Online. www.tandfonline.com/doi/pdf/10.1080/03069885.2017.1413706?needAccess=true (accessed 14 August 2018).

Rusch, F.R., Hughes, C., Agran, M., Martin, J.E. and Johnson, J.R. (2009) 'Toward self-directed learning, post-high school placement, and coordinated support: Constructing new transition bridges to adult life'. *Career Development for Exceptional Individuals*, 32 (1), 53–9.

Skipp, A. and Hopwood, V. (2016) *Mapping User Experiences of the Education, Health and Care Process: A qualitative study.* London: Department for Education.

Sloper, P., Beecham, J., Clarke, S., Franklin, A., Moran, N. and Cusworth, L. (2010) *Models of Multi-Agency Services for Transition to Adult Services for Disabled Young People and Those with Complex Health Needs: Impact and costs*. York: Social Policy Research Unit.

Stevens, T., Lewis, A. and Thind, R. (2017) *Into Further Education 2017*. London: Disability Rights UK.

Thom, G. and Agur, M. (2014) *Special Educational Needs and Disability Pathfinder Programme Evaluation: Thematic report: Provision for older young people, aged 19–25*. London: Department for Education.

Thomson, G.O.B. and Ward, K.M. (1995) 'Pathways to adulthood for young adults with special educational needs'. *British Journal of Education and Work*, 8 (3), 75–87.

UK Parliament (2010) 'Equality Act 2010'. Online. www.legislation.gov.uk/ukpga/2010/15/contents (accessed 25 August 2018).

UK Parliament (2014) 'Children and Families Act 2014'. Online. www.legislation.gov.uk/ukpga/2014/6/contents/enacted (accessed 25 August 2018).

Ward, L., Mallett, R., Heslop, P. and Simons, K. (2003) 'Transition planning: How well does it work for young people with learning disabilities and their families?'. *British Journal of Special Education*, 30 (3), 132–7.

Yates, S., Harris, A., Sabates, R. and Staff, J. (2011) 'Early occupational aspirations and fractured transitions: A study of entry into "NEET" status in the UK'. *Journal of Social Policy*, 40 (3), 513–34

Chapter 3

Educational psychologists working with universities

Garry Squires

Entry to university is based on merit, but what happens if you have a disability or a learning difficulty? While each university should have a policy in place to take disability into account there are competing agendas that can mean university practices are sometimes unclear. It is important for educational psychologists (EPs) to understand how these agendas are similar to or different from those encountered when conducting local authority work. EPs have transferable knowledge and skills to help students at university, whatever the age of the student. This chapter will start to address these questions and is intended to inspire colleagues to develop the potential role for EPs in higher education. In writing this chapter, I am drawing on my experiences as a practitioner educational psychologist who has moved from local authority work to working with students in university and using my experiences as a lecturer thinking about teaching and learning in an adult environment and being involved in working groups to help a university become more inclusive.

The chapter will be split into three main sections; an introduction that provides the context; a focus on individual assessment; then a section on thinking more inclusively about university teaching.

Contextual conflicts and agendas

Educational psychologists are experienced in working in systems that contain ideological and political tensions creating competing agendas. Higher education, like other complex systems, has competing agendas that will affect attitudes towards inclusion and support. Understanding these tensions and agendas provides some protection from the frustration that would otherwise arise in trying to work with the system as an outsider and it also provides opportunities for change for the system.

Having a well-educated workforce is an important consideration for governments in all developed countries and underpins economic activity. This political 'participation agenda' has driven a move towards encouraging an increasing number of young people to attend university. In the 1950s just over 3 per cent of young people attended university. Recent government statistics show that in 2016 the number of 17–30 year olds who participate in education had increased to 49 per cent. However, participation is not even. There is a gender gap of nearly 12 per cent with females outnumbering males (Department for Education (DfE), 2017b). Those who are disadvantaged as indicated through free school meals (FSM) are less likely to participate in university, with 22 per cent of 15 year olds eligible for FSM in 2010 reaching university (DfE, 2016). So it seems that opportunity is as important as academic ability and students do not simply arrive at university based on merit or individual hard work. Social differences such as these have led some authors to claim that the system is elitist and there is a hierarchy between the pre-1992 and post-1992 universities in terms of access for working-class students (Reay *et al.*, 2010). This is reflected in the 'widening participation agenda' that has led to an increase in students from state schools attending university and in 2016 this accounted for 89.8 per cent of English students, an increase from 84.4 per cent in 1998 (Higher Education Statistics Agency (HESA), 2017b). There is some evidence that the nature of the university itself determines its overall approach to the widening participation agenda. For instance, newer universities (post-1992) are more likely to recruit students from working-class backgrounds than the older established universities (Greenbank, 2006). Some authors argue that this is simply a result of the measures taken to improve access by elite universities that end up having the opposite effect, because they replicate the inequalities that the widening access agenda was meant to overcome, for example by focusing on pupils in the top 5 per cent of educational attainment (Rainford, 2017).

There is a tension between widening the participation rate and the view that standards might become diluted if weaker students are admitted to programmes (Riddell and Weedon, 2006; Riddell *et al.*, 2007). At the same time, universities are being held more accountable and increased tuition fees are accompanied by comparators such as the National Student Survey. This not only measures degree success, but it also asks about quality of teaching and academic support. One way of ensuring students have greater satisfaction and more positive experience of university life is to make the tuition more personal by increasing staff access through reducing student numbers on large undergraduate programmes. One consequence of this response to the 'accountability agenda' is that it increases demand relative to supply for the programmes. Universities can then increase the grades needed to enter the programme, which has the potential to act against the widening participation agenda and make universities less inclusive. At the same time, the introduction of fees has led to students treating university education like any other consumer item and expecting good returns for their money. How can they ensure they get a good grade? What can the university be expected to do to ensure they get a good grade? Are there any processes that can give them an advantage? Universities have responded to this and are active in developing access courses and induction programmes that teach students some of the skills needed for success at university. Students can access learning support materials through short programmes delivered on virtual learning environments. The way teaching is done has changed and includes the traditional lecture, online learning, blended learning, project work, collaborative working, the flipped classroom in which the students lead and develop content and then bring it into the classroom, etc. A lot of learning occurs outside the lecture room and while it may be directed, it requires good personal organization, high levels of motivation and self-organized learning.

Students with special educational needs and/or disabilities (SEND) are less likely to be in a position to apply for university in the first place. This may be because they are more vulnerable to leaving school early (Dyson and Squires, 2016; Squires, 2017; Squires and Dyson, 2017) or, if they remain in education, may have their opportunities limited by default transition pathways to further education (FE) at age 16 with a greater risk of drop-out or reduced qualifications (Young *et al.*, 2015a; Young *et al.*, 2015b). There is a clear role here for EPs working with schools to increase opportunities for children with SEND so they are in a position to apply for higher education. Those who do reach university successfully may face additional challenges compared with students who do not have SEND. So, given the tensions created by widening access, maintaining standards and improving student satisfaction, how successful have universities been in recruiting students with SEND?

HESA collects data on student disability and it can be seen that the proportion of students reporting they have a disability attending university at any level has been increasing from 2.6 per cent of the student population in 1994/5 to 11.8 per cent of the student population in 2015/16 (Armstrong and Squires, 2015; HESA, 2014, 2017a). The data suggest universities are becoming more successful in attracting students with disabilities. The most recent data from HESA give a breakdown of the types of disability: blind or visual impairment (1.2 per cent of disabled students); deaf or hearing impaired (2.34 per cent); physical impairment (3.34 per cent); social communication/autistic spectrum disorder (3.76 per cent); two or more conditions (9.23 per cent); mental health (17.16 per cent); and specific learning difficulties

(SpLD) (44.23 per cent). While these numbers represent the self-declared disabilities of students and may be an under-representation of actual numbers of students with each disability, they do give an idea of the kind of disabilities that students at any level of study have at university. The high number of students with a specific disability (such as dyslexia or dyspraxia) within the disabled population suggests that it might either be easier for universities to meet their needs or that it is easier for these students to access university compared with the other subgroups of disabled students. Previous analysis shows that students with SpLD represent an increasing proportion of disabled students and accounts for most of the rise in disabled students at university (Armstrong and Squires, 2015; Riddell and Weedon, 2006). The data are useful in thinking about EPs' role within higher education institutions (HEIs) and it is most likely that individual student-based work is going to involve students with either SpLD or mental health difficulties, such as anxiety or depression. There is some evidence to suggest that students who are found to have SpLD are more likely than students without SpLD to suffer from anxiety (Carroll and Iles, 2006).

While the *Special Educational Needs and Disability Code of Practice* (DfE and Department of Health (DoH), 2015) indicates that Education, Health and Care Plans (EHCPs) cover the age range 0–25, and covers FE and apprenticeships, they do not apply in universities (DfE and DoH, 2013). Universities are required to take into account the Equality Act 2010 and make reasonable adjustments for students who have a recognizable disability. Disability is defined within the Act if the student has 'a physical or mental impairment' that has a 'substantial and long term adverse effect on the person's ability to carry out normal day-to-day activities' (UK Parliament, 2010, Part 2, Chapter 1, Point 6). What counts as disability here is quite limited and a medical model of disability is applied; it is not simply that the student is different from other students. The kinds of disabilities that fall under the Act are specific learning disability (such as dyslexia, dyspraxia or attention deficit hyperactivity disorder (ADHD)) but not general learning disability; hearing impairment; visual impairment; physical disability; social communication disorder and autism; mental health difficulties; other long-term disabilities or illnesses (for example traumatic brain injury, chronic heart disease, cancer, HIV). Universities provide access to various services to provide support for students although these go under different names depending on the university in question. There will be access to student counselling services that support students with mental health problems and these will provide support for students who have academically related emotional problems such as procrastinating or being prone to perfectionism or imposter syndrome (Clance and Imes, 1978). There are also staff who provide more general advice around disability and accessing support at Manchester and this is called the Disability Advice and Support Service. English students who require additional support at university need to apply for a Disabled Students' Allowances from Student Finance England.

This puts an emphasis on individual within-student assessment to which I will return in the second part of the chapter. The student cannot be treated unfavourably for something that arises as a consequence of their disability (UK Parliament, 2010, Point 15). For example, a student with dyslexia cannot be penalized for not completing an examination within the specified time if their slow speed in that examination is a consequence of slow reading or writing speed linked to their dyslexia if the dyslexia is made known to the university. Section 20 of the Act sets out the notion of making reasonable adjustments, for instance in the example given, allowing the student to have 25 per cent or 50 per cent additional time in examinations would be considered a reasonable adjustment to the normal way of working that takes into account their disability. There is a tension between making reasonable adjustments while also maintaining academic standards through the continued use of assessment processes such as timed examinations that are discriminatory (Riddell and Weedon, 2006). There is also a tension arising from making reasonable adjustments for a student on a professional training route such as nursing or medicine or educational psychology and protecting the public once that person has qualified by passing their programme. Section 53 (7) discusses the exemption of the Act in relation to professional competencies. For example if a medical student has to perform a procedure within a particular time frame to prevent loss of life then they cannot be allowed longer to do it on the basis of poor processing speed. Of course, a reasonable adjustment might be to allow them longer to practise and develop fluidity in carrying out the procedure prior to assessment so they reach the correct level of competency to be fit to practise. Based on this, one of the goals of individual assessment might be to work out what kinds of adjustments can be provided that are clearly related to the tasks the individual carries out on a daily basis within their programme of study.

Individual assessment

The background context has established that some students who may have a disability could be able to apply for Disabled Students' Allowances from Student Finance England or through the NHS Student Bursary. These students and others who may have a disability can request that the university make reasonable adjustments to their programme of study, teaching or assessment. The students will self-refer through the university's support services and seek an assessment by an EP. The students may have to pay the assessment fee, or the fee may be subsidized by the university. At one level, it could be argued that the assessment has a bureaucratic purpose and follows a medical model. To assist with this purpose there are guidelines that have been established by the SpLD Assessment Standards Committee originally set up by the Department for Education and Skills (DfES) in 2005. The guidelines discuss which tests are suitable and set out a template for writing an assessment report (DfES, 2005; SpLD Assessment Standards Committee, 2010; SpLD Test Evaluation Committee, 2009, 2016). One of the challenges of assessing these students is there is a lack of referral information or prior assessment and the reason the student is seeking the assessment is not always known in advance. This needs to be obtained through a clinical interview before using psychometric assessment instruments so that the assessment can be tailored to the reported difficulties. For many of these students the reason they want the assessment is pragmatic; they just want additional time in examinations. For other students the assessment has greater meaning and they are trying to understand themselves and to understand why they have always struggled relative to their peers in education. For other students the goal is to develop strategies to be able to cope independently with their studies. These different goals require slightly different approaches to the assessment and the choice of methods used. Understanding why the student has been referred and what they want out of the assessment is an important starting point. Good professional practice should recognize this and not simply offer a 'quick one assessment fits all' package. For those who simply want the assessment to serve a bureaucratic function, then it could be argued that the simplest, quickest approach to meet that need is the one to select as it places less burden on the student. But for those who want a deeper understanding of their strengths and weaknesses, a more sophisticated and time-consuming assessment might be needed. For those wishing to become more independent learners, there may be a need to link psychometric assessments to the tasks they need to do by undertaking some level of functional task analysis supported through clinical observation and trying alternative ways of responding to set problems to identify the best approach to learning and study.

A good clinical interview should allow enough time for these reasons to be explored and for hypotheses to be generated that can explain why the student is struggling. This should also allow for the possibility that the reason the student has asked for the assessment may not be the actual problem. For example, the student who says, 'I came along because one of my friends is dyslexic and I thought I might be as well' may turn out to not be dyslexic but to have performance anxiety, or to be depressed, or autistic, or dyspraxic, or to have no disability at all. Understanding what the student is struggling with in academia is one goal, another is to understand how the problems affect them in life more generally and to explore how students are able to support themselves or other services to which they might need referring. We also need to understand how long the problem has been evident and what support arrangements have existed in the past that have been useful or not helpful. For some students, the problems will have been evident since starting primary school, with support provided or extra teaching undertaken and access arrangements in place for all examinations prior to university. For other students, the problems have only emerged since starting university and become evident as the pace of work increased, quantity of work increased and the move to independent study started. Some of the principles used in functional assessment might help by breaking the task down into parts that can be completed and parts that cannot.

The working definition of dyslexia produced by the British Psychological Society (BPS, 1999) is useful in that it summarized all the main research undertaken to look at models of causation of dyslexia and drew out the commonalities. It is not helpful, however, when we think about individuals and why reading, spelling and writing skills might not be as easy for them as for their peers. We need to return to the theories that explain how information is processed and what this means in neurological models and consequently in psychometric models such as the Cattell-Horn-Carroll (CHC) model of intelligence that underpins modern intelligence tests such as the Wechsler Adult Intelligence Scale. We also need to compare like with like; that is, we are comparing university students with university students and not with the wider population. We might also want to look at alternative models of interpreting such test results that allow us to understand aspects of verbal processing, visual processing, working memory, speed of processing, long-term memory, etc. In using these models to underpin our assessment, we can go beyond scores (which are subject to standard error or measurement and to cultural biases) by supplementing the assessment with clinical observations and hypothesis-testing questions. By this I mean that the theoretical CHC model guides our data collection which comprises three elements that can be triangulated to provide the interpretation: test score, observation, reflective interview questions. The test score is treated cautiously as a hypothesis related to the underlying cognitive processes that are implicit in completing the subtest (described in the technical manual and in underlying cognitive psychology research). To do this effectively, the student's performance on subtests needs to be scored immediately and during the ongoing assessment. Observations about how the student undertook the tasks are just as important. For instance, this can lead to process questions such as: How did they use space? Did they plan? Was the problem solved through trial and error? How was attention sustained or redirected? Were they resilient in the face of difficulty? If they did stop, and were prompted to continue with the task, did they re-engage and were they successful? A reflective interview question can be as simple as, 'In this artificial test that I gave you, you seemed to cope well with X and not so well with Y. I wonder whether there are examples of times when you experience this at home or in your studies?' Using all three sources of information together with information gleaned in the clinical interview provides a better interpretation than over-relying on the psychometric score alone (which could be wrong for lots of reasons). This kind of triangulated information can lead us to understand emotional components, for example giving up when things seem hard, even though they may be within the student's capabilities; performance anxiety; low self-esteem. It can also lead observations of cognitive components, for example attentional control, focus, perseverance, distractibility, co-ordination skills, planning and execution; tip-of-the-tongue phenomena, verbal dyspraxia, word-finding difficulties, etc. It may also be that during this process there is evidence of mental health difficulties and this can then lead to screening tools being used, for example for depression or anxiety. To do this properly obviously takes time and goes beyond the purely bureaucratic function of the assessment, but it can then lead into more precise description of strengths and difficulties and how these difficulties can be overcome by the student or through reasonable adjustments being made to teaching and assessment or for referral on to other services. It is worrying that test manufacturers are trying to encourage psychologists to move towards systems that employ electronic assessment and reduce the opportunity for clinical observation.

There is another group of students that may be referred by the university, those following professional courses where there is a question of fitness to practise and the board want to know if there are hidden disabilities (such as dyslexia or autism) that should have been taken into account and may explain the circumstances that have arisen and could in future be managed through reasonable adjustments in training or through the use of technology. The psychologist's job here is not to decide on fitness to practise but to make an assessment of the individual student that can then inform the fitness to practise board and assist in their decision-making. Usually, there is a lot of information available in advance of seeing the student and this will have been collected over time by the fitness to practise board. This is a useful source for generating hypotheses that can then be tested in the ways described above.

Having completed the assessment, there now needs to be an interpretative report written. The exact format depends on why the student was referred and the reasons for the assessment. If the report is to be used for seeking financial support in the form of Disabled Students' Allowances, then it has to follow a set format. The guidelines for this are available from the SpLD Assessment Standards Committee website. This format is also useful for students who are asking the university for reasonable adjustments to be made. A fitness to practise assessment is going to be more complex and the format will need to be developed to match this. The psychologist needs to state their qualification and experience on the report and that they are registered with the Health and Care Professions Council (HCPC) and that the report conforms to the appropriate format required. The psychologist also needs to make a clear statement of the difficulties and say whether these are disabilities as defined by the Equality Act 2010. Some students will have difficulties that are not so defined and will not be entitled to reasonable adjustments – while this point is frustrating and does not make logical sense, it is what it is and a different approach is needed, which is the focus of the third part of this chapter.

If the report is to be used to make reasonable adjustments, then it goes back to the disability office and team and the staff will co-ordinate with lectures and programme directors. Each university has its own system for doing this. In a large university there will be a disability co-ordinator in each faculty who links with disability co-ordinators in each school who send information to each programme director. The amount of information reaching lecturers is minimal because of data protection concerns and will usually state what the disability is and what reasonable adjustments are required. All of the information needed to reach that point and contained within the psychologist's report is retained by the disability office. This means that the psychologist has to take time explaining strategies that the student will need to use to the student themselves – good professional practice would expect this anyway. The report needs to speak to the student in terms of self-support and encourage independent learning and self-understanding, identify self-help skills and identify other sources of help or the need for referral to other services.

The organization: Helping universities become more inclusive

The system based around individual assessments attempts to treat students fairly, yet it is not equitable. Poorer students cannot afford the assessment; students from other countries may not be able to participate in the assessment fully or the results may be unclear due to cultural or language or normative issues; some students will have cognitive weaknesses but not meet the criteria for one of the recognized disabilities; not all students who do meet the criteria seek assessment. A better system is one that would see universities trying to become more inclusive and removing barriers to learning and participation. Ideologically, this leads to the possibility that there would be no need for individual assessments because support would be available as needed and potential barriers reduced; in short, lecturers would have greater reach in their teaching. For example, if most students who are assessed have as one of their suggested adjustments an additional 25 per cent time in examinations, either the time constraint or the method of assessment is a barrier to participation. Suppose there was no time limit or suppose there were no exams, then that barrier has been removed. This is possible. In designing a new BSc Psychology of Education programme we have taken the decision to have no written examinations in the programme. Instead, we have a range of assessments that include: producing a user's guide to the brain for teachers; essays; reflective fieldwork portfolio; research plan; lab report; critical review of a school-based intervention; mini research report; collaboratively produced poster; and a small-scale research project dissertation. We have also considered getting students to produce a ten-minute video guide for teachers on a topic as an alternative to an essay. We did experience some resistance to this move and have had to compromise by having online self-assessments built into the programme instead of formal exams that 'test that students have learnt some facts'. In some ways this fits in well with the Equality Act 2010 and its predecessor the Disability Discrimination Act, both of which expect employers and educators to anticipate what needs might require reasonable adjustments and to act to make these adjustments in advance of any assessments or disclosure of disability (Sanderson-Mann and McCandless, 2005).

In January 2017, DfE published a report to encourage universities to be more inclusive (DfE, 2017a). The report is driven by the Equality Act 2010 but goes further in promoting inclusive teaching by providing guidance to HEIs and starts by outlining the benefits to institutions. These fall under four areas: providing evidence to external scrutiny that steps are taken to address differential outcomes for students from different backgrounds; inclusive teaching means that adjustments are no longer necessary since barriers to participation are removed; cost savings by enabling students to thrive without the need for interventions when they do not; improving the reputation of the institution as a provider of quality teaching and learning. These arguments should be familiar to most EPs who have worked with schools pursuing inclusion kitemarks such as Dyslexia Friendly status, the Inclusion Chartermark, Inclusion Quality Mark, Autism Friendly status, etc. The principles are the same: audit what barriers exist to participation and then set about finding ways to remove them. As a result of this and pressures to reform Disabled Students' Allowances, many universities have developed their own inclusive or accessible teaching policy. Examples of how teaching can be made more accessible involve planning in advance such as: having lectures recorded or podcast automatically; allowing students to record lectures on their mobile phones; placing course materials and lecture slides on a virtual learning environment in advance of the lecture; having the library buy digital copies of books that can be downloaded for screen readers or for extended time periods; and having an organization PowerPoint template that reduces interference patterns and has an easily readable font. There may be resistance to such approaches and this needs to be managed within the institution, for example lecturers may want to defend their intellectual property rights; however, research and PowerPoints have been paid for by the employer. Lecturers may worry about unscrupulous use of video material by students; however, it is possible to allow lecturers to edit podcasts prior to release. It could be argued that individually tailored reasonable adjustments are better than globally rethinking how teaching and assessment are conducted because they take into account specific differences. However, it has been shown that when a raft of adjustments are presented to groups of disabled students they find that some are supportive of their learning and adopt these in favour of adjustments that are not helpful (Jansen *et al.*, 2017). This suggests that more general approaches can be anticipatory and supportive, although not all of the approaches will work for all of the students. Perhaps there is a role for EPs in thinking about how to audit and reduce potential barriers to learning (for instance see Moriña, 2017); how to overcome resistance from a few lecturers; and how to champion the creativity of the most inclusive lecturers and departments within the university.

Conclusions

There are different agendas at play that lead to some students being described as disabled while others with the same levels of ability and the same presenting difficulties are not categorized in this way. There are pressures for some students to seek individual assessment in order to have reasonable adjustments made so they can participate more fully in higher education while other students are unable or unwilling to seek the same assessments. Similarly, for Disabled Students' Allowances, these only apply to English students and only to difficulties that can be described as disabilities under the Equality Act 2010. Universities have been trying to widen participation and there is evidence that more students from poorer backgrounds are being successful in finding university places. Equally there are agendas at play that counteract the widening participation agenda. For students with disabilities, there has been an increase in accessing university places, but this can be accounted for by large increases in students with specific learning difficulties (SpLD) and mental health difficulties. There is a need for psychologists to work individually with these students so that reasonable adjustments can be made and students can apply for Disabled Students' Allowances if applicable. However, the reasons for asking for an assessment might be wider than this and psychologists should ascertain these reasons before deciding how best to assess. Assessment needs to go beyond a standard package of psychometrics to include clinical interview, clinical observation and task analysis. Inequity in the system is causing concern and this has reached the national agenda. There is clearly a role for EPs to develop in helping universities become more inclusive. This will inevitably involve working alongside other professionals and support structures within the university. The skills needed for this kind of work are the same skills that EPs have traditionally used in schools and local authorities. The time is right to do this and the wider political context is favourable. The challenge now is one of how to position EPs in that role.

References

Armstrong, D. and Squires, G. (2015) *Key Perspectives on Dyslexia: An essential text for educators*. London: Routledge.

BPS (British Psychological Society) (1999) *Dyslexia, Literacy and Psychological Assessment: Report by a working party of the Division of Educational and Child Psychology*. Leicester: British Psychological Society.

Carroll, J.M. and Iles, J.E. (2006) 'An assessment of anxiety levels in dyslexic students in higher education'. *British Journal of Educational Psychology*, 76 (3), 651–62.

Clance, P.R. and Imes, S.A. (1978) 'The imposter phenomenon in high achieving women: Dynamics and therapeutic intervention'. *Psychotherapy: Theory, Research and Practice*, 15 (3), 241–7.

DfE (Department for Education) (2016) *Widening Participation in Higher Education, England, 2013/14 Age Cohort.* London: Department for Education.

DfE (Department for Education) (2017a) *Inclusive Teaching and Learning in Higher Education as a Route to Excellence.* London: Department for Education.

DfE (Department for Education) (2017b) *Participation Rates in Higher Education: Academic years 2006/2007–2015/2016 (provisional).* London: Department for Education.

DfE (Department for Education) and DoH (Department of Health) (2013) *Implementing the 0 to 25 Special Needs System: Government advice for local authorities and health partners.* London: Department for Education and Department of Health.

DfE (Department for Education) and DoH (Department of Health) (2015) *Special Educational Needs and Disability Code of Practice: 0 to 25 years: Statutory guidance for organisations which work with and support children and young people who have special educational needs or disabilities.* London: Department for Education. Online. https://assets.publishing.service.gov.uk/government/uploads/system/uploads/attachment_data/file/398815/SEND_Code_of_Practice_January_2015.pdf (accessed 23 August 2018).

DfES (Department for Education and Skills) (2005) *Assessment of Dyslexia, Dyspraxia, Dyscalculia and Attention Deficit Disorder (ADD) in Higher Education: Final report of the SpLD Working Group.* London: Department for Education and Skills.

Dyson, A. and Squires, G. (eds) (2016) *Early School Leaving and Learners with Disabilities and/or Special Educational Needs: A review of the research evidence focusing on Europe.* Odense: European Agency for Special Needs and Inclusive Education.

Greenbank, P. (2006) 'Institutional admissions policies in higher education: A widening participation perspective'. *International Journal of Educational Management*, 20 (4), 249–60.

HESA (Higher Education Statistics Agency) (2014) HE student enrolments by personal characteristics 2012/13 to 2016/17. Online. www.hesa.ac.uk/data-and-analysis/sfr247/figure-4 (accessed 25 September 2018).

HESA (Higher Education Statistics Agency) (2017a) 'Yearly overviews: Table 14 – First year UK domiciled HE students by level of study, sex, mode of study and disability 2015/16'. Online. www.hesa.ac.uk/data-and-analysis/students/overviews?keyword=All&breakdown[0]=581&year=620&page=1 (accessed 25 August 2018).

HESA (Higher Education Statistics Agency) (2017b) *Widening Participation Summary: UK performance indicators 2015/16.* Cheltenham: Higher Education Statistics Agency.

Jansen, D., Petry, K., Ceulemans, E., van der Oord, S., Noens, I. and Baeyens, D. (2017) 'Functioning and participation problems of students with ADHD in higher education: Which reasonable accommodations are effective?'. *European Journal of Special Needs Education*, 32 (1), 35–53.

Moriña, A. (2017) 'Inclusive education in higher education: Challenges and opportunities'. *European Journal of Special Needs Education*, 32 (1), 3–17.

Rainford, J. (2017) 'Targeting of widening participation measures by elite institutions: Widening access or simply aiding recruitment?'. *Perspectives: Policy and Practice in Higher Education*, 21 (2–3), 45–50.

Reay, D., Crozier, G. and Clayton, J. (2010) '"Fitting in" or "standing out": Working-class students in UK higher education'. *British Educational Research Journal*, 36 (1), 107–24.

Riddell, S. and Weedon, E. (2006) 'What counts as a reasonable adjustment? Dyslexic students and the concept of fair assessment'. *International Studies in Sociology of Education*, 16 (1), 57–73.

Riddell, S., Weedon, E., Fuller, M., Healey, M., Hurst, A., Kelly, K. and Piggott, L. (2007) 'Managerialism and equalities: Tensions within widening access policy and practice for disabled students in UK universities'. *Higher Education*, 54 (4), 615–28.

Sanderson-Mann, J. and McCandless, F. (2005) 'Guidelines to the United Kingdom Disability Discrimination Act (DDA) 1995 and the Special Educational Needs and Disability Act (SENDA) 2001 with regard to nurse education and dyslexia'. *Nurse Education Today*, 25 (7), 542–9.

SpLD Assessment Standards Committee (2010) SpLD assessment tools. Online. www.sasc.org.uk/%28S%28ybkovhztjga40545wyg5y1zs%29%29/Default. aspx?id=2 (accessed 25 August 2018).

SpLD Test Evaluation Committee (2009) *Suitable Tests for the Assessment of Specific Learning Difficulties in Higher Education (Revised October 2009)*. London: Department for Education and Skills.

SpLD Test Evaluation Committee (2016) *Suitable Tests for the Assessment of Specific Learning Difficulties in Higher Education (Revised March 2016)*. London: Department for Education and Skills. Online. www.sasc.org.uk/ SASCDocuments/REVISED%20guidelines-March%202016%20a.pdf (accessed 25 August 2018).

Squires, G. (ed.) (2017) *Early School Leaving and Learners with Disabilities and/ or Special Educational Needs: Final summary report*. Odense: European Agency for Special Needs and Inclusive Education.

Squires, G. and Dyson, A. (eds) (2017) *Early School Leaving and Learners with Disabilities and/or Special Educational Needs: To what extent is research reflected in European Union policies?* Odense: European Agency for Special Needs and Inclusive Education.

UK Parliament (2010) 'Equality Act 2010'. Online. www.legislation.gov.uk/ ukpga/2010/15/contents (accessed 25 August 2018).

Young, A., Oram, R., Squires, G. and Sutherland, H. (2015a) *Identifying Effective Practice in the Provision of Education and Education Support Services for 16–19 Year Old Deaf Young People in Further Education in England*. London: National Deaf Children Society.

Young, A., Squires, G., Oram, R., Sutherland, H. and Hartley, R. (2015b) 'Further education as a post-secondary destination for deaf and hard of hearing young people: A review of the literature and analysis of official statistics in England'. *Deafness and Education International*, 17 (1), 49–59.

Chapter 4

Informed consent: Considerations and issues

Brian Davis

Introduction

This chapter explores the issue of informed consent as it relates to educational psychology practice; it considers matters as they apply to children and young people both under 16 and over 16, since there is a need for some consistency of approach as well as understanding some differences to be identified during transition.

Through reading this chapter the reader will gain an understanding of a number of factors that need be considered as they affect decision-making by educational psychology services and individual educational psychologists (EPs) on issues of required and appropriate informed consent related to different elements of practice and some of the information governance requirements to be considered. However, there is not scope in this chapter to address the latter comprehensively and a key issue for further consideration would be the relationship between informed consent for involvement and informed consent for data storage, sharing and use.

The fundamental questions relating to consent are what are the legal parameters and professional guidance considerations: on when consent is required, who is required to consent, what are they consenting to, what are the limits to that consent and the associated controls? In addition there is a need to consider the processes that services and individuals will need to adopt to help ensure educational psychology practice stays within appropriate guidelines at a time when data management law is changing and legislation and guidance affecting those working in health, social care and education is undergoing a period of apparent change and convergence.

What elements of work might this relate to?

The primary elements of practice for the consideration of consent requirements for EPs are the provision of consultation including problem solving, assessment (both individual and environmental/ecological), individual and joint single agency or multiple agency assessment, planning, provisions and interventions, the delivery of therapies, research including auditing and evaluation, training and professional development, critical incident type responses and operation from individual to strategic and community levels (Davis and Cahill, 2006; Farrell *et al.*, 2006; Beaver, 2011; MacKay, 2002, 2006)

This of course represents a combination of direct applied psychology-based work with people we might call 'clients' and also a great range of activity, which may affect 'clients' indirectly and be carried out without face-to-face contact.

Who is the client?

Because of the unique contractual and engagement arrangements for EPs working with almost every school, college, local authority children's and adults' services and many multi-agency teams, it could be said that the educational experience of almost every child and young person in the country is affected by the educational psychology profession, its service delivery and its research and recommendations; as is almost every teacher or person who works with children and young people, and every parent or carer.

A key related question is who is the client at any time and how does this affect the boundaries and processes for informed consent. It is helpful that the British Psychological Society (BPS) indicates that the word 'client' is used for and refers to any person or persons with whom a psychologist interacts on a professional basis. For example, the client may be a couple, a family group, an educational institution, a community organization or group, a private or public organization including a court, or an individual (sometimes referred to as, for example, athlete, child/young person, patient, prisoner, coachee, service user, stakeholder, leader, or student) who is in receipt of the services of the psychologist (BPS, 2017a).

The Practice Guidelines (BPS, 2017a), in considering the issue of working with multiple clients, note that psychologists will sometimes be in situations where their client will not be one clear individual or group; for example, a psychologist may be employed by an organization to provide assessment or psychological support for employees. Psychologists need to consider and be mindful of the demands that this might place on their ethical practice and how this might lead to conflicts of interest (particularly when services are traded or part traded to service users). A client hierarchy is suggested as follows:

- Primary client: the person or persons with whom the psychologist is interacting directly: the recipient of a psychological service.
- Commissioning stakeholders: the organization or overall commissioning body that has sought the psychologist.
- Others affected by the primary client's actions: the customers of the organization or service, or the personal acquaintances, friends and family of the primary client. In some circumstances this will be the general public or larger groups interested in the outcomes of the intervention. (BPS, 2017a)

The psychologist's role is described to be mainly to the primary client and then the commissioning stakeholder. It is noted that it is paramount that issues around boundaries and sharing of information are made explicit and addressed appropriately through a clear contracting agreement. It would appear arguable, however, that EPs might frequently be operating at the tertiary or third (other) level. Examples might be in the development of social language groups, in promoting peer support, or in developing inclusive policies.

The guidance goes on to note that within each of the levels of the hierarchy, varying allegiances to associates (friends, family, acquaintances, colleagues) will need to be attended to, as will consideration of the impact of professional activity on the reputation of the profession and all those concerned. The nature of the relationship (hired or supplied) might be important information to share.

All of the aforementioned elements (not an exhaustive list) of applied psychological skills and knowledge may occur in direct contact with a young person or persons and in most cases their family, or be carried out indirectly, for example through contact with those responsible for planning and delivery of efficient education, care and health provision and possibly, if rarely, without meeting the children and young people concerned.

In the former case of direct contact, this is usually in effect working from a collaborative basis, with young people and the people whom they live with and who care for them, work with them and for their benefit, and plan and provide resources for them. This might be focused on achieving improved outcomes in these domains for individual young people and their families. However, in the latter case the focus might be on teachers or other providers of services, groups of young people provided for in a range of settings or organizations, or populations, both local and national.

Educational psychologists then will ply their trade at individual, group, organizational, systems and strategic levels; this will often then raise the question 'who is/are the clients at any particular time?' There is just as legitimate a role in working with school and college staff on the issues that affect the quality of their service delivery, for example developing inclusion and policy, maintaining accessibility and improving educational outcomes and well-being of staff and pupils, as there is in the delivery of direct individual-level work to young people.

There are of course further levels to this, for example a particular school head teacher or other commissioner might prefer EPs working with them on the promotion of emotional well-being and positive mental health, or learning and teaching to achieve impact, rather than solely maintaining a focus on individual young people, which might limit beneficial impact on the school population.

It should also be remembered that many EPs hold positions of influence through specialist lead roles, for example for age groups or particular special or additional needs, and can contribute to the development of strategy, joint working protocols and new provision through the application of psychological knowledge including that gained through research.

Through collaborative multi-agency working, for example through implementation science (Kelly *et al.*, 2017) and leading-edge groups (which can include the voluntary sector and parents), professionals including EPs can bring an evidence base to universal provision and the meeting of special educational or additional need. The author has experience of facilitating leading-edge groups through EP service deployment, for example in the areas of speech and language and autism. By bringing key partners together in this way, up-to-date research and outcomes can be reviewed and improvements made that have the support of many key stakeholders.

With regard to supporting schools, colleges and local authorities to be learning and developing organizations, EPs can draw on their knowledge of local needs and how they can be met. This might include analysis of individual case studies, the inclusion of children, young people and parents sharing their stories, analysis of aggregated data on population outcomes and evaluations of services that are commissioned, and assisting in the development of new provision.

A number of EPs occupy strategic management positions in local authorities and schools and colleges, such as principal educational psychologists, heads of service, deputies and directors of services for children and adults. These roles, as well as sometimes the senior and main grade roles, often bring them into the information-sharing loops for decision-making, planning and provision for young people in need, with special educational needs (including those who are disabled), those who are at risk and require safeguarding and protection, and those offending, posing a risk to others or to themselves.

There may be individuals or groups for whom there is conflict or indecision, or major resourcing requirements related to decisions on how to progress. This can bring ethical and other professional considerations related to the information sharing, the professional's behaviour 'in role' or multiple roles and the expectations. Are there times when a psychologist is not acting as a psychologist? One might maintain an expectation that when working in most of the situations (i.e. professionally) described in this chapter, the normal standards of a practitioner psychologist would generally apply. It is incumbent on the psychologist to make clear their professional background and the role in which professional skills are being applied.

What is the other primary legislation and guidance affecting informed consent and associated information management?

This is a difficult question to answer; undoubtedly there are primary areas of legislation that shape the guidance that can be made available to professionals on this matter. However, there remains a question of how far one can cast the net in trawling the legislation for relevance. A very broad range of legislation pertaining to adults and children might affect to some extent the areas of investigation here.

In addition to the Data Protection Act (UK Parliament, 1998), in 2018 superseded by the General Data Protection Regulation (EU) (Information Commissioner's Office (ICO), 2018) concerning information management, some of the legislation affecting this area would include: the Equality Act (2010); Freedom of Information Act (2000); Health and Safety at Work Act (1974); Mental Capacity Act (2005); Mental Health Act 1983 (amended 2007); Children and Families Act (2014); in relation to whistle-blowing, The Public Interest Disclosure (Prescribed Persons) (Amendment) Order (2018); Children Act (1989); Children Act (2004); Children and Social Work Act (2017); Safeguarding Vulnerable Groups Act (2006); Female Genital Mutilation Act (2003); Working Together to Safeguard Children (DfE 2015; note no specific adult equivalent but a combination of Act, Code of Practice and guidance expectations); Counter-Terrorism and Security Act 2015, Section 26; and the Health and Social Care Act (2008). This list is not exhaustive!

Educational psychologists are required to know the relevant law. The BPS (2017b) expected outcomes for an EP completing training include the ability to:

- demonstrate professional and ethical practice that adheres to the British Psychological Society's Code of Ethics and Conduct and the Health and Care Professions Council (HCPC) Standards of Conduct, Ethics and Performance
- apply knowledge of, and demonstrate the ability to operate effectively within, the legal, national and local frameworks for educational psychology practice
- synthesize, use and share assessment information to negotiate and develop action plans to address learning, social, physical and mental health outcomes for children and young adults with diverse abilities and needs
- demonstrate knowledge of the legislative context for service delivery
- identify and understand policies, structures and accountability systems in a range of educational settings (e.g. early years, school, further education, youth justice) to ensure effective service delivery for all children.

The HCPC standards of proficiency (SOPS), against which the ability to practise is judged, demand that psychologists be able to know about and practise within the legal and ethical boundaries of the profession (HCPC, 2015).

A significant recent development for EPs is the publication by the BPS of the aforementioned Practice Guidelines (BPS, 2017a, third edition replacing the second edition of 2009). Legislation, practice and technology are acknowledged to have moved on since 2009 and there is an attempt to address these changes in the new guidance. This is a 'must read' for practitioner psychologists if they are to ensure their practice remains secure.

This edition of the guidelines was produced through the BPS's Professional Practice Board by a working group of almost 30 members, drawn from the range of member networks across the society whose members are engaged in professional practice, as well as representatives from relevant expert reference groups of the society, in particular areas of practice. There is consideration of the requirements of the devolved nations, Scotland and Northern Ireland.

It is a large and very encompassing document and it is doubtful it has achieved full impact yet. The first part of the guidance (Sections 1–3) sets out considerations for psychologists on different contexts of practice. The second part of the guidance (Sections 4–8) sets out guidance for psychologists on how to manage work with clients. It is still recognized that in addition to the extensive guidance, psychologists may require more detailed advice for some particular roles and responsibilities or for particular situations in which they work and these might be local in nature.

The Society expects that the guidelines will be used to form a basis for consideration, with the principles being taken into account in the process of decision-making, together with the needs of others and the special circumstances. It is stated that no guidance can replace the need for psychologists to use their own professional judgement: 'Effective practice means exercising this professional judgement in a defensible way that does not put clients or the public at risk, or undermine, or call into question the reputation of the profession as a whole' (BPS 2017a: 3).

It is hoped that this chapter can assist psychologists in making those judgements.

Given the recency, significance and sheer extent of the new BPS Practice Guidelines, content relating to consent is drawn on heavily in this chapter. Psychologists working with the Practice Guidelines are advised they should do so in conjunction with the BPS Code of Ethics and Conduct (BPS, 2018) and the BPS Code of Human Research Ethics (BPS, 2014), as necessary. There is not the scope to consider this other documentation fully in this chapter. However, it is important to remember that it may be extremely helpful and impactful in a strategic way to ask clients to consent to involvement, required information sharing and the use of data for evaluation and for effective education, health and care planning, for example in planning requiring upcoming provision.

The BPS Practice Guidelines include the clinical psychology perspective, as well as the educational psychology perspective and those of other areas of psychology; this means that EPs will now need to review their position on a number of issues regarding consent and information governance, as they may have previously related more to the health sector. The guidelines appear to blur the picture with regard to the education and health professional divide.

It would seem advantageous to consider the legislation, but primarily the legislation-informed professional guidance (as this is a much easier starting position); however, it should also be borne in mind that health services and local authority children's and adults' services have legal teams for a reason and drawing on their guidance can be invaluable in determining a professional course of action. Inevitably sensible drafting of policy, supporting documentation and practice guidelines locally will ensure preventative good practice and relatively testable clarity and reduce challenge and vulnerability to challenge for services and individual psychologists. This is a task educational psychology services should not shy away from.

Preparing to get it right for a new mental health agenda

A clinical psychology perspective in particular is also contained within another interesting development: the publication of 'What good looks like in psychological services for schools and colleges: Primary prevention, early intervention and mental health provision' (Faulconbridge *et al.*, 2017; referred to hereafter as WGLL). This reviews the evidence and discusses the practical ways in which psychological well-being can be addressed in school settings, as well as the implications for commissioning and delivery of provision.

Although it appears the content may have been put together as early as 2015, this publication precedes the Green Paper *Transforming Children and Young People's Mental Health Provision* (DoH and DfE, 2017) by just a few months, and clearly informs its content. It follows the *Future in Mind* (DoH, 2015a) document developed by the Children and Young People's Mental Health and Well-being Taskforce, which made recommendations for the future development of children's mental health services in the NHS that were later incorporated into the Five Year Forward View for Mental Health. The government's response outlined a £1.4 billion investment in child mental health over the 2017–20 period, including:

- making mental health first-aid training available to all secondary schools, with the aim of having trained at least one teacher in every secondary school by 2019
- evaluating different approaches that schools can use for mental health promotion and prevention
- launching a pilot programme on peer support for young people in schools and online
- possible Care Quality Commission and Ofsted joint inspections on children's mental health and well-being.

In addition £20 million is being provided to the 'Time to Change' anti-stigma programme, probably largely based in schools, improving the attitudes of young people towards mental health and reaching 1.75 million young people and 1.5 million parents each year by 2020. There will also be reporting on the prevalence of mental health conditions in children and young people during 2018.

WGLL shares and informs some ambitions within the Green Paper in terms of multi-agency mental health teams in schools. Clearly psychologists working in this way would now need to be following the BPS Practice Guidelines (BPS, 2017a).

WGLL contains some recommendations EPs would find interesting.

Recommendation 16:

While enhanced training for teachers is recommended, commissioners, service providers and employers should recognize it is essential that it is not seen as a stand-alone solution. Effective training requires adequate follow-up in terms of ongoing access to consultation, support and supervision from more highly trained and experienced staff. (WGLL: 3)

Recommendation 17:

The development of psychologically healthy schools that support the well-being of staff and students should be a priority for all including commissioners, service providers and employers. Use of community psychology models and methods would be a positive way to approach this jointly with staff, students, families and local communities. (Ibid.)

The WGLL report indicates that every school or college should now adopt a whole-school approach to promoting emotional health and well-being (from Lavis and Robson, 2015).

The WGLL report recommends that schools be expected to work actively with parents and carers, to embed clear systems for identifying mental health needs and develop a cycle of support for vulnerable pupils using an assessment, plan, do, review process. This process would be consistent with that described in the *Special Educational Needs and Disability Code of Practice: 0 to 25 years* (DfE and DoH, 2015). The WGLL report indicates that pupils will be identified in different ways: by their presentation in school, through parental concerns, by the presence of known risk factors, through mental health screens and via multi-agency discussions, for example in Team Around the School meetings.

The WGLL review is written by clinical psychologists and this perspective rather than an educational psychology perspective is evident in the writing. The review also implies full involvement of children and families (implying informed consent) when there is direct work, but little is said about informed consent and involvement in relation to the extensive indirect work and group face-to-face work, with a range of clients, that might be carried out.

The above information is included as clearly there could be greater presence of psychologists in schools and colleges of a number of practice persuasions, probably needing to work together rather than in 'silos' or antagonistically. None of those groups would want to be disadvantaged in being able to provide preventative, consultative and development work and direct work in education and mental health because information on services, consent pathways and data management related to both aspects are not clear.

In working for improved outcomes for children and young people both under 16 and over 16, EPs are constantly in a position of determining what activities they intend to carry out, whether they have provided the necessary information for consent, need specific consent and of what type, don't need consent or don't have a choice and what the limitations and boundaries are.

A recent informal review by the author, of educational psychology service informed consent arrangements/forms for EP involvement, both pre- and post-16, indicates a wariness, a sense of not being well informed and a need for review at service, school and local authority levels. Consent forms would appear to be largely lacking in information about what was being consented to, both in activity and in information management. Some examples indicated that there would be a discussion with an EP prior to referral; some indicated that there was confidentiality but others that there were circumstances when information would be shared or that the parent was agreeing for information to be shared. None of the forms seen at the time indicated a place for a child or young person to consent. Specific forms for young people aged 16 plus appeared largely absent. These observations are not based on formal research, simply an opportunity to view a few examples.

It can be seen from the above that there is a need to identify, determine and further debate, and respond by developing the required consenting and consensual basis and platform to maximize the potential contribution of educational psychology practice from supporting professionals at early stages of prevention and concern to intense direct work; this, so practice can operate at multiple levels in meeting the needs of all young people and particularly the vulnerable, including those in need, those requiring protection, those requiring special educational and other provision and not being erroneously constrained or made vulnerable to challenge through poor joint planning for consent issues.

It is not a primary intention of this chapter to explore how large local authorities provide information about personnel and overall systems involved in, for example, the arrangements for the statutory assessment of special educational needs of young people and their provision, or other large systems such as multi-agency public protection arrangements (Ministry of Justice, National Offender Management Service and HM Prison Service, 2012 updated 2017) or Early Help (information at www.gov.uk/government/publications/early-help-whose-responsibility). However, there are significant issues for EPs to address about themselves in these and other local authority systems.

Suffice it to say that local authorities should take care to have robust arrangements to inform all parties appropriately about what the processes are, who is involved and their professional backgrounds, and how information is managed and shared. Parents and young people would need to provide initial and ongoing consent for the whole process or particular aspects of it.

It is hoped, however, to help ensure service leads and EPs themselves are aware of the issues they need to take into account, particularly when some of the reliance for the mechanisms for informed consent might lie jointly with other parties. This might include reviewing the information the local authority and schools are providing in relation to the processes and personnel involved and the information/data-related issues that affect them.

It is also an intention to bring some helpful observation on consent issues as they affect direct work and there is a further intention to clarify consent issues as they might apply to the provision of consultation and indirect work at the levels identified above once those that relate to direct work are first explored.

The right to make decisions and be involved in decision-making

The *Special Educational Needs and Disability Code of Practice* (DfE and DoH, 2015), referred to hereafter as 'SEND COP', indicates that children and young people with special educational needs and/or disabilities (SEND) should be involved in decisions that affect them. It is of course desirable that a child or young person of any age would be agreeing to work with an EP, through informed consent. This would also be true of other professionals asked to work with psychologists, especially those in the primary client position.

The BPS Practice Guidelines (2017a) state 'Psychologists should always ensure that they have sought and received the consent of those they work with, given of their own free will, without undue influence' (Section 6, p. 48). It further states that the concept of informed consent relates to the client's right to choose whether to receive psychological services, and to make this choice on the basis of the best information available presented in the most appropriate way. The principles apply whether the psychologist works in the public, private or voluntary sector or in independent practice. It should be remembered that the client might be a teacher in a school or other professional, as well as a child or young person.

Following the guidelines psychologists should obtain the informed consent of the client in an appropriate manner prior to undertaking any assessment, intervention or research activities. It is stated that 'In all circumstances, common sense and ethical practice should apply when considering the approach to gaining informed consent from those with whom the psychologist is working' (ibid.).

Ethical matters can often present a dilemma but the BPS does provide specific guidance on this. However, the practice guidance raises the question of 'what is common sense?' in the common vernacular, but also and in parallel is the question 'what is reasonable, given the law?' This is a more pertinent legal question should practice become legally challenged. In this respect the guidance still appears to miss the mark in some way.

The Mental Capacity Act 2005 and associated Mental Capacity Act Code of Practice (Department for Constitutional Affairs, 2007) and the Children and Families Act 2014 and the SEND COP (DfE and DoH, 2015) indicate that a young person will make their own decisions with regard to health issues from their 16th birthday. The SEND COP indicates that a young person will make their own decisions with regard to education from the end of the academic year during which they become 16. The Children Act 1989 indicates that young people can make their own decisions relating to care from the age of 17. Section 6 of the BPS Practice Guidelines (2017a) refers, in the main, to consent with adults with capacity.

Further information on informed consent with discrete communities where further consideration may be needed is available in Sections 6.1 to 6.4 of the BPS Practice Guidelines (2017a).

Mental capacity assessments that may apply to young people 16 and over are dealt with fully in Chapter 5.

Parental responsibility and limitations to confidentiality

BPS Practice Guidelines (2017a, Section 7.5, Confidentiality with children and young people) indicate that when beginning direct work with a child or young person, the psychologist should discuss and agree who will have access to the information arising from the work, with direct reference to principles of 'Gillick competence' for young people under 16.

In undertaking this discussion it is helpful to acknowledge that there may be those adults (e.g. parents/carers, other relevant professionals such as teachers, social workers, counsellors) who may have a supportive interest in the work and may wish to have appropriate access to information, but the wishes of a Gillick-competent young person should take precedence unless there are safeguarding concerns.

Parents or those with legal responsibility should be made aware of this agreement if appropriate, although a young person deemed to be Gillick competent is able to agree to work with a psychologist independently. Those with parental responsibility do not have an automatic right of access to the psychologist's records by making a subject access request under data protection legislation.

The nature and purposes of any work will vary and this will determine how and with whom information will be shared; however, the child or young person should always be made aware of who will have access to what and for what purpose, and due consideration should be given to the wishes of a Gillick-competent young person about who can have access to information about any involvement with a psychologist.

The child or young person should be fully aware of the content of any shared information, including, as appropriate, copies of the documents. Whatever is agreed about information sharing, including work where information is confidential, the psychologist must ensure the child or young person knows and understands that if there is a risk of harm the psychologist must follow safeguarding procedures and that there would be other legal limits to confidentiality.

Under the terms of the Children Act 2004, a local authority can secure parental responsibility as can a guardian. Although not explored here, some parents will lose parental responsibility under certain circumstances. In a small minority of cases some parents may not have any rights to information.

Young people under 16 are not covered by the Mental Capacity Act. The understanding would be that a young person under 16 *lacks* competence unless proved otherwise. The level for this is set by the Gillick case (1985; see NSPCC, 2018) as the child having 'sufficient understanding and intelligence to enable him or her to understand fully what is proposed'. In determining this, the key questions of the Mental Health Act Code of Practice (DoH, 2015b) may be helpful:

- Does the child understand the information that is relevant to the decision that needs to be made?
- Can the child hold the information in their mind long enough so that they can use it to make decisions?
- Is the child able to weigh up that information and use it to arrive at a decision?
- Is the child able to communicate their decision (by talking, using sign language or any other means)?

Even an adult with parental responsibility could not agree to medical treatment if their Gillick-competent child refused it. Such a case would be likely to be referred to the courts.

With reference to the above it is clear that many young people under 16 with whom EPs work should be treated as if they are Gillick competent when it comes to issues of consent. This being the case their informed consent for involvement should be obtained and the limits of their control explained to them. Parental responsibilities and rights to information must be carefully checked to avoid challenges further down the line. After the age of 16 in most cases the young person would be deemed competent to consent unless formally assessed otherwise (see Chapter 5 on mental capacity assessment). It would seem logical that good practice prior to age 16 would lead to good practice with clients post-16.

Further confidentiality limitations and the potential involvement of others

As previously stated, psychologists have an obligation to ensure that prospective clients are informed of the extent and limitations of confidentiality with respect to anticipated services, the purposes of any assessment, the nature of the procedures to be employed or the intended uses of any product such as notes or recordings, before the assessment or intervention starts (BPS Practice Guidelines, 2017a).

In general the guidance steers psychologists towards agreeing with clients the nature of any assessment or intervention, who would be informed of this and any outcomes or responses or further details that they might wish to share. In some cases the sharing of information may appear essential, e.g. in relation to the requirements of a court or in relation to child protection or the protection of vulnerable adults. There may be circumstances where information must be shared as part of the counter-terrorism legislation and in both protection and counter-terrorism and other criminal issues there may be an obligation to pass information on without 'tipping off'. It is generally desirable, however, that where appropriate the clients have access themselves to the information that is shared.

If it is deemed necessary to move from individual contact to include others, this should also be done where possible with the client's prior consent (BPS, 2017a). This would imply that the client has been informed of all the parties who might have a part to play in an assessment or information-gathering process or be considered having a 'need to know', for example, in the interests of making appropriate provision. Further information is available in BPS, 2017a Section 7: Managing data and confidentiality.

The BPS Practice Guidelines (2017a) note that a psychologist may be asked to provide consultancy or advice to colleagues about an identified client without that person's knowledge or when the client has indicated that they do not want to have direct contact with the psychologist. In these circumstances the psychologist will need to consider their potential involvement and the need for consent. However, there is no further clarification on this point in the guidance.

This relates to a key point about consultative services that will be picked up later in relation to EPs working at different organizational levels and what young people and parents might know about it. For example, if a teacher were having both an emotional difficulty and a skills issue in delivering on a plan for a young person, might they expect a consultation where information about the content is not shared with a young person? This would be an area for skilled navigation, based on a sound and established footing or contractual agreement to ensure appropriate uptake of a required service.

It would generally be regarded as appropriate for one professional psychologist to consult with another psychologist involved with a client. It would seem appropriate to draw on reports that they have provided. A psychologist who draws upon the work of other professionals in preparing a report should seek their consent where possible and if not already in disclosed records, to include that material and acknowledge its source in the report (BPS, 2017a).

This would seem straightforward in the event that the psychologist and the client are in agreement with the report. It might be less straightforward if either the psychologist or the client disagree with the content or findings identified in the report. If the duty of candour applies to EPs as HCPC-registered health and social care professionals then one might expect a frankness in professional reports to reflect the duty, including reporting on differences of opinion (with the client included) and negative as well as positive outcomes of involvement.

If a report is requested that draws upon previous or concurrent investigations of a client in other contexts, for example NHS records in the preparation of a report for the court, the client's consent or relevant authority's consent for that information to be used should be sought. If psychologists wish to use reports on clients that have been compiled by other professionals, they should do so only with the consent of those professionals and use the reports only in the context for which the report was specifically provided (BPS, 2017a).

Provision of information to inform consent

An important precursor to the obtaining of informed consent is the provision of information about what the service user or client is consenting to.

It is more than just good practice to provide potential clients and service users with clear and full information, in a format accessible to them and about what exactly the person is consenting to. Most educational psychology services now would probably have service information designed for young people and parents related to direct contact activity. Some will have information about other activity they carry out but this might not have progressed to supporting informed consent for consultancy-level work not involving direct contact with children and young people.

The BPS Practice Guidelines (2017a) are particularly clear about this in relation to some aspects of EPs' practice, in what would appear to be largely a clinical model for direct work in the application of psychology to particular aspects of applied practice, namely, assessment, intervention and treatment.

Information would include:

- what the psychological activity involves, as far as this is consistent with the model of interaction, for example there will be limits in the use of some non-directive therapies and psychometric assessments
- the benefit of the activity, either directly to the client in the case of assessment or intervention, or indirectly in the case of systemic intervention, or to potential theoretical advances or service improvement
- any alternative assessment or treatment options and their known availability
- foreseeable risks and how minor or serious they may be, for example the potential to feel worse at stages during therapeutic interventions
- what might be the benefits and potential costs and risks to them of engaging or not engaging in the proposed psychological activity; and

- the client's right to withdraw their consent from assessment, treatment or intervention at any stage, along with information about any likely consequences of such withdrawal (BPS, 2017a).

The above of course covers some of the case-specific involvement of what an EP might do and some of the allied activity that might emanate from involvement with a young person or their family.

Every psychologist should consider how they can (with children and young people):

- provide an accessible explanation to the child or young person about their work as a psychologist
- offer a clear reason for their possible involvement
- provide an opportunity for the child or young person to talk about what working with the psychologist might involve
- discuss and agree how information is recorded and possibly shared with others with an awareness that young people who are Gillick competent can consent to information not being shared with parents
- discuss how the child or young person will be kept safe
- ensure that the child or young person has understood the psychologist's role and has given their informed consent
- ensure the child or young person understands they can withdraw their consent at any point
- ensure their practice acknowledges and respects the culture, community and context of the child or young person (BPS, 2017a).

Express specific consent must be sought in advance in particular for the use of video, audio recording or one-way screens, with a clear explanation of the purpose of these. Further information is available in BPS Practice Guidelines (2017a, Section 7.1: Information governance). This also of course applies to EPs in training.

A young person or a parent may express a desire to have someone with them during an assessment. This is barely dealt with in the guidelines. Many educational psychology services indicate to parents that they could be present during such professional activity. However, there may be occasions when the professional might think this may preclude effective dialogue and it would make sense to have pre-agreed rationales for when this might be suitable and applicable.

Brian Davis

Task- and time-limited consent

There is an indication in the BPS Practice Guidelines (2017a) that consent might be given specific to a particular task, which might also be specific to a purpose and even a specific time (that might lapse and need to be reviewed). This could question the validity of consent given for the general and ongoing involvement of a professional psychologist or service with imprecise boundaries to services being provided and time limits (depending on the initial agreement). Consideration must be given to suggesting time spans for involvement.

> Obtaining informed consent involves a process which is dynamic and is relevant to the specific assessment, intervention or decision being made at that time. (BPS, 2017a: 48)

> When there are substantive changes in the intervention or when the psychologist has reason to consider the client may no longer consent, consent should be reviewed. Psychologists should ensure that their clients are enabled to play an active role in this process. Clients should be encouraged to ask questions whenever they are in doubt. (BPS, 2017a: 48)

Influencing initial and ongoing consent

Psychologists need to be aware of the role they play in promoting and maintaining consent and motivations for this that might include evoking feelings of compliance and conflict avoidance, need or desire in a client or a psychologist's personal need to feel required, valued or to be gainfully employed (BPS, 2017a). This would link with the notion of the application of undue influence or coercion.

> Psychologists should be aware that a client's desire for help, and the immediate impact of the psychologist's supportive listening, may affect the client's ability to make informed choices about the help they wish to receive. They should also be aware that their own desires to help a client may bias their presentation of information, such as the probability of successful outcomes. (BPS, 2017a: 48)

Power imbalances need to be considered. The BPS Practice Guidelines indicate:

> Psychologists should be aware of the complexities of obtaining informed consent to treatment due to the perceived power, status and authority of the professional psychologist. It may not be clear if the consent given is freely given by the client or, for example, is part of a pattern of compliance towards authority figures. (BPS, 2017a: 48)

Particular care would be required if the young person is detained or the work is related to their employment.

Equally, it is described that a client may say that they understand the explanation given by the psychologist, and accept a plan for intervention, in order to avoid the discomfort of being seen not to understand the psychologist's complex language and ideas.

The guidance promotes ongoing dialogue between client and psychologist, as part of the process of joint decision-making, stating that at any point the client should feel free to ask questions about the impact of the treatment and withdraw consent to continue. Psychologists are advised that they should attempt to intervene against the express wish of a client only after careful consideration and in line with relevant legislation, policies and professional practice (BPS, 2017a).

Informed consent for activities such as consultancy, which do not involve direct assessment, intervention and treatment of children and young people

This is an area where one might consider the legislation and guidance to be seen wanting. This might bring us into the area of the application of 'common sense' (BPS, 2017a) and local organizational procedures.

Educational psychologists play an enormous role in the development of early years, school, college and other institutions' policy and procedures, staff continuing professional development and development of competency and skills, curriculum development and developing teaching and behaviour management skills. They play a large part in providing consultancy to help meet the needs of individuals, managers and groups of staff, parents, and children and young people.

For example, in helping a teacher to develop classroom management skills, or become aware of children and young people who can be helped in their classroom and how to do it, a school head teacher might ask an EP to work with that teacher. This is a legitimate role that would bring the EP as part of a team in the school into the classroom. It might mean also that following such a classroom visit a teacher might want to discuss the EP's observation, the teacher's approach to a group of young people or a young person about whom they have a concern.

This appears to have become an area of concern for some educational psychology services in terms of informed consent and information management; to be fair the BPS professional practice guidance does not appear to deal with the related issues, although it does allow for a flexible view on who is the client. This provides a potential and undesirable barrier to effective consultative support from EPs to schools and colleges.

If we first approach the issue of information available to young people and parents, it becomes apparent that there are many opportunities for this working relationship to be explained so that all understand it.

These include the publication of the local offer (facilitated by the Children and Families Act 2014) by the local authority. This is a means by which all parents can access information about what happens in schools and colleges about how EPs are legitimately involved in helping organizations to deliver improved services and what activities in schools or colleges this might involve.

In addition, there is the school comparison tool and the SEN Information Report (information at www.gov.uk/school-performance-tables). From September 2016, the school comparison tool would include the complaints procedure, the behaviour policy, the Pupil Premium report, Dashboard figures for governors regarding vulnerable children, and a statement about values and ethos.

The SEN Information Report has been a requirement on schools detailed in the SEND COP (DfE and DoH, 2015) that should be updated annually. The SEN Information Report should contain everything Ofsted, any other agency, parent, student or professional could want to know in terms of SEND identification, provision and support. It can also act as a guide through SEND provision for all members of staff, whatever their career profile.

It must include:

- Details on where the local authority's local offer is published (each one drawn on by the school) and links to the area local offer(s) – working with more than one local authority requires links to all of the local offers for those authorities.
- In relation to mainstream schools and maintained nursery schools, the name and contact details of the special educational needs co-ordinator (SENCo). Best practice would be to also include the same details for

your head teacher and your SEND governor, as well as how parents can make a complaint or raise a concern.

- Information about the expertise and training of staff in relation to children and young people with SEND and about how specialist expertise will be secured.
- How provision is made for pupils with SEND, whether or not they have Education, Health and Care Plans (EHCPs).
- What interventions have been implemented and their impact.
- The additional learning opportunities for pupils with SEND.
- Procedures, in a mainstream school or nursery, for the identification and assessment of pupils with SEND.
- The approach to teaching pupils who have SEND.
- How the curriculum and the learning environment are adapted for those who have SEND.
- How the school enables pupils with SEND to engage in the activities of the school (including physical activities) together with children who do not have SEND.
- Details of the support that is available for improving the social, emotional and mental health and development of pupils with SEND.
- How students and their parents are involved in decision-making.
- How effectiveness of provision is evaluated, including securing feedback and the views of pupils and their parents.
- The arrangements for consulting parents of children with SEND about, and involving such parents in, the education of their child.
- The arrangements for consulting young people with SEND about, and involving them in, their education.
- How the governing body involves other bodies, including health and social services bodies, local authority support services and voluntary organizations, in meeting the needs of pupils with SEND and in supporting the families of such pupils.
- The contact details of support services for the parents of pupils with SEND, including those for arrangements made in accordance with Section 32.

Together the local offer, the school comparison report and the SEN Information Report, as well as educational psychology service websites and documentation, provide ample opportunity for schools, colleges and educational psychology services to accurately provide the required information on how EPs form part of the staff or multi-agency team of the provision and the activities they carry out to support the organization.

Schools and colleges could easily ensure parents and young people confirm that they have seen these descriptions and accept them through, for example, the signing of a home–school agreement (even if these are no longer compulsory). However, it seems schools will need to have a sign-up arrangement for provision and student and parent data management with the advent of new data protection arrangements. Of course all staff in the school would need to sign up in some way to working with psychologists wherever required and this may not currently routinely happen.

Under the arrangements for mental health, well-being and SEND, it needs to be acknowledged that a young person who is competent can self-refer to services on the basis of information that is provided about what is available to them on or off site.

In mental health, the government is committed to shared decision-making and the principle 'no decision about me without me'. This applies from work with an individual client through to changes in government policy relevant to the services provided by psychologists. Psychologists should develop services, policies and guidelines in collaboration with the people who use their services or have lived experience. For schools and colleges this could involve policy and practice development groups that involve parents and young people.

Summary

It has been demonstrated that there have been significant legislation and guidance changes in recent years related to informed consent for professional involvement and information management, along with increased work with young people past the age of 16; this is now an important and key time for EPs working in services or independently to review their arrangements to ensure practice remains sound and within acceptable legal and guidance boundaries.

It is important that this review includes consideration of the information provided to service users on the full range of EPs' activity and encompasses the principle of informed consent for all such activity, by the key service users.

If service delivery is not to be restricted and limited to individual assessment and intervention work then a particular area of focus should be on the provision of preventative consultative activity, based on sound consent and governance arrangements. This is now even more important with the proposed strategic changes in the provision of mental health promotion and support services, if educational psychology services are to play a key role in this area.

References

Beaver, R. (2011) *Educational Psychology Casework: A practice guide.* 2nd ed. London: Jessica Kingsley Publishers.

BPS (British Psychological Society) (2014) *BPS Code of Human Research Ethics.* 2nd ed. Leicester: British Psychological Society. Online. www.bps.org.uk/ news-and-policy/bps-code-human-research-ethics-2nd-edition-2014 (accessed 25 August 2018).

BPS (British Psychological Society) (2017a) *Practice Guidelines.* 3rd ed. Leicester: British Psychological Society. Online. www.bps.org.uk/sites/bps.org.uk/files/ Policy%20-%20Files/BPS%20Practice%20Guidelines%20(Third%20Edition). pdf (accessed 25 August 2018).

BPS (British Psychological Society) (2017b) *Promoting Excellence in Psychology: Standards for the accreditation of Doctoral programmes in educational psychology in England, Northern Ireland & Wales.* Leicester: British Psychological Society. Online. www.bps.org.uk/sites/bps.org.uk/files/ Accreditation/Educational%20Accreditation%20(England,%20NI,%20 Wales)%202017_WEB.pdf (accessed 25 September 2018).

BPS (British Psychological Society) (2018) *Code of Ethics and Conduct.* Leicester: British Psychological Society. Online. www.bps.org.uk/sites/bps. org.uk/files/Policy%20-%20Files/BPS%20Code%20of%20Ethics%20 and%20Conduct%20%28Updated%20July%202018%29.pdf (accessed 25 August 2018).

Davis, B. and Cahill, S. (2006) 'Challenging expectations for every child through innovation, regeneration and reinvention'. *Educational and Child Psychology*, 23 (1), 80–91.

Department for Constitutional Affairs (2007) *Mental Capacity Act 2005: Code of practice.* Norwich: The Stationery Office. Online. https://assets. publishing.service.gov.uk/government/uploads/system/uploads/attachment_ data/file/497253/Mental-capacity-act-code-of-practice.pdf (accessed 25 August 2018).

DfE (Department for Education) (2015) *Working Together to Safeguard Children.* Online. www.gov.uk/government/publications/working-together-to-safeguard-children--2 (accessed 25 August 2018).

DfE (Department for Education) and DoH (Department of Health) (2015) *Special Educational Needs and Disability Code of Practice: 0 to 25 years: Statutory guidance for organisations which work with and support children and young people who have special educational needs or disabilities.* London: Department for Education. Online. https://assets.publishing.service.gov.uk/government/ uploads/system/uploads/attachment_data/file/398815/SEND_Code_of_Practice_ January_2015.pdf (accessed 23 August 2018).

DoH (Department of Health) (2015a) *Future in Mind: Promoting, protecting and improving our children and young people's mental health and wellbeing.* London: Department of Health. Online. https://assets.publishing.service.gov.uk/ government/uploads/system/uploads/attachment_data/file/414024/Childrens_ Mental_Health.pdf (accessed 25 August 2018).

DoH (Department of Health) (2015b) *Mental Health Act 1983: Code of practice.* Norwich: The Stationery Office.

Brian Davis

DoH (Department of Health) and DfE (Department for Education) (2017) *Transforming Children and Young People's Mental Health Provision: A Green Paper*. London: Department of Health. Online. www.gov.uk/government/uploads/system/uploads/attachment_data/file/664855/Transforming_children_and_young_people_s_mental_health_provision.pdf (accessed 25 August 2018).

Farrell, P., Woods, K., Lewis, S., Rooney, S., Squires, G. and O'Connor, M. (2006) *A Review of the Functions and Contribution of Educational Psychologists in England and Wales in Light of "Every Child Matters: Change for children"* (Research Report 792). London: Department for Education and Skills.

Faulconbridge, J., Hickey, J., Jeffs, G., McConnellogue, D., Patel, W., Picciotto, A. and Pote, H. (2017) 'What good looks like in psychological services for schools and colleges: Primary prevention, early intervention and mental health provision'. *Child and Family Clinical Psychology Review*, 5, 1–32.

HCPC (Health and Care Professions Council) (2015) *Standards of Proficiency: Practitioner psychologists*. London: Health and Care Professions Council. Online. www.hcpc-uk.org/assets/documents/10002963SOP_Practitioner_psychologists.pdf (accessed 24 August 2018).

ICO (Information Commissioner's Office) (2018) 'Guide to the General Data Protection Regulation (GDPR)'. Online. https://ico.org.uk/for-organisations/guide-to-the-general-data-protection-regulation-gdpr/ (accessed 25 August 2018).

Kelly, B., Woolfson, L.M. and Boyle, J. (eds) (2017) *Frameworks for Practice in Educational Psychology: A textbook for trainees and practitioners*. 2nd ed. London: Jessica Kingsley Publishers.

Lavis, P. and Robson, C. (2015) *Promoting Children and Young People's Emotional Health and Wellbeing: A whole school and college approach*. London: Public Health England. Online. www.gov.uk/government/publications/promoting-children-and-young-peoples-emotional-health-and-wellbeing (accessed 25 August 2018).

MacKay, T. (2002) 'The future of educational psychology'. *Educational Psychology in Practice*, 18 (3), 245–53.

MacKay, T. (2006) 'The educational psychologist as community psychologist: Holistic child psychology across home, school and community'. *Educational and Child Psychology*, 23 (1), 7–15.

Ministry of Justice, National Offender Management Service and HM Prison Service (2012) 'MAPPA guidance 2012 (version 4.2)'. Online. www.gov.uk/government/publications/multi-agency-public-protection-arrangements-mappa--2 (accessed 25 August 2018).

NSPCC (2018) 'Gillick competency and Fraser guidelines'. Online. https://learning.nspcc.org.uk/research-resources/briefings/gillick-competency-and-fraser-guidelines/ (accessed 5 September 2018).

UK Parliament (1974) 'Health and Safety at Work etc. Act 1974'. Online. www.legislation.gov.uk/ukpga/1974/37 (accessed 25 August 2018).

UK Parliament (1983, amended 2007) 'Mental Health Act 1983'. Online. www.legislation.gov.uk/ukpga/1983/20/contents (accessed 25 August 2018).

UK Parliament (1989) 'Children Act 1989'. Online. www.legislation.gov.uk/ukpga/1989/41/contents (accessed 25 August 2018).

UK Parliament (1998) 'Data Protection Act 1998'. Online. www.legislation.gov.uk/ukpga/1998/29/contents (accessed 25 August 2018).

UK Parliament (2000) 'Freedom of Information Act 2000'. Online. www.legislation.gov.uk/ukpga/2000/36/contents (accessed 25 August 2018).

UK Parliament (2003) 'Female Genital Mutilation Act 2003'. Online. www.legislation.gov.uk/ukpga/2003/31/contents (accessed 25 August 2018).

UK Parliament (2004) 'Children Act 2004'. Online. www.legislation.gov.uk/ukpga/2004/31/contents (accessed 25 August 2018).

UK Parliament (2005) 'Mental Capacity Act 2005'. Online. www.legislation.gov.uk/ukpga/2005/9/contents (accessed 25 August 2018).

UK Parliament (2006) 'Safeguarding Vulnerable Groups Act 2006'. Online. www.legislation.gov.uk/ukpga/2006/47/contents (accessed 25 August 2018).

UK Parliament (2008) 'Health and Social Care Act 2008'. Online. www.legislation.gov.uk/ukpga/2008/14/contents (accessed 25 August 2018).

UK Parliament (2010) 'Equality Act 2010'. Online. www.legislation.gov.uk/ukpga/2010/15/contents (accessed 25 August 2018).

UK Parliament (2014) 'Children and Families Act 2014'. Online. www.legislation.gov.uk/ukpga/2014/6/contents/enacted (accessed 25 August 2018).

UK Parliament (2015) 'Counter-Terrorism and Security Act 2015'. Online. www.legislation.gov.uk/ukpga/2015/6/contents/enacted (accessed 25 August 2018).

UK Parliament (2017) 'Children and Social Work Act 2017'. Online. www.legislation.gov.uk/ukpga/2017/16/contents/enacted (accessed 25 August 2018).

UK Parliament (2018) The Public Interest Disclosure (Prescribed Persons) (Amendment Order). Online. http://www.legislation.gov.uk/uksi/2018/795/contents/made (accessed 25 August 2018).

Chapter 5

Mental capacity assessments

Brian Davis

Introduction

This chapter introduces mental capacity assessments, which relate to a person's capacity to make decisions about significant matters that will have an impact on them. Through reading this chapter professionals working in education, including educational psychologists (EPs), will gain an understanding of the purpose of such capacity assessments, when and how they might be planned for and carried out, and the various carer and professional roles and responsibilities that will need to be considered.

The chapter considers the relevant legislation and guidance underpinning mental capacity assessments for young people with special educational needs and those who are disabled. It goes on to consider how we build independence and choice before the age of 16, how to prepare for and carry out mental capacity assessments, who does the assessment, and 'scaffolding the assessment' to provide the best opportunities for young people to contribute. Decisions that cannot be made for others are highlighted. What happens following the decision on capacity is then explored. Consideration is given to the role of the EP and other education professionals throughout and there is a section on training and support for EPs and their services. Finally the chapter is summarized to consider what has been learnt.

Relevant legislation and guidance

The Mental Capacity Act 2005 (UK Parliament, 2005; MCA enacted in 2007) is legislation for England and Wales and is applicable to young people from the age of 16. Protected within this Act is the right of young people to make their own decisions wherever possible. The Act forms part of UK legislation relating to human rights. There is a related Mental Capacity Act Code of Practice (Department for Constitutional Affairs, 2007; the MCA COP) that applies to professionals working in education as well as health and social care. This statutory guidance aims to assist parents and professionals in supporting young people in making decisions. It also clearly lays down the required steps in determining when a young person may lack the capacity to make a particular decision. This determination is critical as the assessment of capacity allows or denies a right. In Scotland the Adults with Incapacity (Scotland) Act 2000 (Scottish Parliament, 2000) applies and in Northern Ireland the Mental Capacity Act (Northern Ireland) 2016 (Northern Ireland Assembly, 2016) applies. (Differences are not explored in this chapter.) National Institute for Health and Care Excellence (NICE) guidelines on 'Decision making and mental capacity' have been produced during October 2018.

Professionals in education would want to avoid any confusion between the MCA and the Mental Health Act 1983 as amended in 2007 (UK Parliament, 1983; MHA). The main purpose of the MHA is to allow compulsory action to be taken, where necessary, to ensure that people with mental disorders receive the care and treatment they require for their own health or safety, or for the protection of other people. In Scotland the Mental Health (Scotland) Act 2015 has a similar function.

For professionals working in education, health and social care services it is important to consider the requirements of the MCA alongside the requirements of the other highly relevant legislation, including the Children and Families Act 2014 (UK Parliament, 2014) and the related Special Educational Needs Act 2001 Code of Practice (Department for Education (DfE), 2001; SENDA COP). This last has now been withdrawn and the term 'SEND COP' is used referring to the *Special Educational Needs and Disability Code of Practice* (DfE and Department of Health (DoH), 2015). The Children and Families Act 2014 covers adoption and contact, family justice, children and young people with special educational needs and disabilities (SEND), child care and child welfare. It introduces Education, Health and Care Plans (EHCPs) to replace Statements of Special Educational Need and clarifies that a young person may have an EHCP and be in an education or training provision with special arrangements, up to the age of 25, should the EHCP not have ceased at an earlier appropriate time and the young person have alternative arrangements made.

Local authorities must involve families and children in discussions and decisions relating to their care and education, and provide impartial advice, support and mediation services. These clarifications of a statutory process, along with the transition for the older age group as a priority from Statements of Special Educational Need to the new EHCPs, have brought education professionals including EPs rapidly into closer sustained involvement with these young people, particularly in their duties to provide consultation, assessment leading to intervention, psychological advice and

Brian Davis

support, and strategic developments such as supporting the development of provision.

With regard to applied psychologists, the recently produced British Psychological Society Practice Guidelines (BPS, 2017a: 5) state: 'It is the psychologist's responsibility to ensure they are aware of the legislation and guidelines that govern their particular area of practice.'

Professionals must show regard for both the MCA COP and the SEND COP or provide good reasons for why they have operated differently. In effect the SEND COP incorporates the MCA COP. The intention is clearly to bring about greater consistency and standardization of understanding and practice across professionals in relation to the issues addressed. However, there are some differences between these documents in presentation and subsequent interpretation about which professionals should be aware and these are highlighted below.

There are four key questions detailed in the SEND COP Annex 1, which form the basis of a mental capacity assessment. However, this annex does not include a vital prior, first-step question, which is whether or not the young person meets the criteria for an assessment of their capacity in the first instance. A further inconsistency is that the SEND COP appears to imply that a mental capacity assessment might be enduring and continue to apply for later decisions that need to be made. This is misleading; although prior knowledge might contribute to a subsequent assessment of capacity to make a decision, a related capacity assessment should be carried out or reviewed in the light of the demands of the upcoming decision. Both positions are clearer in the MCA COP.

If there is doubt about a person's mental capacity, consideration needs to be given as to whether the person may lack capacity to make a particular decision, as they may have capacity to make some decisions but not others.

The Children and Families Act 2014 applies to children and young people aged from 0 to 25 years. This brings the legislation closer to the United Nations definition of a young person as aged 15 to 24 (with some variation across countries to which the definition applies). The Children and Families Act establishes the principles of involving young people as far as possible in decisions about their education, developing their independence and preparing them for adulthood.

The MCA COP indicates that a young person will make their own decisions with regard to health issues from their 16th birthday. The SEND COP indicates that a young person will make their own decisions with regard to education from the end of the academic year during which they

76

became 16. The Children Act 1989 (UK Parliament, 1989) indicates that young people can make their own decisions relating to care from the age of 17. These differences might need to be managed effectively to ensure continuity in co-ordinating education, health care and care support, and provision such as that detailed in an EHCP for young people with SEND.

Of course, there is a broader legislative framework within which we operate for young adults. The United Nations Convention on the Rights of the Child (1989) still applies to young people aged 16 and 17. The Children Act 1989 applies to young people up to the age of 19, the Equality Act 2010 (UK Parliament, 2010) applies into adulthood. In relation to the Equality Act 2010, the BPS Practice Guidelines (2017a: 6) states that 'Psychologists, where they operate in an organizational context, must also seek to encourage and influence others in ensuring that equality of opportunity is embedded in all thinking and all practice relating to access to services for client groups.'

The Law Society guidance (2015) considering deprivation of liberty can apply to a range of educational and training environments but particularly residential special schools. References to 'deprivation of liberty' in the MCA have the same meaning as Article 5 of The European Convention for the Protection of Human Rights and Fundamental Freedoms. The substantive rights it guarantees are largely incorporated into UK law by the Human Rights Act 1998 (UK Parliament, 1998). Issues with regard to deprivation of liberty are explored later.

Building independence and choice before the age of 16

The SEND COP and good professional practice foster the building of autonomy and independence. Young children should be encouraged to develop the skills relating to decision-making at an appropriate age and ability level. This might include the ability to choose between educational activities, meals, clothing, entertainment and trips, etc. For children with special educational needs and those who are disabled, professionals and parents who work and live with the child daily will understand how to communicate appropriate options to the child through preferred supported communication channels where required and how the child can indicate their preferences. This will happen on many levels from simple decisions made alone or with adults on which colours to paint with, ingredients to use, or food to eat, to more far-reaching decisions such as the best way to carry out support for learning, learning objectives, intimate personal care or medical treatment and intervention.

The child's view and child/person-centred planning arrangements are paramount in delivering on the intentions of the SEND COP. Children with

EHCPs should be encouraged to contribute to their annual reviews, usually held in their schools.

Professionals such as EPs consider child and parent advocacy as central to their role and they can consult, advise and work with others to ensure the policies and ethos of the education environment promote a child's choice and independence, mediated through, for example, effective augmented communication methods. These principles carry forward into any capacity assessment.

It is very important that young people are informed about key people, including professionals and their roles. It is also important that they are informed from an early age about the role of the local authority and perhaps be able to link names with faces.

We shall see later that contributing to the empowerment of vulnerable children in this way, and understanding what supports them in understanding and communicating, will help ensure that they can make and communicate their decisions past the age of 16. It also helps to ensure that other professionals such as teachers and mental health professionals, and also the parents, continue to be well placed to make assessments of capacity, perhaps supported where needed by the EP.

Preparing for and implementing mental capacity assessments

'A capacity assessment is an interaction between the assessor and the young person. It is not a test or exam, nor is it something done to the young person; it is an enabling process' (Sinson, 2016: 83).

A capacity assessment must follow the MCA COP procedures and be properly recorded. It would be useful for professionals and their services to have an agreed pro-forma for recording the process and outcome of the assessment, as this could be required at a later stage to evidence what took place (Sinson, 2016). It should be noted that a young person, family members or other professionals could challenge the outcome and the way it came about. The outcome might restrict the human right to self-determination as outlined in the Human Rights Act 1998. Decisions can be referred to the Court of Protection.

The MCA details five key principles that should be adhered to:

1. Presumption of capacity – it should not be presumed that capacity is lacking.
2. Support to make decisions – all reasonable steps are taken to aid understanding and communication.

3.   Able to make unwise decisions – others need not agree with the decision or consider it wise for it to be implemented.
4.   If decisions are made for the young person they should be in their best interests.
5.   The least restrictive options must be explored.

With regard to the last point, in addition to the MCA COP there is the separate guidance on policy and procedure provided by the Law Society (2015) on the deprivation of liberty, which might be particularly applicable to residential schools and colleges. Restrictions must be reasonable, not be overly constraining, and be age appropriate. Of course, there are many forms of restriction that do not involve holding or other physical restriction. However, it is acknowledged that restrictions, including physical intervention, can be applied in the event of a person committing an offence, causing injury or damage, or affecting good order and discipline. The DfE publication *Use of Reasonable Force: Advice for headteachers, staff and governing bodies* (2013) outlines application in schools. The NICE guidelines on *Challenging Behaviour and Learning Disabilities* (2015: 37) state that any restrictive interventions, used as part of a reactive strategy, should be 'accompanied by a restrictive intervention reduction programme, as part of the long-term behaviour support plan, to reduce the use of and need for restrictive interventions'.

In establishing the process for any assessments, including a capacity assessment, it should be remembered that the young person should be communicated with directly in the first instance and throughout with regard to any processes that would affect them.

The SEND COP allows for parents or young people at the end of the academic year they are 16 to appeal with regard to matters of statutory assessment and provision for special educational needs and disability; matters may be dealt with by a SEND tribunal.

The specialist Court of Protection has high court status. Application to the court would usually be a final step after following the dispute resolution process in the MCA COP. In addition, school or college representatives must apply to this court should they be seeking 'Deprivation of Liberty'.

In the event that they are required, independent mental capacity advocates (IMCAs) and deputies can be appointed by the Court of Protection, operating across the remit of managing property and financial affairs, health and welfare. Appointees (from family friends or professionals) can manage income solely from state benefits if approved by the Department for Work and Pensions.

The MCA classifies the types of decisions to be made in three categories:

- about everyday life
- more serious or significant
- decisions with legal consequences.

Although the principles of building autonomy and independence through choice would apply to the first, it is the second and third categories that might require a formal capacity assessment as they might relate to significant matters such as ownership and possessions, placement, identity, treatment, relationships and care.

The MCA COP reveals its medical and health-related origins in the form of language employed and this may affect the accessibility for professionals traditionally placed outside health services. The Children and Families Act 2014 Annex A and the Code of Practice relating to the Mental Health Act (1983) Annex A (DoH, 2015) give further clarification of meaning. According to the Mental Capacity Act (2005), a young person may lack the mental capacity to make a decision if they have an impairment or disturbance that affects the way their mind or brain works and the impairment or disturbance affects their ability to make a specific decision at the time it needs to be made. If this possibility is proposed then it should be evidenced appropriately.

It might be a widely held belief that a young person can be determined not to have capacity to make any decisions and that this is a generalizable condition across all decisions. As highlighted previously, this is not the case and individual assessments of capacity must be made for all major qualifying decisions.

In effect first approaching the need for the assessment and then second the assessment itself form a two-part process.

First it is important to answer the question 'Does the young person meet the criteria for it to be considered that they may lack capacity to make the decision?'. There would be no immediate requirement that every child with a special educational need (including a mental health need) or who is disabled be assessed for this. This then leads us to the question, 'Does the young person have an impairment of, or a disturbance in the functioning of, their mind or brain?' MCA COP (4.11).

Many working in education and involved in decisions affecting young people aged 16 plus would be used to the term 'learning difficulties and disabilities'. Learning difficulty is now defined as 'significantly greater difficulty learning than the majority of others of the same age' (SEND COP:

Introduction, xiv). A learning disability can be described as 'a significantly reduced ability to understand new or complex information, or to learn new skills (impaired intelligence), with a reduced ability to cope independently (impaired social functioning), which started before adulthood, with a lasting effect on development' (DoH, 2001: 14).

The Children and Families Act 2014 introduced mental health difficulties as an area of SEND. The DfE publication *Mental Health and Behaviour in Schools* (DfE, 2016) provides further details of what might be included in Annexes A and C, drawing from accepted classifications including *ICD-10: International statistical classification of diseases and related health problems: Tenth revision* (World Health Organization (WHO), 2004).

In general the language used relating to young people pre- and post-16 is now becoming more similar across health and social care and within different age phases of education. If the answer to the previous question relating to impairment is 'yes' then we are led to the next question, 'Does the impairment or disturbance mean that the young person is unable to make a specific decision when they need to?' (MCA COP: 4.13).

If the above applies then there is the application of four following key questions (SEND COP). To be considered to lack capacity, functionally a young person would not be able to do one or more of the following four things.

Therefore ask and assess, will the young person be able to:

1. understand the information relevant to the decision (might include nature of the decision, reason decision required and likely effects of decision or no decision)
2. retain the information long enough to make the decision (given the principle of providing support, this might involve reinforcing learning and prompts and aids)
3. use and weigh the information to arrive at a choice (could be supported through photographs, counters, Talking Mats, etc.)
4. communicate their decision in any way (might involve communication aids).

The decision as to whether the young person has capacity to make a decision is 'yes' or 'no' with no indication of degree. If the answer to one of the four questions is 'no' then on the balance of probabilities the young person lacks the mental capacity at this time to make the decision.

Who does the assessment?

An assessor does not require formal qualifications although many health professionals, and particularly clinical psychologists and psychiatrists, might see this as a familiar expectation of their role. However, it would seem necessary that an assessor have experience of working directly with those who may lack capacity. The assessor may be a professional or a parent or family member, or someone with a designated responsibility. It is desirable that the young person has met and knows the assessor. From MCA COP 4.43 we are informed that 'any assessor should have the skills and ability to communicate effectively with the person; if necessary they should get professional help to communicate with the person' (p. 54). The assessor will want to be sure the young person is provided with the right help and support to make and communicate a decision. Services and individuals would be advised to seek out training, support and resource materials. Some sources are detailed at the end of this chapter.

Sinson in her book (2016: 81) suggests that 'whilst formal qualifications are not required, experience of working directly with those who may lack capacity, training in the MCA principles and capacity assessments are essential'. Services should consider how experience can be obtained for EPs.

The assessor of capacity is usually the person who needs the young person to make the decision and this would depend on the type of decision to be made. It could be that different people are required for different decisions. The assessor may seek advice in this assessment from a specialist such as an EP, for example preferred communication methods, ways of presenting and indicating choices, and meeting the emotional well-being needs of the young person so they feel safe and secure in the process. Formal records must be kept (MCA COP: 4.61).

It is highly likely that the assessor will need to take into account the views of other professionals and the parents (should it not be the parent assessing). These may be expressed in reports or in person. Thus a professional such as an EP might hold in mind that reports such as statutory advice towards an EHCP or input to an annual review of such may support the process.

In determining the parental responsibility it is useful to consult the government website www.gov.uk/parental-rights-responsibilities/who-has-parental-responsibility

When working with children and young people, psychologists are advised to ensure that they have ascertained who has parental responsibility and that those with parental responsibility are aware of their planned involvement, if this is appropriate (BPS, 2017a). With regard to access to other services, but of course also to the educational psychology service, the BPS Practice Guidelines (2017a) provide guidance relating to the Equality Act 2010: 'Providers of service to the public must also make reasonable adjustments for people who have a disability under the Act. This requirement is anticipatory so requires consideration, and adjustment where reasonable, of any barriers which may prevent a person with a disability from using a service.'

An EP would be seeking to help ensure that the process is as inclusive a possible while also helping to ensure that the young person is at the centre of the process and that their views are paramount.

'Scaffolding' the assessment

The concept of scaffolding is one that many EPs would have worked with (Vygotsky, 1978; Wood *et al.*, 1976). Here the concept seems relevant on two levels. First and generally, it is clear that any approach to obtaining a decision from a young person about something that affects them needs to be thought about carefully in terms of how decisions are planned for, perhaps in terms of how information is presented, how understanding is facilitated, and decisions communicated. This is in order to ensure that the best possible opportunities and support are provided to the young person so that they can make a decision. Furthermore, Bruner (1960) provides a notion of scaffolding relating to a spiralling of levels of understanding from the simple to the more complex, which allows us to think about how young people might achieve a position of being able to make a decision if they are assisted to move up through the levels of complexity required through careful teaching and support.

It has been suggested earlier that helping children when they are younger to understand key roles of adults and to make decisions can be an important step towards decision-making as an older young person. Providing appropriate help with decision-making should form part of care planning processes for people receiving health or social care services. Examples include person-centred planning (White and Rae, 2016) for people with learning disabilities (MCA COP: 3.5). Within the person-centred planning processes, EPs will be familiar with techniques such as MAPS and PATHS (O'Brien and Pearpoint, 2002; Pearpoint *et al.*, 2001); these processes can be incredibly supportive in building a holistic approach but with critical decision-making points being identified and addressed.

In general it would be important to ensure the young person is prepared for the meeting or event. They should be presented with information in their preferred format and be able to understand the language used. It would be necessary to ensure that their communications can be understood by professionals or local authority officers in attendance. The young person must be given time to process the information. The MCA COP (3.9) highlights the importance of providing all the needed information but also not confusing the young person.

The person who assesses an individual's capacity to make a decision will usually be the person who is directly concerned with the individual at the time the decision needs to be made (MCA COP: 4.38). In general the young person should be communicating in a familiar place, with someone to support them if they wish, in addition to the adult who may be seeking the decision (Sinson, 2016).

The quality and range of the communication strategies and the associated mediating language facilitating understanding and communication of intent are extremely important. The presentation of information needs to take account of the young person's favoured ways of receiving information. This could include use of pictures and objects (MCA COP: 3.10) among other approaches.

Medical or other needs may mean that there are times of the day when the young person can best function in the assessment; comfort, fatigue, hunger and mood are other factors worthy of consideration.

Particular consideration should be given to the role of any interpreter to ensure as accurate a representation of the young person's view as possible. Some adults may believe they know the young person best, but they could be projecting their view. There is a need to consider that as a young person moves to greater independence they may consider options in how they interpret or work within or outside cultural or religious norms, within which others might expect them to remain. Strategies for some degree of verification might therefore be required.

Scheduling of the assessment could be considered alongside other key planning events for a young person. Where a young person has an EHCP the assessment could take place within or as part of a contribution to the preparation, carrying out and reporting on the annual review and proposals for decisions that need to be considered by the local authority in relation to the needs and provision detailed in the EHCP. Person-centred planning and review approaches could help to bridge the requirements of a mental capacity assessment and the identifying of ongoing special educational needs and required provision.

In such circumstances, however, the young person would need to understand fully that it is the local authority (possibly represented by people the young person is made aware of) who will need to agree to consider the recommendations (or proposed decisions and actions) and make the decision to amend the plan, for example for a change in provision.

The young person should be required where possible to give consent for parents and other relevant people to be present for an assessment and allied review and planning activity to be carried out. Person-centred planning is recommended often and within this process the young person is encouraged to place themselves at the centre of a process over which they have some control, including over who might be invited to contribute. Adults including professionals around the young person may need to adapt their ways of working to accommodate this positioning.

The MCA COP (4.51) indicates that a multi-agency approach is beneficial. Clinical psychologists might often find themselves leading on capacity assessments and they report that information sharing by educational psychologists is seen as helpful by (Walji, 2014, in Sinson, 2016). The point here is that ensuring there is consent to share information that is relevant across professionals with an interest in the young person can make for a richer and more informed process and outcome.

A formal record of the capacity assessment should be agreed, preferably in a standardized format, with the relevant parties and be distributed and retained on an agreed 'need to know' basis. The record and distribution can be agreed with the young person when they have capacity; otherwise it is the person making the decision who would decide.

Specialist teachers, health professionals and EPs are all well placed to help the local authority, schools and colleges with new or signposted resource materials, to consult on strategies and to provide training.

Multi-agency strategic planning for and tracking of young people's upcoming transitions can help to ensure appropriate timescales for effective support for a young person's decision-making are in place alongside appropriate and timely assessment of capacity where required. This is good practice and it aids the authorities in meeting statutory compliance.

Decisions that cannot be made on another's behalf

Decisions that cannot be made on another's behalf are detailed in the MCA COP (1.10). Decisions others cannot make include those on marriage, civil partnership, sexual relations and the placing of a child for adoption. Forced marriage is a criminal offence in England and Wales. Sexual intercourse is illegal with a young person who does not understand the nature of the act or reasonably foreseeable consequences. Female genital mutilation is illegal. Professional applied psychologists could be in a position of contributing to an assessment of capacity in relation to capacity to consent to sexual relations or marriage as part of an EHCP, which might also consider semi-independent living arrangements.

Following the decision on capacity

An EP might have been involved in the planning to support a young person in making a decision and/or helping an assessor to determine if a young person has capacity to make a decision. This determination might then be a contributory factor to subsequent actions.

A resulting decision made on the young person's behalf or by the young person might lead to a disagreement on how to proceed. This might include a young person aged 16 plus or their parents wanting to change a decision made by a local authority. In some cases this may lead to a SEND tribunal as detailed in the SEND COP.

The process of making life-shaping decisions can introduce strong emotions and conflict. The young person has the right to make a decision that others might think is unwise, as long as they have the capacity to do so.

Conflicts can occur between the young person, and parents and any family member, and the local authority or health services. In the three-way relationship of the young person, the parents and the local authority, it is possible that the young person's account of what they want to happen does not match that of either of the others. Parents can seek a SEND tribunal should it be apparent that the young person is providing consent. Educational psychologists can provide objective assessment information through reports and in person, for example at planning meetings, or at tribunals. They can support a degree of advocacy for the young person and/or the parents and perhaps help them to problem solve their way through conflict or to access mediation arrangements.

In the event that a young person does not have the capacity to make a decision, the SEND COP (Annex 1) indicates that the young person's parent(s) or representative will make the decision. Educational psychologists and other professionals could be consulted on best interest decisions, by those making the decision. This could include professionals or parents. Where a decision made on the young person's behalf does not seem to be in their best interests, professionals should be prepared to raise the matter with the assessor and decision-maker.

The BPS has produced *Best Interests: Guidance on determining the best interests of adults who lack the capacity to make a decision (or decisions) for themselves [England and Wales]* (Joyce, 2008).

The aims and objectives of this guidance are as follows:

- to raise awareness of the different ways in which people can make decisions on behalf of those who lack capacity and how these are relevant to the Mental Capacity Act 2005
- to enable those working with individuals who lack capacity to increase their understanding of what is meant by best interests
- to enable people who are required to make judgements about best interests, or who are required to participate in best interests meetings, to do this in a structured way; this is in order to ensure that decision-makers consider and weigh all relevant factors in making decisions that are in the best interests of the adult who lacks capacity
- to provide chairs of best interests meetings with additional guidance on the process, content and structure of best interests meetings.

Best interest decisions weigh up a range of factors (including the wishes or preferences of the person, and the views of their families and carers) and decide what is, on balance, the best for the person both now and in the future. Less restrictive options must always be considered.

Training and support

With professionals in education, including EPs, extending their involvement with young people to age 25, they are becoming more aware of the need to address the onset of mental health difficulties. Through related professional activity the Chief Medical Officer Report 2013 (Davies, 2013) indicates that 75 per cent of mental health illnesses are apparent by age 18. Adolescence to young adulthood is the greatest period for these illnesses to become apparent, with perhaps one in four experiencing a mental health problem in a year.

Indications of a high level of occurrence lead us to consider the roles of schools, colleges and professionals in determining what high-level impact can be achieved through strategic thinking. Included in this would be the need for professionals to understand the neuropsychological aspects that affect adolescent brain development and subsequent risk-taking and decision-making.

At the time of writing there is a consultation on the Green Paper, *Transforming Children and Young People's Mental Health Provision* (DoH and DfE, 2017). This was preceded by and very much appears to draw on the document 'What good looks like in psychological services for schools and colleges: Primary prevention, early intervention and mental health provision' (Faulconridge *et al.*, 2017), produced by a team of clinical psychologists from the BPS.

Educational psychologists will need to scope out the nature and range of a portfolio of professional activity they can offer in the area of mental health across age phases including 16–25, developed and informed by an evidence and research base considering issues such as impact. This might include the role they play in understanding the educational and training contexts they operate in and assisting young people in being involved in planning and decision-making, as well as providing direct support and intervention where appropriate.

Educational psychologists are trained within the competency requirements of the BPS (BPS, 2017b) and the standards of proficiency requirements to obtain and maintain registration with the Health and Care Professions Council (HCPC, 2015). In general these 'standards' apply to all work relating to the 16–25 age group.

Atkinson *et al.* (2015) found very high levels of agreement from EPs responding to an enquiry about the MCA, considering whether it should be included in the initial training of EPs. The authors included a proposed augmenting 16–25 competency framework, which could be used to inform training and develop practice. This framework encompasses the domains of context, legislation, assessment, interventions and outcomes, development and transitions. The framework and the detail therein sits well with the BPS general competency and HCPC requirements and amplifies and details trainee performance expectations in the 16–25 age range.

Educational psychology initial training courses have responded quickly to the revised expectations to work with young people up to the age of 25. Course developments include extending the age range applicability for subject matter, extended professional placement requirements, the introduction of training from EPs in 16-plus specialist roles, reviews of 16-plus provision, the establishment of links with further education (FE) providers, considerations of funding and resourcing in FE, input on complex needs of young adults, person-centred planning and the role of the EP in such, and training sessions on the MCA and advocacy. It could be said that the MCA COP questions relating to capacity do perhaps depend on the person making the judgements to have some knowledge about mental health.

In considering the BPS guidance at the time (now superseded) and the study of Walji *et al.* (2014), who looked particularly at the needs of clinical psychology practitioners and how EPs could assist in assessments, Sinson (2016) an educational psychologist herself, suggests EPs would benefit from training sessions and resources that:

- ensure an understanding of the MCA principles
- have a focus on undertaking capacity assessments, including assessment approaches
- discuss the implications of a capacity assessment in relation to the young person and their parents
- present relevant education-focused case studies
- enable appropriate supervision
- facilitate a shared understanding of the MCA with other education professionals
- provide an awareness of 'best interests'
- explore the implication of the Law Society guidance on deprivation of liberty for EP practice, including safeguarding responsibilities.

The HCPC states that, once registered, practitioner psychologists must continue to meet the standards of proficiency that are relevant to their scope of practice – the areas of their profession in which they have the knowledge and skills to practise safely and effectively. BPS competencies and the HCPC proficiencies for trainee and qualified EPs have been kept under revision. There is of course also a continuing professional development (CPD) requirement on practitioners and audit arrangements for this. CPD can be across the board or be more specific, for example in relation to new legislation and guidance such as the MCA COP. Ongoing CPD is a requirement on practitioner psychologists and these expectations for quality of practice would seem to be very helpful in this function, alongside the 16–25 competency suggestions of Atkinson *et al.* (2015).

Summary

Educational psychologists are required to have a knowledge of legislation and guidance related to their work. In relation to the Mental Capacity Act it means understanding the implications of the Act and the guidance for practice in the Mental Capacity Act Code of Practice.

Educational psychologists may, if only occasionally, be asked to be the assessor of mental capacity, but they certainly will be frequently involved in facilitating, understanding and supporting mental capacity assessment by others and best interest decision-making.

Their role is important in working alongside parents and professionals in ensuring effective advocacy, understanding and communication are facilitated for young people to enable them to overcome barriers to choice and independence. Educational psychologists need to further develop their skills in this area by accessing appropriate training and supervision, and developing their portfolio of activity to support young people who are disabled or have special educational needs including mental health needs, or who are otherwise vulnerable, across the 16–25 range.

References

Atkinson, C., Dunsmuir, S., Lang, J. and Wright, S. (2015) 'Developing a competency framework for the initial training of educational psychologists working with young people aged 16–25'. *Educational Psychology in Practice*, 31 (2), 159–73.

BPS (British Psychological Society) (2017a) *Practice Guidelines*. 3rd ed. Leicester: British Psychological Society. Online. www.bps.org.uk/sites/bps.org.uk/files/Policy%20-%20Files/BPS%20Practice%20Guidelines%20(Third%20Edition).pdf (accessed 28 August 2018).

BPS (British Psychological Society) (2017b) *Promoting Excellence in Psychology: Standards for the accreditation of doctoral programmes in educational psychology in England, Northern Ireland and Wales*. Leicester: British Psychological Society. Online. www.bps.org.uk/sites/bps.org.uk/files/Accreditation/Educational%20Accreditation%20(England,%20NI,%20 Wales)%202017_WEB.pdf (accessed 25 August 2018).

Bruner, J.S. (1960) *The Process of Education*. Cambridge, MA: Harvard University Press.

Davies, S.C. (2014) *Annual Report of the Chief Medical Officer 2013: Public mental health priorities: Investing in the evidence*. London: Department of Health. Online. https://assets.publishing.service.gov.uk/government/uploads/system/uploads/attachment_data/file/413196/CMO_web_doc.pdf (accessed 28 August 2018).

Department for Constitutional Affairs (2007) *Mental Capacity Act 2005: Code of Practice* [MCA COP]. Norwich: The Stationery Office. Online. https://assets.publishing.service.gov.uk/government/uploads/system/uploads/attachment_data/file/497253/Mental-capacity-act-code-of-practice.pdf (accessed 25 August 2018).

DfE (Department for Education) (2001) *Special Educational Needs Code of Practice*. Online. https://assets.publishing.service.gov.uk/government/uploads/system/uploads/attachment_data/file/273877/special_educational_needs_code_of_practice.pdf (accessed 26 October 2018).

DfE (Department for Education) (2013) *Use of Reasonable Force: Advice for headteachers, staff and governing bodies*. London: Department of Education. Online. www.gov.uk/government/publications/use-of-reasonable-force-in-schools (accessed 28 August 2018).

DfE (Department for Education) (2016) *Mental Health and Behaviour in Schools: Departmental advice for school staff*. London: Department for Education. Online. https://assets.publishing.service.gov.uk/government/uploads/system/uploads/attachment_data/file/508847/Mental_Health_and_Behaviour_-_advice_for_Schools_160316.pdf (accessed 28 August 2018).

DfE (Department for Education) and DoH (Department of Health) (2015) *Special Educational Needs and Disability Code of Practice: 0 to 25 years: Statutory guidance for organisations which work with and support children and young people who have special educational needs or disabilities* [SEND COP]. London: Department for Education. Online. https://assets.publishing.service. gov.uk/government/uploads/system/uploads/attachment_data/file/398815/ SEND_Code_of_Practice_January_2015.pdf (accessed 23 August 2018).

DoH (Department of Health) (2001) *Valuing People: A new strategy for learning disability for the 21st century: A White Paper*. London: The Stationery Office.

DoH (Department of Health) (2015) *Mental Health Act 1983: Code of practice*. Norwich: The Stationery Office.

DoH (Department of Health) and DfE (Department for Education) (2017) *Transforming Children and Young People's Mental Health Provision: A Green Paper*. London: Department of Health. Online. www.gov.uk/government/ uploads/system/uploads/attachment_data/file/664855/Transforming_children_ and_young_people_s_mental_health_provision.pdf (accessed 25 August 2018).

Faulconbridge, J., Hickey, J., Jeffs, G., McConnellogue, D., Patel, W., Picciotto, A. and Pote, H. (2017) 'What good looks like in psychological services for schools and colleges: Primary prevention, early intervention and mental health provision'. *Child and Family Clinical Psychology Review*, 5, 1–32.

HCPC (Health and Care Professions Council) (2015) *Standards of Proficiency: Practitioner psychologists*. London: Health and Care Professions Council. Online. www.hcpc-uk.org/assets/documents/10002963SOP_Practitioner_ psychologists.pdf (accessed 24 August 2018).

Joyce, T. (2008) *Best Interests: Guidance on determining the best interests of adults who lack the capacity to make a decision (or decisions) for themselves [England and Wales]*. Leicester: British Psychological Society. Online. www1.bps.org.uk/system/files/Public%20files/Policy/rep_67_best_interests_web. pdf (accessed 27 August 2018).

Law Society (2015) *Identifying a Deprivation of Liberty: A practical guide*. London: Law Society. Online. www.lawsociety.org.uk/support-services/advice/ articles/deprivation-of-liberty/ (accessed 28 August 2018).

NICE (National Institute for Health and Care Excellence) (2015) *Challenging Behaviour and Learning Disabilities: Prevention and interventions for people with learning disabilities whose behaviour challenges* (NICE Guideline NG11). London: National Institute for Health and Care Excellence. Online. www.nice. org.uk/guidance/ng11/resources/challenging-behaviour-and-learning-disabilities- prevention-and-interventions-for-people-with-learning-disabilities-whose- behaviour-challenges-1837266392005 (accessed 28 August 2018).

NICE (National Institute for Health and Care Excellence) (2018) *Decision-making and Mental Capacity* (NICE Guideline NG108). London: National Institute for Health and Care Excellence. Online. https://www.nice.org.uk/guidance/ng108/ resources/decisionmaking-and-mental-capacity-pdf-66141544670917 (accessed 26 October 2018).

Northern Ireland Assembly (2016) 'Mental Capacity Act (Northern Ireland) 2016'. Online. www.legislation.gov.uk/nia/2016/18/contents/enacted (accessed 25 August 2018).

O'Brien, J. and Pearpoint, J. (2002) *Person-Centered Planning with MAPS and PATH: A workbook for facilitators*. Toronto: Inclusion Press.

Pearpoint, J., O'Brien, J. and Forest, M. (2001) *PATH: A workbook for planning positive possible futures*. 2nd ed. Toronto: Inclusion Press.

Scottish Parliament (2000) 'Adults with Incapacity (Scotland) Act 2000'. Online. www.legislation.gov.uk/asp/2000/4/contents (accessed 25 August 2018).

Scottish Parliament (2015) 'Mental Health (Scotland) Act 2015'. Online. www.legislation.gov.uk/asp/2015/9/contents/enacted (accessed 25 August 2018).

Sinson, J.L. (2016) *Applying the Mental Capacity Act 2005 in Education: A practical guide for education professionals*. London: Jessica Kingsley Publishers.

UK Parliament (1983) 'Mental Health Act 1983'. Online. www.legislation.gov.uk/ukpga/1983/20/contents (accessed 25 August 2018).

UK Parliament (1989) 'Children Act 1989'. Online. www.legislation.gov.uk/ukpga/1989/41/contents (accessed 25 August 2018).

UK Parliament (1998) 'Human Rights Act 1998'. Online. www.legislation.gov.uk/ukpga/1998/42/contents (accessed 27 August 2018).

UK Parliament (2005) 'Mental Capacity Act 2005'. Online. www.legislation.gov.uk/ukpga/2005/9/contents (accessed 25 August 2018).

UK Parliament (2010) 'Equality Act 2010'. Online. www.legislation.gov.uk/ukpga/2010/15/contents (accessed 25 August 2018).

UK Parliament (2014) 'Children and Families Act 2014'. Online. www.legislation.gov.uk/ukpga/2014/6/contents/enacted (accessed 25 August 2018).

United Nations (1989) *Convention on the Rights of the Child*. Online. www.ohchr.org/Documents/ProfessionalInterest/crc.pdf (accessed 27 August 2018).

Vygotsky, L.S. (1978) *Mind in Society: The development of higher psychological processes*. Cambridge, MA: Harvard University Press.

Walji, I., Fletcher, I. and Weatherhead, S. (2014) 'Clinical psychologists' implementation of the Mental Capacity Act'. *Social Care and Neurodisability*, 5 (2), 111–30.

White, J. and Rae, T. (2016) 'Person-centred reviews and transition: An exploration of the views of students and their parents/carers'. *Educational Psychology in Practice*, 32 (1), 38–53.

WHO (World Health Organization) (2004) *ICD-10: International statistical classification of diseases and related health problems: Tenth revision*. 2nd ed. Geneva: World Health Organization.

Wood, D., Bruner, J.S. and Ross, G. (1976) 'The role of tutoring in problem solving'. *Journal of Child Psychology and Psychiatry*, 17 (2), 89–100.

Educational psychologists delivering psychological therapies to young people aged 16–25: Considerations for practice

Cathy Atkinson and Dorota Martin

The current context for young people's health and well-being

The mental health and well-being of young people aged 16–25 has received increasing prominence in recent times. This is perhaps not surprising, given the estimated annual economic cost in the United Kingdom of adolescent and child mental illness to society, which in 2005/6 figures ranged from £1,500 to £245,921 for an individual child (Clark *et al.*, 2005). The draft Green Paper on *Transforming Children and Young People's Mental Health Provision* (Department for Education (DfE) and Department of Health (DoH), 2017) acknowledged an increasing incidence of mental health problems among student populations, highlighting the need for strategic partnerships to co-ordinate support and improve longer-term outcomes for young people experiencing mental health problems. However, the report has received criticism (e.g. British Psychological Society (BPS), 2018) for paying insufficient attention both to preventative strategies, and to the wider social and political contexts that might be contributing to the high incidence of children and young people experiencing diagnosable mental health difficulties within the United Kingdom (Green *et al.*, 2005).

Rothì and Leavey (2006) explored mental health help-seeking behaviour of young people in the United Kingdom. Their review revealed that often young people's needs only become recognized when their mental health difficulties are serious, missing the opportunity for earlier interventions. The same issue was investigated by Warwick *et al.* (2006) and later by Warwick *et al.* (2008). They carried out interviews, postal surveys of 150 further education (FE) colleges and five FE case studies, and found that in terms of identifying need, there was often a misconception about mental health problems, associated with stigma and misidentification of mental difficulties as behavioural issues. They also found that a positive college ethos, environment and good links with services were crucial in delivering effective help to students. This had a positive impact on students' work, helping them to continue with their studies. Staff development, FE leadership, funding, and national policies and guidelines also contributed to supporting mental health and well-being of students, thus putting this in a wider context of increasing awareness of mental health nationally.

Evidence that young people experience stigma is supported by a recent review by the Children's Commissioner (Apland *et al.*, 2017), which concluded that children and young people's conceptualizations of mental health tend to be stereotyped and limited; and that they have limited awareness of the range and type of mental health needs or the support that may be available. The report indicated that young people with mental health difficulties perceive these as attracting significant stigma and make them feel different from other young people. On the positive side, findings suggested that services are most effective when they offer agency and are participatory; and that meaningful and supportive relationships with professionals can foster a sense of autonomy and independence.

Embedding mental health support at a school level can be a complex issue. Connelly *et al.* (2008) surveyed a large number of teachers in Scotland about how they responded to mental health difficulties. They found that teachers working with children and young people with mental health needs sometimes felt overwhelming difficulties in providing appropriate support. Furthermore, they felt challenged in their roles as educators while providing support. Working with specialist services in school can be an effective way for an early intervention; however, as revealed from evaluation studies of the Targeted Mental Health in Schools (TaMHS) UK pilot project (Cane and Oland, 2015; Wolpert *et al.*, 2013), this is not always straightforward. Findings were mixed, and although in general had positive impact for children in primary schools, addressing their behavioural and emotional needs, the impact was greater when targeting behavioural rather than emotional difficulties in primary school children (Wolpert *et al.*, 2013).

Support for young people with mental health needs, such as anxiety, depression and obsessive compulsive disorder

Frameworks for mental health assessment are prominent within mental health support for young people, for example *Diagnostic and Statistical Manual of Mental Disorders (DSM-V)* (American Psychiatric Association, 2013). However, it should also be noted that there is ongoing debate regarding social construction of depression, value-laden labelling and medicalization of depression, serving pharmaceutical companies' interests (cf. Horwitz and Wakefield, 2007; Moncrieff and Timimi, 2013). For example, Timimi (2010, 2014) argues that labelling of depression in children is unhelpful and excludes contextual factors, such as sociocultural family changes, family circumstances and work patterns. Anxiety is one of the most common mental health needs for children and young adults (Merikangas *et al.*, 2010) and it is widely acknowledged that depression can co-exist with anxiety and obsessive compulsive disorder (OCD) (Alvarenga *et al.*, 2016; Goodwin, 2015).

In terms of intervention, to take these three conditions as an example, the National Institute for Health and Care Excellence (NICE, 2005b) recommended first-line treatment for children and young people with OCD as cognitive behavioural therapy (CBT) with elements of exposure and response prevention, including for family and/or carers. Similarly, the guidelines recommend CBT for anxiety (NICE, 2014) and, in some cases, for depression (NICE, 2005a). However, budget cuts and increasing waiting times for child and adolescent mental health services (CAMHS) have put more pressure on educators to provide support and early intervention in schools, colleges and universities. Bullock *et al.* (2015) recently explored a range of practices and programmes to meet mental health needs of children and young people worldwide, including strategies that could be implemented within the school environment. They postulated that cultural diversity, beliefs and attitudes regarding parenting or child development should also be considered when implementing interventions.

Educational psychologist support for children and young people with mental health needs

The UK government-ratified Children and Families Act 2014 (UK Parliament, 2014) and the *Special Educational Needs and Disability Code of Practice* (DfE and DoH, 2015) saw educational psychologists (EPs) working with a wider age range, and supporting young people up to the age of 25. As part of research with EPs experienced in working with post-school learners, Atkinson *et al.* (2015) found that two-thirds of respondents thought mental health assessment should be an essential element of EP training. Furthermore, in undertaking appreciative inquiry with EPs and FE commissioners, Morris and Atkinson (2018) found that participants felt EPs could make an important contribution to post-16 mental health strategy in three areas: offering support at transition, building capacity and offering individual therapeutic support.

While the role EPs could offer in supporting young people's mental health could potentially span all five areas identified in the Currie Report (Scottish Executive, 2002) – assessment, consultation, intervention, research and training – the primary focus of this chapter will be on assessment and intervention, and work at the individual, rather than group or systemic, level. Specifically, the study will explore the experiences of a young person, 'Eric', who lived with anxiety and depression during his student years. This student was interviewed as part of doctoral research (Martin, 2017) that explored university students' retrospective experiences of living with depression during their educational career. An additional pseudonym has been used to protect the young person's identity.

In order to structure this chapter and to explore the potential role of EPs, the authors have used the recent Division of Educational and Child Psychology (DECP) report (Dunsmuir and Hardy, 2016) *Delivering Psychological Therapies in Schools and Communities*, which offers guidance to EPs in developing and offering therapeutic services. The section headers below relate specifically to the seven chapters of the report: theoretical frameworks and key principles; ethical practice; the evidence base; training and supervision; delivering psychological therapies: the practicalities; commissioning and service delivery; and evaluation.

The case study has been chosen because it charts the experience of a young person, Eric, who dealt with complex mental health problems, including anxiety and depression, and physical health problems, during his education. Discussions will be based around the testimony of this young man, who experienced a traumatic, school-based event at high school, received therapeutic support at sixth form that did not meet his needs, and then found life extremely difficult at university, eventually having to have time out, after experiencing what he described as a mental and physical breakdown. It should be noted that Eric did not work directly with an EP at any time during his school or university career. The authors feel that examining his experiences from the perspective of the Dunsmuir and Hardy (2016) guidance will allow opportunities for EPs to consider possibilities for supporting a post-school young person with complex mental health needs. The next section will offer a short biography of Eric.

Eric

This case study charts Eric's experiences from his childhood until his student years. As a child, Eric witnessed domestic violence and had a difficult relationship with his father. However, he remembers primary school fondly, where he had a small circle of friends. He had good relationships with his teachers, with his mum and sibling. Eric's father had some mental health problems, including experiencing bipolar disorder and depression. Eric was sometimes harshly punished and was scared of his father.

In Year 6, Eric was anxious about his standard attainment tests (SATs), although he performed well and dreamt of becoming a writer. He looked forward to high school, where for the first few days of transition, only Year 7 students attended, which led Eric 'into a false sense of security'. However, when another 1,200 students joined in, who were 'taller, broader, deeper voices, it was just overwhelming'.

Eric's friendship group began to drift away during secondary school, as his friends discovered new interests and 'keeping friends became less important and academic success became more important'. In Year 7 or 8, a teacher mentioned that Eric should be thinking about going to university, and this spurred him to work harder, both in academic terms, but also 'piling up and piling up' extra-curricular activities. At secondary school Eric reports instances of fire setting by other students, physical violence, false accusations against teachers, and anti-social behaviour in general. The school was in special measures and teachers were focusing more on managing behaviour than teaching.

Soon after starting secondary school, Eric was singled out by a group of Year 11 boys who kept bullying him. Eric kept hiding in a computer classroom during lunchtime; however, this was not supervised by any teacher. Mid-way through Year 7 during a computer break Eric describes being sexually assaulted; and how some of the bullies put pornography on his computer. After a few months he managed to report it to an adult. However, this was not handled sensitively and Eric was not supported during making the disclosure statement. He got very stressed and could not remember any names or recognize photographs. The incident was not reported to the police as Eric wanted to forget about his ordeal.

After the sexual assault in secondary school, Eric became 'an incredibly paranoid person', believing that this was his fault and living in fear about being arrested for having pornography on his school computer.

The perpetrator was not punished, and eventually left the school. Eric's situation did not improve and the bullying continued. Eric began to withdraw from life, giving up Scouts and other clubs he enjoyed.

When Eric moved to a sixth form, he met some new people and made new friends. Eric started experiencing more severe emotional difficulties and, as he describes, 'low points were getting lower and the length of them was increasing and there were a few times where it came close to just being a full breakdown'. At this time problems were also escalating at home. To combat his increasing anxiety Eric took on more and more work as well as other activities. He was suffering from 'heart strain', blackouts, weakness and numbness, and almost fainting but without losing consciousness.

With the support of a member of his new friendship group, Eric went to the doctors and following a medical investigation, he was offered therapy from a National Health Service (NHS) counsellor, to help with stress: 'but it still wasn't for help with sort of the depression and the anxiety, it was just the stress component and so I did some work with a therapist ... and got a little bit better with managing stress, but it didn't really help the other side of things; it didn't really help the depression or the anxiety'.

Only two of Eric's teachers knew he had to leave school to access therapy sessions. This was the first time school staff were made aware about some of Eric's difficulties. Eric felt unable to talk to anyone in school, friends after school or at home. During sixth form, he was offered special exam arrangement for AS-levels (first full year of Advanced A-level) but 'that was really as far as it went, there wasn't any extra help during lessons'. Later, Eric found out that a teacher in his sixth form was a trained counsellor but this support was not advertised: 'by sixth form I was aware that the system [of support] should have been there but wasn't ... or rather was but I didn't know it was there'. Eric felt the support was a bit 'patched up', without addressing the root cause.

When Eric started university, things got much worse for him in terms of his mental health and well-being. He 'stopped showering, stopped eating ... there was a period of about six days at one point where I just never left my room for food or water'. A friend supported him to see a doctor 'and then I ended up with a doctor, a counsellor, at one point a psychologist ... and ... I was put on medication and that's when ... sort of ... a proper ... support system got in place and ... the university, the counselling service contacted my department and my department started getting involved and being like 'Do you need anything for lectures? Do you need any extra support in that kind of thing?' And these were all things that I really could have done with like during school.' Unfortunately for Eric, the support came just too late, and shortly afterwards he experienced a 'breakdown' and had to take more than a year out to recover.

During his time out Eric received support and medication. He was back at university completing his studies when the research (Martin, 2017) was conducted.

Delivering therapies in school and communities

Eric's case will now be considered in relation to the *Delivering Psychological Therapies in School and Communities* guidance (Dunsmuir and Hardy, 2016), in accordance with the respective chapters, which form the section headers. It is hoped that this will highlight the potential role and contribution of the EP, as well as proposing suggestions for effective practice.

Chapter 1: Theoretical frameworks and key principles

An issue overlooked in mental health policy (DoH and DfE, 2017) has related to the determinants of mental health from a social and political context (BPS, 2018). Dunsmuir and Hardy (2016) advocated the consideration of ecological and systemic perspectives (e.g. Bronfenbrenner, 2005) in offering a holistic perspective on the mental health issues experienced by young people.

Dunsmuir and Hardy (2016) urged EPs to consider the role that environmental factors have, not only on shaping and maintaining difficulties, but also on possibilities for change. In this case, early experiences and home factors may well have increased Eric's vulnerability. More significantly, the bullying and assault, coupled with an inadequate and inappropriate response from his high school, were the main antecedents for his subsequent mental health difficulties.

From an EP perspective, consideration of the balance of risk and protective factors might have allowed a more systemic response to Eric's needs. In the excerpt below, Eric describes how community and home factors both supported him, and made him more vulnerable, at the time he was experiencing depression.

' ... community got a bit easier because among the extra things that I'd been doing, I met a really nice group of people and they were among the ones who sort of noticed this and sort of ... recommended that I do something about it; because it was clearly having a big effect on me and a lot of them ... a lot of them, the same people, remained the solid support for sort of the next few years.'

'Home … was a bit more difficult because as well as mine [depression] getting worse, my dad's had got significantly worse … around the same time, so home … when I was at home it was never really about … my depression, which was a worry, it was about my dad's and sort of the way that was making him behave … '

A systematic literature by NCH (2007) not only identified resilience factors specific to adolescence, but also detailed effective strategies for promoting resilience in adolescence and young adulthood (13–19 years). Strategies that may have been particularly helpful to Eric include: 'Positive school experiences'; 'A committed mentor or other person from outside the family'; and 'Participation in a range of extra-curricular activities' (p. 9).

STIGMA

'It wasn't something that came easily, I wasn't … very open in talking about this, even though some of it had been happening for years and years … '

A systematic literature review by the Children's Commissioner (Apland *et al.*, 2017) revealed that mental illness is perceived as attracting stigma by young people. The report revealed that young people often have 'highly stereotyped' (p. 7) conceptualizations of mental health difficulties and that self-stigma is often reinforced by interactions with others. While the DoH and DfE (2017) proposed 'the school environment is non-stigmatising, making interventions offered in this context more acceptable to children and young people, and their parents' (Section 23), EPs can work with young people to break down the stigma around getting or accepting support (Atkinson *et al.*, 2018).

Chapter 2: Ethical practice

'I didn't really understand much about the treatment options available, the, the therapy and the medication side, I wasn't really … in the know and so – and just who I was as a person. I didn't think it was something I'd be able to realistically change, not even in a big way, just in a small way, just managing it. I didn't think it was something I'd be able to get to and even though it was something I really wanted to happen. I didn't know how to get there or even how to start getting there; I just sort of lived with it.'

Central to this section is the BPS (2009) *Code of Ethics and Conduct* and its four principles of respect, competence, responsibility and integrity. These aspects will be explored in relation to the work undertaken with Eric, and the possible role an EP might undertake in working with him.

The quote at the beginning of this section raises issues about considerations EPs must make to the *integrity* of their therapeutic work with young people. Eric did not understand the treatment options available to him. His statement suggests he had limited self-efficacy for change. It also appears that preferred outcomes were not discussed and that Eric had no sense of what a successful therapeutic intervention might look like.

Dunsmuir and Hardy (2016) proposed that one question that should form part of the ethical basis for working with young people is: 'What knowledge and understanding does the child or young person have about the therapeutic approach offered?' (p. 10). Eric's apparent confusion about the nature and aims of the therapy might have been alleviated by clear and detailed information, presented in a young-person-friendly format, and as many times as required. This would have allowed him to participate in decision-making and allowing choice and autonomy in selecting treatment options. It would also have ensured that he was at the centre of setting and evaluating outcomes.

Had Eric been seen by an EP at sixth form, and a formulation made about the difficulties he was experiencing, one plausible explanation might have been that he was suffering from post-traumatic stress after the assault at high school. Although there is some evidence of EPs undertaking specialist work with individuals around trauma (e.g. Yates, 2009), this would typically require additional resources, including access to additional training and specialist supervision (see Chapter 4: Training and supervision). So, while from a *competence* perspective the individual EP may not have been best placed to assume the role of a therapist, they might have been able to act as keyworker (Cryer and Atkinson, 2015), thus enacting their *responsibility* towards acting in the young person's best interests, by enabling multi-agency practice (Section 2.2).

In the event that individual therapy (e.g. through CAMHS, or adult mental health services) was deemed appropriate, the EP acting in their capacity as caseworker could have looked at systemic solutions for reducing his emotional arousal, or using something like the human emotional needs framework (Griffin and Tyrrell, 2003) to audit his emotional needs, and established simple, practical and pragmatic strategies to support his mental health. Finally, *respect* would be observed by ensuring confidentiality and informed consent within all interactions.

Chapter 3: The evidence base

Evidence-based practice (EBP) has its roots in medicine and health-related professions, such as physiotherapy and occupational therapy (Kratochwill, 2007). According to the American Psychological Association (2006), 'evidence-based practice in psychology (EBPP) is the integration of best available research with clinical expertise in the context of patient characteristics, culture, and preferences' (p. 273).

The Health and Care Professions Council (HCPC, 2015) professional standards regarding EBP indicate that psychologists should draw upon scientific evidence in their professional practice. There are, however, some issues associated with EBP in educational psychology, as the research, and knowledge produced as a result of it, is a product situated in time and culture and not completely value-free (cf. Hollway, 2012; Kennedy and Monsen, 2016). Moreover, there are proposed frameworks for practice for EPs (Kelly, 2008, 2012) and BPS (2002) codes of practice and guidelines that require collaboration with service users to enable their involvement in the process of planning, assessing, implementing and reviewing interventions.

Lane and Corrie (2006) propose that as modern scientist-practitioners, psychologists should act within the following framework:

- the ability to think effectively;
- the ability to produce a formulation or a story, based on gathered information, that is grounded in psychological knowledge;
- the ability to act effectively, including creative and inventive solutions to produce intervention plans;
- the ability to critique own work, including evaluation and reflections upon own actions and 'the use of scientific inquiry to guide and evaluate own work'. (p. 3)

In Eric's case, once his needs had been established, one aspect of an EP intervention would have been to ascertain which evidence-based approaches might have been appropriate to support him. However, the implementation of this approach would need to be cognisant of cultural, contextual and individual factors; and utilize practice-based evidence in making judgements about its effectiveness.

THE THERAPEUTIC RELATIONSHIP

Miller and Rose (2009) highlighted the importance of considering both the relational (relating to the relationship with the client) and technical (relating to delivery of the specific intervention) components of therapeutic work. For instance, Moyers and Miller (2013) found that low therapist empathy was associated with poor client outcomes. It is argued that some therapeutic modalities, such as person-centred counselling and motivational interviewing, define the relational features of therapeutic interventions coherently; while others offer a clearer technical intervention, such as CBT and solution-focused brief therapy (SFBT) (e.g. Driessen and Hollon, 2011). It is therefore suggested for EPs that explicit consideration of relational factors accompanies technical delivery of any evidence-based approach. For example these are defined as empathy, genuineness and unconditional positive regard by Rogers (1951); or acceptance, compassion, evocation and partnership by Miller and Rollnick (2012).

Chapter 4: Training and supervision

' ... around May time I had a proper full breakdown in which I just – it was during an exam ... which my department had nicely let me sit in a room pretty much on my own to do this exam ... and I just had a breakdown and ... sort of went home to recover for a year and a few months.'

' ... it had just ... it had gone too far and unchecked and ... I needed some proper time to just focus on fixing it and nothing else.'

The excerpts above describe Eric's experiences during his first year at university. The support he had received at sixth form had been insufficient in preparing him for the transition to university and to independent living. The quotes illustrate how accessing the right support is of paramount importance; and can determine future outcomes. The HCPC standards of proficiency for practitioner psychologists state that:

> Your scope of practice is the area or areas of your profession in which you have the knowledge, skills and experience to practise lawfully, safely and effectively, in a way that meets our standards and does not pose any danger to the public or to yourself. (HCPC, 2015: 4)

It is important that practitioners working therapeutically are mindful of BPS (2009) standards highlighted by Dunsmuir and Hardy (2016). Specifically, essential elements of therapeutic work are cited as follows:

- have successfully undertaken additional training
- be actively working in therapeutic practice
- undertake regular supervision from an appropriately qualified supervisor

- be committed to developing the evidence base of the therapeutic practice
- be actively engaged in gaining further training and development in therapeutic practice. (Dunsmuir and Hardy, 2016: 19)

While EPs have skills and knowledge transferable to working with post-16 populations (Clifford, 2013), it is also important to note that Atkinson *et al.* (2015) found that EPs with post-16 expertise highlighted specific competencies, which included mental health assessment, for which there should be specific post-16 training within doctoral programmes.

As EPs potentially respond both increasingly to young people's mental health needs (BPS, 2018) and to working with post-16 learners, it is important for educational psychology services to reflect on these developments, and ensure that training and supervisory structures are in place to support and protect both young people and the EPs working with them. Dunsmuir and Leadbetter (2010) proposed that in addition to generic supervision, EPs might need specialist supervision for certain aspects of their work, including therapeutic practice.

Chapter 5: Delivering psychological therapies: The practicalities

' ... really all they had to go on was that I was just a very stressed ... and ... stressed person and they probably came to the conclusion that it was the stress that was making me sad and just fix the stress and I'll stop feeling sad and that didn't really happen, but ... the therapy didn't end ... really when I left ... the therapy didn't really come to a natural close. I sort of went from therapy and just came to university afterwards; they ended a few months before I think because I'd got exams and things. But it was more ... we didn't have like the opportunity to carry on with it, so I just took the tactics I'd got for dealing with stress and ... ran with them and used them for what I could.'

Under *appropriateness of the intervention*, Dunsmuir and Hardy (2016) described steps that might be taken to assist decision-making about therapeutic work (Figure 4, p. 24). In Figure 6.1 below, this flow chart is recreated, this time with consideration to Eric's experience.

Step 1: Referral As part of Step 1, different referral routes, including self- and third-party referrals, are described (Dunsmuir and Hardy, 2016). School-based self-referral was not an available option to Eric, or at least not something he was aware of. This is despite the fact that there was a trained person in school who could have helped him. Following his GP referral, no consultation with school was evident; and there was no signposting to alternative services.

Step 2: Triage Dunsmuir and Hardy (2016) suggested preliminary, comprehensive, multi-agency triage assessment. This did not happen in Eric's case. Because of this, his therapeutic support was targeted purely at managing stress, and did not address any of the underlying issues, including the traumatic events he had experienced at high school.

Step 3: Acceptance for therapy Eric received support from an NHS counsellor. However, he was not given information about the therapy (see quote at start of Chapter 2 section). It is plausible that he met criteria for stress/anxiety-based support, but because a detailed case history was not taken, nor a psychological formulation carried out, the support he received did not address his problems, or prepare him for university.

Step 4: Agree contract A contract was not agreed with Eric at the start of the therapy. He did not have information about the therapeutic approach or any choice about treatment options. Expected outcomes were not discussed with him. When he went to university, although he needed support, next steps were not clarified nor support at university contracted or signposted.

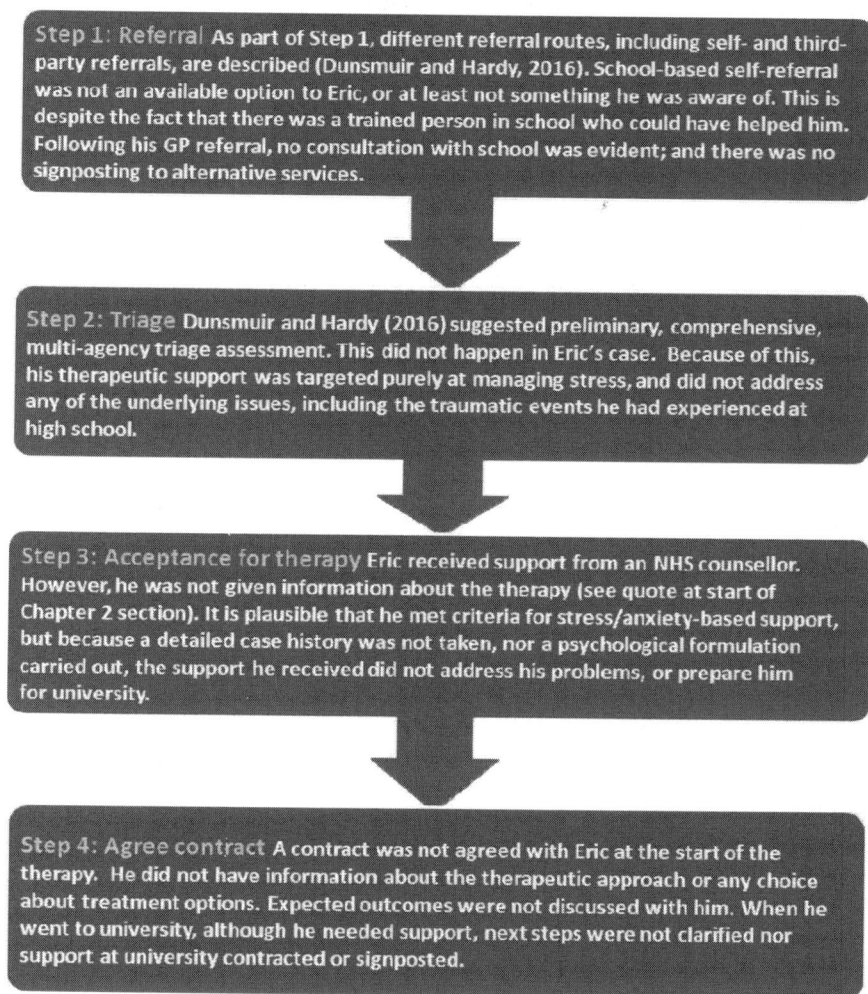

Figure 6.1: Procedures for acceptance of therapy considered from Eric's experience

Source: Dunsmuir and Hardy (2016)

As is clear from Figure 6.1, there was a distinct lack of transparency within the referral process, acceptance for therapy and contracting within this case. Eric's recollection of the support notes: 'I think they got the impression that I was a very stressed person and that there was possibly some anxious elements in there, but they'd not really picked it up that it was a problem in itself.' It is possible that triage, a multi-agency forum and a clear case formulation may have enabled more appropriate and holistic support for Eric.

Within Chapter 5, Dunsmuir and Hardy (2016) also discussed *criteria/conditions for discontinuation of therapy*. A range of reasons for this are described, but one that is not mentioned is transition. In this case, Eric's therapy ended when he moved to university. From Eric's statement at the beginning of this section it is clear that there was not any closure or ending to the therapeutic support he received. In fact, on going to university and his therapy finishing, Eric said, 'There was quite a lot that was not being tied up or dealt with at that point, just a lot of open ... open problems.' This raises issues for EP practice, in that it is perfectly plausible that a young person could make a transition, to college or university, to another FE setting, to independent living, or to paid employment, before the therapeutic intervention is complete. However, it is important that if ongoing support is required, as it was in Eric's case, this is negotiated and contracted with the involvement of the young person. In this case it would have been potentially helpful to ensure, towards the end of the therapy, that on moving to university there would be, at the very least, a key person in place to support Eric to settle him in and access ongoing support. With Eric's permission, or maybe even with him taking the lead, it may have been better to ensure this support was already in place before he left home.

In sharing any information with other agencies, it would be important to adhere to the Caldicott principles (Caldicott Committee, 1997) as well as the new General Data Protection Regulation (GDPR). In Eric's case it would appear that principles of information sharing and confidentiality were upheld, in that only a couple of his teachers knew that he was receiving therapy. However, given the fact that he was a capable student and at sixth form, it may have been useful to involve him more directly in these discussions.

There was no evidence that *communication protocols for feeding back and reporting to children and young people and parents/carers* (Dunsmuir and Hardy, 2016: Section 5.5) were used to document either the initial contracting of the therapy, or to convey to Eric areas of progress or ongoing need. Dunsmuir and Hardy (2016) suggested these can take many forms, including letters and emails, and can help to strengthen the therapeutic alliance and to provide a permanent record of progress. They can also help support psychoeducation and communicate strengths and needs to adults supporting the young person.

Chapter 6: Commissioning and service delivery

'I'd just spent all of school and then all of sixth form ... with no support network and then the first semester of university not reaching out to the support network that was there ... and ... it had just ... it had gone too far and unchecked and ... I needed some proper time to just focus on fixing it and nothing else. So not trying to fix it and also do work ... I just ... and that was when I properly started using support networks which was way too late.'

Lee and Woods (2017) noted that following the development of traded services, some services (therapy is the example provided) might be viewed as an effective use of EP time by some schools, but not by others. This can potentially lead to differential access to therapeutic support from EPs for young people in different schools. Dunsmuir and Hardy (2016) proposed putting citizens at the heart of commissioning. Indeed, in Morris and Atkinson's (2018) exploration of how EPs might work effectively in FE settings to support mental health, one of the proposed suggestions was for a self-referral system for young people, to ensure that they were not reliant on third-party referrals. Creating this kind of system within post-16 settings might improve both access to and the timing of the therapeutic interventions.

Alongside the actual commissioning of the EP services should come consultation about the joint responsibilities of all parties involved. This is particularly important in ensuring a holistic response to young people's needs. Snape and Atkinson (2017) highlighted the need for systemic factors to be considered alongside therapeutic work, acknowledging that where these were not recognized and addressed they could potentially jeopardize the effectiveness of the therapeutic intervention. This links in with assertions by Asay and Lambert (1999) that up to 40 per cent of therapeutic change is due to extra-therapeutic factors. It also highlights the need to use 'the ability of EPs to spot potential "levers for change" outside the therapeutic relationship which may be instrumental in improving outcomes' (Cryer and Atkinson, 2015: 68). In Eric's case: 'I think at one point the idea was suggested that I could possibly have extra time in exams ... but that was as far as it went, there wasn't any extra help during school lessons and that kind of thing.' A more co-ordinated and responsive approach may have enabled him to feel more settled at school and helped promote the positive school experiences advocated in promoting resilience (NCH, 2007). Furthermore, having a key person he could talk to in sixth form might have meant that Eric opened up about his problems before going to university, instead of recalling, 'I wasn't ... very open in talking about this [his mental health problems], even though some of it had been happening for years and years.'

Finally, responsibility lies beyond therapeutic interventions and EPs can also work systemically with school staff, empowering them to provide early intervention and promote the building of resiliency within school communities.

Chapter 7: Evaluation

> ... I'd just find a quiet space and just sit there for a while, so at sixth form that tended to be the – there was a common room that they built in the science department and no one used it but everyone just went and used the main common room.
>
> ... I'd just be sat in silence, so that was ... that was ... yeah, that was an interesting one, but for most of them it was just finding a quiet space to sit for a while and just away from stress and ... and ... on reflection I should have taken more of those breaks and longer ... to sort of ... think more about how I needed to deal with it rather than just ... doing it to deal with the symptoms and then ... going back straight into it ... so ... it was more ... doing what I needed to do to keep going rather than ... trying to fix it.

Eric's quote in the 'Chapter 2' section illustrates his low expectations of the therapeutic support he received. The statements above reveal not only his isolation and withdrawal at sixth form, but also how the therapy he was receiving was only offering superficial support for addressing his problems.

Hobbs *et al.* (2000) discussed the role of the EP in terms of consulting with and gaining the views of young people. They asserted:

> The process of psychological assessment should not only provide the educational psychologist with a fuller understanding of the child's educational world (and other worlds), it should also provide the child with a greater understanding of their own situation and what actions may be open to them to undertake positive change. (p. 113)

Chapter 7 of Dunsmuir and Hardy's (2016) guidance provides comprehensive advice on evaluating therapeutic outcomes. What is particularly striking in

Eric's case, and which has implications for post-16 practice, is that desired outcomes do not appear to have been discussed with Eric. It could have been that there was consensus with his counsellor that the aim would be to reduce stress. However, using session-by-session measures (Duncan *et al.*, 2003) or self-set measures using Target Monitoring and Evaluation (Dunsmuir *et al.*, 2009) might have allowed Eric a greater sense of agency, and revealed a more sophisticated, and outcomes-focused response to his needs. Furthermore, EPs are becoming increasing adept at using the Preparing for Adulthood (2013) outcomes – paid employment, good health, independent living and community inclusion – in helping young people think about transition to adulthood. Retrospectively, it becomes clear that on leaving home for university, arrangements for at least three of these outcomes were insufficient to enable him to complete his programme without a significant interruption to his studies. It is therefore advocated that Preparing for Adulthood (2013) is also used within post-16 therapeutic casework.

Conclusions

Schools and educational environments are 'ecologically valid settings' (Fox *et al.*, 2014: 356) when it comes to helping students. The recent Green Paper (DoH and DfE, 2017: Section 23) suggested that mental health provision offered *in situ* for students can help provide a graduated response, potentially be cognisant of educational triggers, and reduce stigma. However, within this document, the role of EPs in supporting the mental health of young people was largely overlooked. Subsequently, the BPS (2018) called for a greater role for applied psychologists, including EPs, to work directly with educational settings in promoting mental health.

This chapter charts the retrospective student experiences of Eric, a young man who experienced mental health problems during his educational career. The problems persisted into adulthood and ultimately jeopardized the completion of his university degree. Eric's experiences are benchmarked against Dunsmuir and Hardy's (2016) DECP guidance for *Delivering Psychological Therapies in Schools and Communities*. In summary, key recommendations arising from this case study, which may be useful for EPs to consider, are highlighted in Table 6.1.

Table 6.1: Recommendations arising from the retrospective case study

Chapter	Key recommendations
1. Theoretical frameworks and key principles	• Assess and be cognisant of systemic factors that may have an impact on the young person's mental health • Identify risk and resilience factors that may support or inhibit the effectiveness of the intervention • Consider adolescent-appropriate strategies for promoting resilience • Look at provision-wide approaches for reducing stigma
2. Ethical practice	• Ensure that the young person has agency in discussions about the intervention • Check that the young person is fully informed about the nature and aims of therapy • Allow participation in decision-making and choice and autonomy in selecting treatment options • Practise within levels of competence, and seek advice and supervision appropriately • Adopt a 'keyworker' role where therapy is delivered by external agencies • Ensure confidentiality and consent in accordance with professional guidelines
3. The evidence base	• Refer to research to inform good practice • Be mindful of cultural and contextual factors • Adopt a scientist-practitioner approach to therapy • Be attentive to both relational and technical aspects of therapy
4. Training and supervision	• Ensure sufficient training has been received • Consider the application of knowledge to post-16 practice • Access generic and specialist supervision, as appropriate
5. Delivering psychological therapies: The practicalities	• Ensure that a psychological formulation and, where appropriate, triage and multi-agency discussions inform access to therapy • Be especially mindful of endings and follow-up • If the young person is transitioning to independent life, ensure ongoing needs are supported • Be aware of information-sharing protocols • Use written artefacts to communicate progress and outcomes to the young person

Chapter	Key recommendations
6. Commissioning and service delivery	• Consider equality of provision within traded models of service delivery • Try to encourage self-referral pathways • Advocate for holistic and systemic support around the therapeutic intervention • Empower school staff to support young people
7. Evaluation	• Put the young person at the centre of outcomes evaluation • Consider using sessional and self-set measures • Think about Preparing for Adulthood (2013) outcomes

Source: Related to Dunsmuir and Hardy (2016)

It should be noted that the chapter does not set out to criticize the actions of others and the support Eric received. Indeed, the case study is based on Eric's testimony alone, and not substantiated by or triangulated by the adults involved. Furthermore, it is noted that some of the events in school date back more than ten years, and it is very much hoped that school-based responses to safeguarding, bullying and mental health are more robust and supportive in the current era.

Nevertheless, the experience through Eric's eyes makes salutary reading. It is hoped that considering it here, with reference to guidelines that were published subsequent to his 'breakdown', might help EPs to pre-empt issues and protect against problems. Perhaps most significantly, it seems to illustrate the need to place the young person at the centre of decision-making, contracting, intervention, evaluation, outcomes-planning and preparation for adulthood. It is also hoped that it helps raise the profile of Dunsmuir and Hardy's (2016) guidance, which offers multiple dimensions by which to establish safe and effective therapeutic practice.

References

Alvarenga, P.G., do Rosario, M.C., Cesar, R.C., Manfro, G.G., Moriyama, T.S., Bloch, M.H., Shavitt, R.G., Hoexter, M.Q., Coughlin, C.G., Leckman, J.F. and Miguel, E.C. (2016) 'Obsessive-compulsive symptoms are associated with psychiatric comorbidities, behavioral and clinical problems: A population-based study of Brazilian school children'. *European Child and Adolescent Psychiatry*, 25 (2), 175–82.

American Psychiatric Association (2013) *Diagnostic and Statistical Manual of Mental Disorders: DSM-5*. 5th ed. Arlington, VA: American Psychiatric Association.

American Psychological Association Presidential Task Force on Evidence-Based Practice (2006) 'Evidence-based practice in psychology'. *American Psychologist*, 61 (4), 271–85.

Apland, K., Lawrence, H., Mesie, J. and Yarrow, E. (2017) *Children's Voices: A review of evidence on the subjective wellbeing of children with mental health needs in England*. London: Children's Commissioner for England.

Asay, T.P. and Lambert, M.J. (1999) 'The empirical case for the common factors in therapy: Quantitative findings'. In Hubble, M.A., Duncan, B.L. and Miller, S.D. (eds) *The Heart and Soul of Change: What works in therapy*. Washington, DC: American Psychological Association, 23–55.

Atkinson, C., Dunsmuir, S., Lang, J. and Wright, S. (2015) 'Developing a competency framework for the initial training of educational psychologists working with young people aged 16–25'. *Educational Psychology in Practice*, 31 (2), 159–73.

Atkinson, C., Thomas, G., Goodhall, N., Barker, L., Healey, I., Wilkinson, L. and Ogunmyiwa, J. (2018) 'Student-led, whole school mental health initiatives: An example from practice'. Paper presented at the Division of Educational and Child Psychology Conference, Brighton, 11–12 January 2018.

BPS (British Psychological Society) (2002) *Professional Practice Guidelines: Division of Educational and Child Psychology*. Leicester: British Psychological Society.

BPS (British Psychological Society) (2009) *Code of Ethics and Conduct*. Leicester: British Psychological Society.

BPS (British Psychological Society) (2018) 'Child mental health green paper is a missed opportunity'. *BPS News*, 5 March. Online. www.bps.org.uk/news-and-policy/child-mental-health-green-paper-missed-opportunity?utm_source=BPS_Lyris_email&utm_medium=email&utm_campaign= (accessed 16 August 2018).

Bronfenbrenner, U. (ed.) (2005) *Making Human Beings Human: Bioecological perspectives on human development*. Thousand Oaks, CA: SAGE Publications.

Bullock, L.M., Zolkoski, S.M. and Estes, M.B. (2015) 'Meeting the mental health needs of children and youth: Using evidence-based education worldwide'. *Emotional and Behavioural Difficulties*, 20 (4), 398–414.

Caldicott Committee (1997) *Report on the Review of Patient-Identifiable Information*. London: Department of Health. Online. http://webarchive. nationalarchives.gov.uk/20130124064947/http://www.dh.gov.uk/ prod_consum_dh/groups/dh_digitalassets/@dh/@en/documents/digitalasset/ dh_4068404.pdf (accessed 25 August 2018).

Cane, F.E. and Oland, L. (2015) 'Evaluating the outcomes and implementation of a TaMHS (Targeting Mental Health in Schools) project in four West Midlands (UK) schools using activity theory'. *Educational Psychology in Practice*, 31 (1), 1–20.

Clark, A.F., O'Malley, A., Woodham, A., Barrett, B. and Byford, S. (2005) 'Children with complex mental health problems: Needs, costs and predictors over one year'. *Child and Adolescent Mental Health*, 10 (4), 170–8.

Clifford, V. (2013) 'Applying psychology to education and learning for 16 to 25-year-olds: New horizons, opportunities and challenges 2013'. Training session presented to Bolton EPS, 19 December 2013.

Connelly, G., Lockhart, E., Wilson, P., Furnivall, J., Bryce, G., Barbour, R. and Phin, L. (2008) 'Teachers' responses to the emotional needs of children and young people: Results from the Scottish Needs Assessment Programme'. *Emotional and Behavioural Difficulties*, 13 (1), 7–19.

Cryer, S. and Atkinson, C. (2015) 'Exploring the use of motivational interviewing with a disengaged primary-aged child'. *Educational Psychology in Practice,* 31 (1), 56–72.

DfE (Department for Education) and DoH (Department of Health) (2015) *Special Educational Needs and Disability Code of Practice: 0 to 25 years: Statutory guidance for organisations which work with and support children and young people who have special educational needs or disabilities.* London: Department for Education. Online. https://assets.publishing.service.gov.uk/government/uploads/system/uploads/attachment_data/file/398815/SEND_Code_of_Practice_January_2015.pdf (accessed 23 August 2018).

DoH (Department of Health) and DfE (Department for Education) (2017) *Transforming Children and Young People's Mental Health Provision: A Green Paper.* London: Department of Health. Online. www.gov.uk/government/uploads/system/uploads/attachment_data/file/664855/Transforming_children_and_young_people_s_mental_health_provision.pdf (accessed 25 August 2018).

Driessen, E. and Hollon, S.D. (2011) 'Motivational interviewing from a cognitive behavioral perspective'. *Cognitive and Behavioral Practice,* 18 (1), 70–3.

Duncan, B.L., Miller, S.D., Sparks, J.A., Claud, D.A., Reynolds, L.R., Brown, J. and Johnson, L.D. (2003) 'The session rating scale: Preliminary psychometric properties of a "working" alliance measure'. *Journal of Brief Therapy,* 3 (1), 3–12.

Dunsmuir, S., Brown, E., Iyadurai, S. and Monsen, J. (2009) 'Evidence-based practice and evaluation: From insight to impact'. *Educational Psychology in Practice,* 25 (1), 53–70.

Dunsmuir, S. and Hardy, J. (2016) *Delivering Psychological Therapies in Schools and Communities.* Leicester: British Psychological Society.

Dunsmuir, S. and Leadbetter, J. (2010) *Professional Supervision: Guidelines for practice for educational psychologists.* Leicester: British Psychological Society.

Fox, J.K., Herzig, K., Colognori, D., Stewart, C.E. and Warner, C.M. (2014) 'School-based treatment for anxiety in children and adolescents: New developments in transportability and dissemination'. In Weist, M.D., Lever, N.A., Bradshaw, C.P. and Sarno Owens, J. (eds) *Handbook of School Mental Health: Research, training, practice, and policy.* 2nd ed. New York: Springer, 355–68.

Goodwin, G.M. (2015) 'The overlap between anxiety, depression, and obsessive-compulsive disorder'. *Dialogues in Clinical Neuroscience,* 17 (3), 249–60.

Green, H., McGinnity, Á., Meltzer, H., Ford, T. and Goodman, R. (2005) *Mental Health of Children and Young People in Great Britain, 2004.* Basingstoke: Palgrave Macmillan.

Griffin, J. and Tyrrell, I. (2003) *Human Givens: A new approach to emotional health and clear thinking.* Chalvington: HG Publishing.

HCPC (Health and Care Professions Council) (2015) *Standards of Proficiency: Practitioner psychologists.* London: Health and Care Professions Council. Online. www.hpc-uk.org/assets/documents/10002963SOP_Practitioner_psychologists.pdf (accessed 24 August 2018).

Hobbs, C., Todd, L. and Taylor, J. (2000) 'Consulting with children and young people: Enabling educational psychologists to work collaboratively'. *Educational and Child Psychology,* 17 (4), 107–15.

Hollway, W. (2012) 'Social psychology: Past and present'. In Hollway, W., Lucey, H., Phoenix, A. and Lewis, G. (eds) *DD307 Social Psychology Matters: Book 1*. 2nd ed. Milton Keynes: Open University, 59–90.

Horwitz, A.V. and Wakefield, J.C. (2007) *The Loss of Sadness: How psychiatry transformed normal sorrow into depressive disorder*. New York: Oxford University Press.

Kelly, B. (2008) 'Frameworks for practice in educational psychology: Coherent perspectives for a developing profession'. In Kelly, B., Woolfson, L. and Boyle, J. (eds) *Frameworks for Practice in Educational Psychology: A textbook for trainees and practitioners*. London: Jessica Kingsley Publishers, 15–30.

Kelly, B. (2012) 'Implementation science and enhancing delivery and practice in school psychology services: Some lessons from the Scottish context'. In Kelly, B. and Perkins, D.F. (eds) *Handbook of Implementation Science for Psychology in Education*. New York: Cambridge University Press, 111–31.

Kennedy, E.-K. and Monsen, J.J. (2016) 'Evidence-based practice in educational and child psychology: Opportunities for practitioner-researchers using problem-based methodology'. *Educational and Child Psychology*, 33 (3), 11–25.

Kratochwill, T.R. (2007) 'Preparing psychologists for evidence-based school practice: Lessons learned and challenges ahead'. *American Psychologist*, 62 (8), 829–43.

Lane, D.A. and Corrie, S. (2006) *The Modern Scientist-Practitioner: A guide to practice in psychology*. London: Routledge.

Lee, K. and Woods, K. (2017) 'Exploration of the developing role of the educational psychologist within the context of "traded" psychological services'. *Educational Psychology in Practice*, 33 (2), 111–25.

Martin, D.I. (2017) 'Support? What Support? An Exploratory Study of Young People's Experiences of Living with Depression during Their Student Years'. Unpublished doctoral thesis, University of Manchester.

Merikangas, K.R., He, J., Burstein, M., Swanson, S.A., Avenevoli, S., Cui, L., Benjet, C., Georgiades, K. and Swendsen, J. (2010) 'Lifetime prevalence of mental disorders in US adolescents: Results from the National Comorbidity Survey Replication – Adolescent Supplement (NCS-A)'. *Journal of the American Academy of Child and Adolescent Psychiatry*, 49 (10), 980–9.

Miller, W.R. and Rollnick, S. (2012) *Motivational Interviewing: Helping people change*. 3rd ed. New York: Guilford Press.

Miller, W.R. and Rose, G.S. (2009) 'Toward a theory of motivational interviewing'. *American Psychologist*, 64 (6), 527–37.

Moncrieff, J. and Timimi, S. (2013) 'The social and cultural construction of psychiatric knowledge: An analysis of NICE guidelines on depression and ADHD'. *Anthropology and Medicine*, 20 (1), 59–71.

Morris, R. and Atkinson, C. (2018) 'How can educational psychologists work within further education to support young people's mental health? An appreciative inquiry'. *Research in Post-Compulsory Education*. In press.

Moyers, T.B. and Miller, W.R. (2013) 'Is low therapist empathy toxic?'. *Psychology of Addictive Behaviors*, 27 (3), 878–84.

NCH (2007) *Literature Review: Resilience in children and young people*. London: NCH.

NICE (National Institute for Health and Care Excellence) (2005a) *Depression in Children and Young People: Identification and management* (NICE Clinical Guideline CG28). London: National Institute for Health and Care Excellence.

NICE (National Institute for Health and Care Excellence) (2005b) *Obsessive-Compulsive Disorder and Body Dysmorphic Disorder: Treatment* (NICE Clinical Guideline CG31). London: National Institute for Health and Care Excellence.

NICE (National Institute for Health and Care Excellence) (2014) *Anxiety Disorders* (NICE Quality Standard QS53). London: National Institute for Health and Care Excellence.

Preparing for Adulthood (2013) *Delivering Support and Aspiration for Disabled Young People*. Bath: Preparing for Adulthood.

Rogers, C.R. (1951) *Client-Centered Therapy: Its current practice, implications, and theory*. Boston: Houghton Mifflin.

Rothì, D.M. and Leavey, G. (2006) 'Mental health help-seeking and young people: A review'. *Pastoral Care in Education*, 24 (3), 4–13.

Scottish Executive (2002) *Review of Provision of Educational Psychology Services in Scotland*. Edinburgh: Scottish Executive.

Snape, L. and Atkinson, C. (2017) 'Students' views on the effectiveness of motivational interviewing for challenging disaffection'. *Educational Psychology in Practice*, 33 (2), 189–205.

Timimi, S. (2010) 'The McDonaldization of childhood: Children's mental health in neo-liberal market cultures'. *Transcultural Psychiatry*, 47 (5), 686–706.

Timimi, S. (2014) 'No more psychiatric labels: Why formal psychiatric diagnostic systems should be abolished'. *International Journal of Clinical and Health Psychology*, 14 (3), 208–15.

UK Parliament (2014) 'Children and Families Act 2014'. Online. www.legislation. gov.uk/ukpga/2014/6/contents/enacted (accessed 25 August 2018).

Warwick, I., Maxwell, C., Simon, A., Statham, J. and Aggleton, P. (2006) *Mental Health and Emotional Well-Being of Students in Further Education: A scoping study*. London: Thomas Coram Research Unit. Online. http://discovery.ucl. ac.uk/10000056/1/Mental_health_in_FE.pdf (accessed 28 August 2018).

Warwick, I., Maxwell, C., Statham, J., Aggleton, P. and Simon, A. (2008) 'Supporting mental health and emotional well-being among younger students in further education'. *Journal of Further and Higher Education*, 32 (1), 1–13.

Wolpert, M., Humphrey, N., Belsky, J. and Deighton, J. (2013) 'Embedding mental health support in schools: Learning from the Targeted Mental Health in Schools (TaMHS) national evaluation'. *Emotional and Behavioural Difficulties*, 18 (3), 270–83.

Yates, Y. (2009) 'The Effectiveness of a Human Givens Therapeutic Intervention with Adolescents Reporting Poor Subjective Well-Being: Multiple case studies in a socially deprived ward'. Unpublished doctoral thesis, University of Manchester.

Part Two

Casework and psychological
interventions

2

Transitions from school to further education

Jayne Manning

Research context

Background

This chapter is primarily based on research completed as part of my doctoral training, during 2015 and 2016. This was the time when we were seeing the implications of the new *Special Educational Needs and Disability Code of Practice* (Department for Education (DfE) and Department of Health (DoH), 2015) coming to fruition, namely the young people interviewed for the research were part of the first cohort to have their additional needs recognized through an Education, Health and Care Plan (EHCP) as opposed to a Statement of Special Educational Needs. Other such features of the Code, such as the emphasis on children and young people's voices and tailoring provision and outcomes to meet their own aspirations, will of course be reflected on. However, it is important to recognize that at this time any impact of the Code on professionals' approaches to supporting young people had not yet come to light and the 'new' way of working was in its infancy.

Area of interest

Transition points within a young person's educational journey are critical times that can evoke challenge, excitement and uncertainty for the individual and those around them.

Arguably, the transition that takes place post-16 may further heighten such emotions due to the greater number of possible destinations available. For instance this can include programmes within schools, colleges, private providers, specialist provisions, training courses and apprenticeships. Equally, within college and school settings there may be further variety within the types of programmes on offer such as the level and style of delivery.

My interest in this topic emerged from my personal experience and work in the education sector to date. Personally, I experienced a number of transitions within education that presented the opportunity for reflection both on who I was and where I was within my educational journey. Each educational setting I attended had its own ethos, culture and approach to the learning environment. A significant shift in ethos could be seen in the move to post-16 education, which is arguably reflected across a variety of settings in the United Kingdom, namely an increase in student autonomy and a clearer focus upon future goals. I consider that education has a central role in preparing young people for their future, which is supported by Wallace (1989) and reflected in the Ofsted framework (2014); the transition into post-16 education therefore is a pivotal point in this process.

Within my previous roles in education I experienced supporting young people in secondary schools and further education (FE) colleges. This experience led to an interest in the challenges facing young people in this age group and the journey they take to develop their goals and aspirations for their future. I was interested in young people's experience of planning for their futures, the extent to which they feel that they had a say and how confident they were in enacting their plans.

Research questions
The following research questions were the focus of the study.

How do young people who have an EHCP experience their preparation for a post-16 transition from secondary school to FE college?

How is the post-16 transition experienced by young people and what does it mean to them?

Approach
Method
Interpretative phenomenological analysis (IPA) was the method selected to explore the young people's experiences. IPA is a qualitative approach to research enquiry that is centred on exploring how individuals make sense of experiences that are significant and important in their lives.

It is understood that there may be more to an experience than an individual conveys in their dialogue alone, therefore within an IPA study the researcher engages in a deeper level of interpretation of what has been said to develop an understanding of the participant's experience (Smith *et al.*, 2009). In this sense IPA adopts an approach whereby the researcher engages in a process of interpreting what the participant has said, which in turn is the participant's own attempt to make sense of their experience (this is termed a 'double hermeneutic'). In this research the phenomenon can be viewed as the experience of transition from secondary school to FE college. This experience is considered significant as it encompasses not only the physical move from spending time in one environment to another, but equally a potential change in friendships, type of learning, independence and looking towards the future.

Design overview

The investigation aimed to explore the experience of transitioning from mainstream secondary school to FE college for three young people who had an EHCP. The secondary schools and FE college were within a large town in the North of England. Semi-structured interviews were completed with three participants using a schedule that enabled the young people to communicate their views and the nature of their experiences of the transition to college. The interview transcripts were then analysed using IPA with the aim of exploring, describing and interpreting how the participants made sense of their experiences. Each participant was interviewed in the June/July during their last few weeks enrolled at their secondary school and during the first few weeks in the September/October when they had begun attending FE college.

The participants were selected based on the following purposive sampling criteria:

- In Year 11 at the start of the study.
- Attending a mainstream secondary school in a particular Northern local authority region.
- Planning on attending the same FE college in the following September.
- Possessing an EHCP.

Pseudonyms were selected to refer to the participants.

Interview

The first interview schedule was composed of questions that related to the key areas of interest that had emerged from completing an initial literature review, such as the process of deciding, planning and preparing to go to FE college. This included the role that school, family and friends have during this time. The second interview schedule was based on the stage of the journey the participants had recently embarked on (the first few weeks at FE college), aspects that had arisen for the individual participants in the first interview and anything that had not been explored in the process to date.

The precise location of the interviews was organized in liaison with a key contact at the participants' schools, the FE college and their parents; however, a prerequisite was that the location be a quiet confidential space where the young people felt comfortable.

Analysis

In order to analyse the data obtained from the semi-structured interviews, I followed the steps outlined by Smith *et al.* (2009).

This process was completed over three phases:

1) analysing and comparing the first set of interviews
2) analysing and comparing the second set of interviews
3) comparing the two interviews for each participant and across participants.

On completion of each interview I spent time noting initial reflections in a research journal; this was felt to be important to enable reflection on the process and to facilitate preparing for the second interviews.

Findings and links to literature

Four superordinate themes were revealed through the analysis of the interview transcripts. These were: self-determination, supportive relationships, college as enabling, and the experience of change. Table 7.1 provides a summary of the themes that emerged and how they related to each research question.

Table 7.1: Summary of research findings

Superordinate theme	Research question 1	Research question 2
	How do young people who have an EHCP experience their preparation for a post-16 transition from secondary school to FE college?	How is this transition experienced by the young people and what does it mean to them?
Self-determination	• Ownership in decision-making. • Exploring the options available (R and S). • Applying self-understanding. • Recognizing what is important to meet own goals (S).	• Demonstrating self-belief by overcoming difficulties. • Opportunity to achieve personal goals.

Superordinate theme	Research question 1	Research question 2
Supportive relationships	• Parental support as part of decision-making. • Friends supporting career exploration (R). • Developing a course interest through school curriculum options. • A mixed experience of school-based support: careers advice (R) and annual reviews (B) were ineffective, having someone to talk to in school was helpful (S).	• Continued parental support. • Dynamics of family relationships. • Developing new and supportive relationships (peers and college tutors). • Reflection on a sense of belonging.
College as enabling	• Confidence that the decision made will facilitate personal goals and enable course enjoyment.	• Expectations being met. • Environment facilitating individual goals, including: a shared approach to learning (R), course enjoyment, developing competence, independence (B), experience of a safe environment, developing friendships (S and B) and a sense of belonging.
The experience of change	• Engaging in activities such as: researching chosen course, visiting college, parental support and annual reviews (S). • Considering personal next steps and taking action to be prepared.	• Active coping strategies applied to overcome potential difficulties. • Overall experience of transition as positive.

Note: S=Sam, B=Bill and R=Rebecca are used where this was elicited for these participants only

Self-determination

Self-determination emerged as a key theme for the participants. Wehmeyer (2004) provides a definition of self-determination that highlights the importance of the individual possessing, 'an understanding of one's strengths and limitations together with a belief in oneself as capable and effective' (p. 24).

In addition, it is suggested that self-determined individuals will apply this self-knowledge to independently strive towards achieving their goals. The young people interviewed demonstrated a sense of their developing self-understanding and self-belief as well as starting to take an active role in decision-making. Such traits can be viewed as fundamental to self-determination.

Palikara *et al.* (2009) and Madriaga and Goodley (2010) argued for the importance of young people having the opportunity to have their voices heard during times of transition in education. In support of recognized good practice (the *Special Educational Needs and Disability Code of Practice*, DfE and DoH, 2015), these authors consider that young people with special educational needs and/or disabilities (SEND) have the right to express their views as part of the decision-making process and reflect on the nature of the support they receive. All the young people interviewed in this study indicated a sense of ownership in making their decision to go to college. They were clear in how they felt their chosen courses matched their interests and aspirations for the future. Palikara *et al.* (2009) also found that the young people they interviewed had a good understanding of their SEND. Although this was not explicitly explored in the current study, two of the participants made reference to having SEND and their reflection on the type of support that they found most helpful.

Carroll and Dockrell (2012) found that personal characteristics including taking an active role in applying for a college course, recognizing one's own skills and talents and displaying self-belief when faced with challenges were factors that enabled successful post-16 transitions. This was considered by the authors as demonstrating self-determination. Similarly to Carroll and Dockrell (2012), the young people in this study expressed their active involvement in planning their transitions, although this differed slightly in the extent to which they experienced autonomy in the process. As indicated above, the young people interviewed were confident in sharing their strengths and interests and exhibited a sense of self-belief. For instance, one participant outlined examples of overcoming difficulties at college, such as getting lost and losing his ID badge, as well as portraying a view that his success had been down to him.

Wehmeyer (2015) purports that: 'Self-determination is a dispositional characteristic manifested as acting as the causal agent in one's life' (p. 20).

The origin of this concept within disability literature was first developed by Wehmeyer in the 1990s as part of numerous projects funded by the US Department of Education, Office of Special Education Programs, with the aim of promoting self-determination as a curriculum for young people with disabilities (Wehmeyer, 2015; Shogren *et al.*, 2015). Through the work of Wehmeyer and others the understanding below was developed.

As highlighted by Cho *et al.* (2012), based on Wehmeyer *et al.* (1996):

> An act or event is self-determined if the individual's action reflects four essential characteristics: (a) the individual acted autonomously; (b) the behaviours were self-regulated; (c) the person acted in a 'psychologically empowered manner', that is, the person acted in the belief that he or she has control over circumstances that are important to him or her; and (d) the person acted in a self-realizing manner, that is, they used reasonably accurate knowledge of themselves and their strengths and limitations to act in such a manner as to capitalize on this knowledge. (p. 19)

Wehmeyer (2015) explained that self-determination is not a process or an outcome that can be achieved but a characteristic and disposition that a person possesses and applies through their motivation and behaviour.

The four essential characteristics of self-determination can be seen on reflection of the analysis of the data gathered. First, being autonomous was a core attribute expressed in the interviews. The participants described how they explored their options and came to a decision about their next steps.

The young people revealed themselves acting in self-regulated and psychologically empowered ways in their approach to challenges they faced as part of their transitions: for instance, how they would go about making friends, deal with any difficulties, and getting involved in activities that were important to them.

Finally, as shown within the subordinate theme of 'self-understanding', the young people all revealed their perceptions of themselves including their strengths, interests and what is important to them now and in the future. Equally, a sense of the areas that they find challenging was also elicited.

To summarize, it can be seen that for the young people who took part in this study their experiences of preparing, making and reflecting on their post-16 transition provided the opportunity to exhibit traits and beliefs linked to the concept of self-determination. It cannot be concluded that the young people were becoming more self-determined through their transition process, but these findings support previous literature that preparing and making a post-16 transition is a crucial time for young people to reflect on who they are, their future aspirations and how they are going to achieve their goals.

Supportive relationships

The young people's experiences of supportive relationships were highlighted throughout their transitions. On a personal level, the support of family members, specifically parents, was received by all the young people (Aston *et al.*, 2005; Palikara *et al.*, 2009; Carroll and Dockrell, 2012). There were differences in how the supportive role of parents was perceived and experienced by each young person. However, this included helping to make decisions, take the next steps to pursue these goals and practical support throughout their transition. Personal support was also received from friends (Palikara *et al.*, 2009) and key support staff (Aston *et al.*, 2005). Peers and key adults in school were described as less supportive in different contexts that contributed to a reflection on the systemic support experienced by the young people in school and in college. Having the opportunity to develop friendships (Aston *et al.*, 2005) and experience belonging was revealed as an integral aspect of their experience of post-16 transition. The drive to experience belonging is supported by Deci and Ryan (2000) who consider that 'relatedness' makes up one of the three innate psychological needs that individuals possess.

College as enabling

There was a sense of the transition to FE college being experienced as enabling. The courses they had chosen to study can be seen to closely match their interests and aspirations, indicating that effective decisions had been made (*Special Educational Needs and Disability Code of Practice*, DfE and DoH, 2015). Moreover, the college environment as a whole was valued for providing a motivated learning culture, goal-orientated opportunities, safety, belonging and the chance to develop new relationships. Allodi (2010) found that these factors had been identified in literature reviews as important for quality learning environments.

The experience of change

The young people all expressed a feeling of being prepared for their transition to college. There were a range of activities that may have contributed to this perception, including finding out about their courses, visiting college and making personal plans. However, it is considered that at the time of the interviews the young people had already reached a level of security about what to expect. Annual reviews were viewed as a mixed experience for the young people, suggesting a difference in both the approach schools may take and the degree to which individuals can be supported to find this effective (DfE and DoH, 2015). As highlighted in Table 7.1, Sam found his annual review to be a positive experience. Kaehne and Beyer (2014) found that having the relevant people present to share their perspectives at person-centred transition reviews is essential. An integral part of this is having the young person and their parents present, which was similar to Sam's experience. However, Kaehne and Beyer (2014) also consider that the attendance of external agencies can have a positive impact on developing the transition plan and considering a wider array of options. The extent to which the young people demonstrated their use of coping strategies, such as social support and cognitive strategies (Cicognani, 2011), to manage their experience of transition was explored and found to be effectively utilized. In addition, a couple of the young people expressed sadness at leaving school and all the young people described the process of getting used to a new environment. This was reflected in an initial feeling of being nervous and followed by a period of time where they became more familiar with people and the environment.

Case example

All of the young people interviewed expressed that they had experienced a positive initial transition to college. Sam's experience is referenced here in more detail to showcase this and demonstrate how the superordinate themes were revealed.

Sam explained that he planned to study catering at college. His interest in this topic had developed through completing the GCSE catering course at school and his experiences of preparing food at home.

Sam can be seen to have acted in a self-determined way through his transition by requesting the kind of support he would like at college and in choosing his preferred next steps. Sam explained how he went to see his mentor at college and requested that any additional support he receives be less visible ('I spoke to her about having private help not visible help'). This can be seen as Sam applying his knowledge about himself, his strengths and needs and feeling empowered to independently act on this. In addition, Sam described how he had independently explored a number of options for what he might do after school, including speaking to the lady at school who co-ordinated apprenticeships and looking for part-time work. There is a sense of Sam's parents helping him in this process, and yet the acknowledgement for him in viewing his future as something of which he wants to take ownership was strongly conveyed ('I have decided').

Sam's experience of supportive relationships during this period can be seen through the actions of his parents and a key individual at school providing ongoing support and encouragement ('me mum and dad helped me out on that', 'staff have been really nice to me and helped me out ... Miss West is the one who helps me out'). Sam explains that this support enabled him to develop his self-confidence over time which now through the fresh start of attending a new educational setting he is able to put into action.

Although Sam reported that he had not had friends at school he felt that, through his interest and ability in cooking and a change in the nature of the additional support he receives in a new educational environment, he will develop friendships. Friendship is very important to Sam and was something that resonated with me as a clear way to reflect on how successful his experience of transition was. He explained in the first interview how he planned to develop friendships at college. He recognized that by having the confidence to approach people who had similar interests to him with a smile on his face, he would be able to start a conversation and demonstrate himself as a friendly guy. In the second interview Sam reported that he had made the friendships that he hoped for (' ... made loads of good friends and it's helped me really settle down, a lot better than I did at school'). Moreover, Sam described how the college environment had met his expectations both through his course choice and the ethos ('it's exactly how I wanted it ... a very grown-up environment').

A combination of the above factors led to Sam feeling prepared for his transition to FE college and Sam also highlighted specific activities that fed into this. For example he explained that both he and his parents found discussing his next steps within his annual review meetings helpful, especially because 'everyone' was together. Sam also explained that he attended a college open evening where he was able to ask questions about his course.

His developing sense of self-belief and self-knowledge combined with the new and 'enabling' environment of college led to a successful experience of transition and the beginning of what Sam felt were his goals being accomplished.

Implications for educational psychologist practice
Self-determination and person-centred planning

There is considerable research evidence indicating the positive impact of developing educational practice to include self-determination (Wehmeyer and Schwartz, 1997; Martorell *et al.*, 2008; Pierson *et al.*, 2008; Powers *et al.*, 2012). However, Wehmeyer (2015) points out that there has not been the take-up that would have been expected in schools. He suggests the main reasons for this are the need for more research evidence and tools to measure the impact of applying self-determination approaches across school systems, a lack of progression towards strengths-based models of disability, and lack of understanding about self-determination. Moreover, the majority of the research evidence around self-determination has been completed in the United States, yet the traits and the skills referred to in this chapter are arguably universal, and therefore applicable within education in the United Kingdom. The lack of research conducted in the United Kingdom is surprising, especially in light of recent legislative developments (DfE and DoH, 2015) championing the inclusion of young people as active agents in planning for their futures. Equally, as highlighted by the literature, student involvement in the decision-making about their futures is a vital part of successful transitions (Palikara *et al.*, 2009; Madriaga and Goodley, 2010; Cameron and Thygesen, 2015). It is considered therefore that, although these studies highlight the importance of supporting young people to be agents of change in their lives, the precise terminology of 'self-determination' had not been referred to in these studies. However, one way in which a comparison can be drawn is through the focus on 'person-centred planning' (PCP) approaches. As outlined by Norwich and Eaton (2015):

> The new Code of Practice expects that the assessment and planning process should be person-centred, defining this as an approach that:
>
> * focuses on the individual
> * enables parents, children and young people to express their views, wishes and feelings and be involved in decisions
> * is easy for them to understand and highlight their strengths and capabilities
> * enables them to communicate their achievements, interests and desired outcomes

- tailors support to their needs and minimises demands on the family; and
- brings together relevant professionals to deliver an outcomes-focused and co-ordinated plan. (p. 121)

The first five bullet points above clearly demonstrate the need for young people to be involved in decision-making about their lives, as well as to understand and communicate their self-knowledge and goals to others. In other words, PCP approaches are providing the opportunity for young people to act as agents of change in their lives. In the current research study Sam and Bill experienced aspects of the above through their involvement in annual review and personal planning during tutorial sessions.

Norwich and Eaton (2015) refer to tools that can be used to facilitate a PCP approach such as 'one page profiles' (Sanderson *et al.*, 2010) and 'Essential Lifestyle Plans' (Smull and Sanderson, 2005). However, this does not take into account the confidence and capacity of young people to engage in such a process. It is acknowledged that through conducting a PCP approach, individual needs are considered and therefore the tools should be adapted accordingly. Nevertheless, the question remains as to what extent have young people been prepared and supported to develop the skills needed to allow them to actively engage in this process. This is where the application of skills related to self-determination would be helpful. As indicated by Pierson *et al.* (2008), the opportunity to develop these skills over time, rather than in isolation, would enable young people to apply the skills they had acquired and act as agents of change within the PCP approach to planning for their futures.

Supporting schools in their approach to PCP through enabling young people to develop self-determination is highly relevant for educational psychologist (EP) practice. In my experience, and through discussion with other EPs, it appears that there is a gap in the knowledge about self-determination. Some professionals are aware of Self-Determination Theory (Deci and Ryan, 2002) and the implication for enhancing student motivation through developing autonomy, relatedness and competence, but there is a gap in understanding of the self-determination construct and how this can be applied to further positive outcomes for young people as they transition through education.

There are a number of implications for EPs. First, through working systemically with schools there is the opportunity to review and develop whole-school approaches and a curriculum linked to self-determination: for instance, considering the opportunities for young people with SEND to develop the traits linked to self-determination, such as autonomy, self-regulation, feeling psychologically empowered and self-realization (Cho *et al.*, 2012; Wehmeyer *et al.*, 1996) and to act in self-determined ways. As highlighted by Algozzine *et al.* (2001) and Pierson *et al.* (2008), a fundamental part of this is developing self and social awareness and becoming more independent through practising to make decisions. Therefore EPs could support schools and colleges to consider the following: how such strategies are taught and used within their settings, what young people's perceptions of this are, and how this would be applied within their wider educational experience. Moreover, as part of a transition process there is a prime opportunity for young people to engage in reflecting on who they are, as well as setting goals and making decisions about their futures. It is suggested that this would be a priority within education from an early age and, at the very least, considering how a young person feels about making their own decisions could be introduced as part of transition planning which officially begins in Year 9. Strategies and interventions to support young people in their journey to becoming more self-determined could be applied as part of this process. EPs have a role in exploring the evidence base and recommending a programme to schools, as well as supporting the implementation and reviewing the impact as part of a project. In addition, within individual casework, it is important that EPs not only elicit and include the voice of the child or young person but also reflect on how comfortable and able the individual was to share their views: for example, a young person's views about the support they receive. As indicated in this research study, the young people talked about the support they had received in school and whether this had been helpful. It is, however, unknown if their views had been shared with other professionals and certainly in the case of Sam it would have been beneficial for his negative experience of teaching assistant support to have been identified sooner. Consequently, as part of the EP involvement, suggestions to build on the child or young person's skills in this area could be shared and discussed with parents and professionals.

School and college practice

I consider that EPs are well placed to support schools and colleges at a systemic level to develop their understanding of the other themes that emerged in this research: namely, the nature of support networks and the role of friendships and activities designed to prepare young people for their transitions. Through reflecting on how such factors may affect students, steps can be taken to improve practice in facilitating positive transition experiences.

First, the interpretative analysis revealed the importance of the various systems and support networks that an individual interacts with during the period of time when they are preparing for and making a post-16 transition: for instance, whether the young person knows where to go for help and advice and whether they have an understanding of activities or spaces designed to support them in school or college. Therefore it is important to consider such factors and what this might look like for the individual in the settings they attend. Furthermore, supportive relationships were viewed as important for the young people interviewed. Exploring how young people experience support both at home and in school or college could be essential in developing understanding about the extent of their support networks: for example, identifying any strengths or gaps that could be enhanced and exploring what the young person finds helpful to incorporate this into their transition plan would be beneficial.

The experience of friendships was also identified as important to the young people. Differences in friendship hopes and expectations were recognized, but there was a strong desire to experience connectedness and belonging through peer relationships. Having the opportunity for young people to explore with a trusted adult what their experience of friendships have been and how they feel about the prospect of developing new friendships at college would be valuable.

Finally, how young people experience planning and preparing for their post-16 transition is crucial. In this study this experience was primarily self-directed, although additional activities and support provided by school and college, such as college visits and careers tutorials, were outlined. Reflecting on the steps that schools and colleges already take to support young people in planning for their transitions and how to improve them is recommended, for example considering what young people who have recently gone through the process found helpful. In addition, the role that annual reviews have in this process could be explored further. Two of the young people interviewed had very different experiences of annual reviews, one positive and one less so. This suggests that young people's perceptions of annual reviews should be investigated to identify the strengths and weaknesses of a school's approach in order to adapt their approach in the future. Equally, including the views of parents and carers in this process could facilitate further good practice.

On an individual casework level, EPs could seek to highlight the importance of the above factors and support professionals to explore these with young people and their parents. In particular, ensuring that young people are given the opportunity to share their views in a way that they find comfortable is essential to tailor a transition plan to best meet their needs.

Further considerations
Limitations of the study

The focus of this research was to explore the experience of transitioning from secondary school to FE college. The positive experiences that were elicited from the young people interviewed are based on their initial experiences of being at college for less than one month and are not claiming to reflect their ongoing experience of attending college as a whole. In addition, it is important to acknowledge the potential impact of researcher effects, how the young people may have perceived me and the interview situation that may have influenced the way they responded to my questions.

As highlighted by Willig (2008), IPA is reliant on language as a means to communicate the essence of experience. It had been considered that eliciting a rich account from the participants in this study might have been a challenge as the participants were identified as having communication difficulties. On reflection, the interviews were shorter than what is typically recommended for IPA studies, a result of the young people not tending to describe their experiences in extensive detail. There was a clear sense of their personal account evoked but I found I was unable to reach the deeper level of interpretation typically required for a robust IPA study.

The participants who took part in this study were, however, able to answer all the interview questions asked. The inclusion criteria that were applied, in particular that the young people were at the onset attending a mainstream secondary school, planning to attend the FE college and interested in taking part, may have facilitated a sample of young people who were able to communicate to a functional level. This research can therefore be criticized for not including the voices of individuals who may have found it more difficult to communicate verbally in a face-to-face interview with an unfamiliar adult. The use of alternative methods such as visuals (Talking Mats, Cameron and Murphy, 2002; Photovoice, Cheak-Zamora *et al.*, 2016) would enable other voices to be included in qualitative research methods and, equally, may have added more richness to the data collected in this study.

Where we are today

Now we are a number of academic years into the 'new' way of working it is helpful to reflect on how our practice has changed. Through my own work and based on discussions with other EPs in the region (Yorkshire and Humber) it can be seen that our approach is constantly evolving as local authorities, schools, colleges and EPs strive to capture young people's views and target appropriate goals within statutory and non-statutory plans. It can be seen that in many places this has had a positive effect on the quality of the plans produced and consequently the type of provision offered to meet need.

With EPs working in a variety of different ways, however, not all provisions have the same access to EP input and therefore may not be in the same place in their journey of working together to improve this process further. Equally, although EPs can now be involved with young people aged up to 25, the extent to which this might be through a one-off piece of work rather than ongoing involvement and support with a particular college or setting means there may be limited impact on the way such settings are guided in developing their practice. In essence it is through working together, sharing and adapting our practice further, that we can ensure that the core values of the new Code of Practice are embedded within our work. Without this there is a danger that we may become stuck in our ways and when striving for a person-centred approach this is not going to be effective. For instance, in the research study detailed here all three young people would have attended annual review meetings, but only one of them found this process helpful. I am sure that the schools would have felt they were doing all they could to actively include the young people, but in practice this was not achieved. Therefore without taking time to listen to their young people an opportunity to develop their approach could be missed. As highlighted in this chapter, it is a person-centred approach, one that takes into account the individuals, self-understanding, goals and support networks, that can be vital for effective post-16 transitions.

References

Algozzine, B., Browder, D., Karvonen, M., Test, D.W. and Wood, W.M. (2001) 'Effects of interventions to promote self-determination for individuals with disabilities'. *Review of Educational Research*, 71 (2), 219–77.

Allodi, M.W. (2010) 'Goals and values in school: A model developed for describing, evaluating and changing the social climate of learning environments'. *Social Psychology of Education*, 13 (2), 207–35.

Aston, J., Dewson, S. and Loukas, G. (2005) *Post-16 Transitions: A longitudinal study of young people with special educational needs (wave three)* (Research Report 655). Nottingham: Department for Education and Skills.

Cameron, D.L. and Thygesen, R. (eds) (2015) *Transitions in the Field of Special Education: Theoretical perspectives and implications for practice*. Münster: Waxmann.

Cameron, L. and Murphy, J. (2002) 'Enabling young people with a learning disability to make choices at a time of transition'. *British Journal of Learning Disabilities*, 30 (3), 105–12.

Carroll, C. and Dockrell, J. (2012) 'Enablers and challenges of post-16 education and employment outcomes: The perspectives of young adults with a history of SLI'. *International Journal of Language and Communication Disorders*, 47 (5), 567–77.

Cheak-Zamora, N.C., Teti, M. and Maurer-Batjer, A. (2018) 'Capturing experiences of youth with ASD via photo exploration: Challenges and resources becoming an adult'. *Journal of Adolescent Research*, 33 (1), 117–45.

Cho, H.-J., Wehmeyer, M.L. and Kingston, N.M. (2012) 'The effect of social and classroom ecological factors on promoting self-determination in elementary school'. *Preventing School Failure: Alternative Education for Children and Youth*, 56 (1), 19–28.

Cicognani, E. (2011) 'Coping strategies with minor stressors in adolescence: Relationships with social support, self-efficacy, and psychological well-being'. *Journal of Applied Social Psychology*, 41 (3), 559–78.

Deci, E.L. and Ryan, R.M. (2000) 'The "what" and "why" of goal pursuits: Human needs and the self-determination of behavior'. *Psychological Inquiry*, 11 (4), 227–68.

Deci, E.L. and Ryan, R.M. (eds) (2002) *Handbook of Self-Determination Research*. Rochester, NY: University of Rochester Press.

DfE (Department for Education) and DoH (Department of Health) (2015) *Special Educational Needs and Disability Code of Practice: 0 to 25 years: Statutory guidance for organisations which work with and support children and young people who have special educational needs or disabilities*. London: Department for Education. Online. https://assets.publishing.service.gov.uk/government/uploads/system/uploads/attachment_data/file/398815/SEND_Code_of_Practice_January_2015.pdf (accessed 23 August 2018).

Kaehne, A. and Beyer, S. (2014) 'Person-centred reviews as a mechanism for planning the post-school transition of young people with intellectual disability'. *Journal of Intellectual Disability Research*, 58 (7), 603–13.

Madriaga, M. and Goodley, D. (2010) 'Moving beyond the minimum: Socially just pedagogies and Asperger's syndrome in UK higher education'. *International Journal of Inclusive Education*, 14 (2), 115–31.

Martorell, A., Gutierrez-Recacha, P., Pereda, A. and Ayuso-Mateos, J.L. (2008) 'Identification of personal factors that determine work outcome for adults with intellectual disability'. *Journal of Intellectual Disability Research*, 52 (12), 1091–101.

Norwich, B. and Eaton, A. (2015) 'The new special educational needs (SEN) legislation in England and implications for services for children and young people with social, emotional and behavioural difficulties'. *Emotional and Behavioural Difficulties*, 20 (2), 117–32.

Ofsted (2014) *School Inspection Handbook: Handbook for inspecting schools in England under section 5 of the Education Act 2005*. Manchester: Ofsted.

Palikara, O., Lindsay, G. and Dockrell, J.E. (2009) 'Voices of young people with a history of specific language impairment (SLI) in the first year of post-16 education'. *International Journal of Language and Communication Disorders*, 44 (1), 56–78.

Pierson, M.R., Carter, E.W., Lane, K.L. and Glaeser, B.C. (2008) 'Factors influencing the self-determination of transition-age youth with high-incidence disabilities'. *Career Development for Exceptional Individuals*, 31 (2), 115–25.

Powers, L.E., Geenen, S., Powers, J., Pommier-Satya, S., Turner, A., Dalton, L.D., Drummond, D. and Swank, P. (2012) 'My Life: Effects of a longitudinal, randomized study of self-determination enhancement on the transition outcomes of youth in foster care and special education'. *Children and Youth Services Review*, 34 (11), 2179–218.

Ritchie, J. and Lewis, J. (eds) (2003) *Qualitative Research Practice: A guide for social science students and researchers*. London: SAGE Publications.

Sanderson, H., Smith, T. and Wilson, L. (2010) *One Page Profiles in Schools: A guide*. Stockport: HSA Press.

Shogren, K.A., Wehmeyer, M.L., Palmer, S.B. and Forber-Pratt, A.J. (2015) 'Causal agency theory: Reconceptualizing a functional model of self-determination'. *Education and Training in Autism and Developmental Disabilities*, 50 (3), 251–63.

Smith, J.A., Flowers, P. and Larkin, M. (2009) *Interpretative Phenomenological Analysis: Theory, method and research*. London: SAGE Publications.

Smull, M. and Sanderson, H. (2005) *Essential Lifestyle Planning for Everyone*. Helen Sanderson Associates.

Wallace, C. (1989) 'Social reproduction and school leavers: A longitudinal perspective'. In Hurrelmann, K. and Engel, U. (1987) *The Social World of Adolescents: International perspectives*. Berlin: de Gruyter.

Wehmeyer, M.L. (2004) 'Self-determination and the empowerment of people with disabilities'. *American Rehabilitation*, 28 (1), 22–29.

Wehmeyer, M.L. (2015) 'Framing the future: Self-determination'. *Remedial and Special Education*, 36 (1), 20–3.

Wehmeyer, M.L., Kelchner, K. and Richards, S. (1996) 'Essential characteristics of self determined behavior of individuals with mental retardation'. *American Journal on Mental Retardation*, 100 (6), 632–42.

Wehmeyer, M. and Schwartz, M. (1997) 'Self-determination and positive adult outcomes: A follow-up study of youth with mental retardation or learning disabilities'. *Exceptional Children*, 63 (2), 245–55.

Willig, C. (2008) *Introducing Qualitative Research in Psychology: Adventures in theory and method*. 2nd ed. Maidenhead: Open University Press.

Chapter 8

From real-world research to the real world: Extending the free association Grid Elaboration Method into applied educational psychologist practice with older students

Jane Park

> It can be easy in many current practices to draw upon theoretical resources that engage only secondarily with the nature of the experiences of the children with whom we work. However, I also argue that any understanding that we might have as professionals of a child's difficulties, and therefore the appropriateness of our advice, may well be dependent on our ability to have some insight or understanding into the child's experience, in particular their experience of intense feelings. (Billington, 2006: 3)

Introduction

The aim for the first part of this chapter is to offer insight into the transition experiences of four young adults on the autism spectrum into further education (FE) from the perspective of the young people themselves, using the free association Grid Elaboration Method (GEM; Joffe and Elsey, 2014). This is followed by exploration of the extension of the GEM into applied educational psychologist (EP) work with young people in the 18–25 age range through two anonymized case studies.

The material in this chapter is situated in the United Kingdom national context of the relatively recent introduction of a new Children and Families Act (UK Parliament, 2014) and updated *Special Educational Needs and Disability Code of Practice* (Department for Education (DfE) and Department of Health (DoH), 2015). These legislative changes continue to influence the context in which EPs practise; prior to the updated Act, EPs broadly worked with the 0 to 19 age range. The extension to age 25 represented an important change to the role of EPs, providing many opportunities to extend both the EP role and service delivery. This chapter both highlights some of the possibilities for EP work in relation to supporting a successful transition to FE for young adults on the autism spectrum and begins to explore ways in which the GEM may be used successfully to gently support young people to have their voices heard.

Contribution to knowledge and practice implications

The views of young people with autism regarding their transition experiences when moving into FE have evidently received scant attention in the research literature. This seems to be related to perceived difficulties in accessing their views. The views of professionals and of parents have been prioritized over the observations and experiences of young people themselves. I felt it was vital to address this gap in the research due to the acknowledged issues these young adults face as they transition into adulthood, such as unemployment, social isolation, lack of independence, mental health needs and general fears for the future (Mitchell and Beresford, 2014; Wehman *et al.*, 2014). According to Ambitious about Autism and their 'Employ Autism' campaign (Ambitious about Autism, 2011), just 15 per cent of adults with autism are currently in full-time paid employment, which the organization attributes to a lack of support and opportunity for young people with autism to transition successfully into the workplace. Since accounts that feature the voices and experiences of this group of young people are scarce, I hoped that my research would facilitate an opportunity for a range of professionals to learn from first-person accounts of the transition experiences of young adults with autism. I was passionate about finding a way to get a real sense of their experiences of transition and to find an effective way to facilitate their voice in the process, spurred on by the following quote from Milton *et al.* (2014: 2650):

> While non-autistic parents and professionals might claim that they are best placed to speak for autistic individuals, especially those who find it difficult to speak for themselves, this cannot be accepted on face value. We believe that human dignity requires us to make every effort to access the views and perspectives of autistic people.

Research with young people with autism has tended to be dominated by the researcher's agenda, for example through the use of questionnaires and structured interviews, which I argue risks presupposing the lines along which the young people should be thinking. Those studies that more directly access the views of young adults with autism have brought about positive change by enabling professionals to develop a deeper understanding of the systems, practices and support that they particularly value. These include support in developing social skills, learning to travel to college independently and receiving empathy and understanding from staff who have accessed autism awareness training, thus demonstrating the rich value that can be gained by accessing young people's views (Browning *et al.*, 2009; Beardon *et al.*, 2009; Mitchell and Beresford, 2014).

In order to learn about the transition experiences of the young people with whom I was privileged to work I used the free association Grid Elaboration Method (GEM; Joffe and Elsey, 2014). As per the opening quote from Billington (2006), by using the GEM to elicit views of a number of young adults with autism currently enrolled in FE, I hoped to discover more about their thoughts, feelings and emotional experiences of transition, while contributing to shifting the inherent power imbalance between participant and researcher to a more equitable position.

What is the Grid Elaboration Method?

The free association GEM is a visually oriented method of data collection based on the principles of free association in which data collection begins with and stems from each individual participant's unique associations to the topic of study. Commonly associated with the clinical work of psychoanalyst Sigmund Freud, in 'free association' the 'patient' says whatever comes to mind without exercising any selectivity or censorship (de Mijoller, 2005: 616). A recently established tool from psycho-social research, the GEM is strongly influenced by Hollway and Jefferson's Free Association Narrative Interview (FANI) method, in which participants are asked to 'tell me about' the topic in question, using a pre-prepared interview schedule (Hollway and Jefferson, 2008, 2013). However, the GEM extends beyond such structured interviewing, recognizing and transcending the possible risks within the FANI (and of other semi-structured interviewing techniques) of constraining interviewees by the assumptions inherent within pre-prepared interview questions.

In the GEM, participants are presented with a blank grid comprising four boxes on a sheet of paper. They are then asked to represent with a word, image or phrase their 'associations' to a given topic, that is, their first immediate responses. Therefore, factors that immediately occur to the participant in association to the issue under study are recorded on the grid before dialogue with the researcher begins. These are limited to one per box, so that once the grid is complete there are four salient associations. The researcher then enquires about these unique associations in turn, encouraging participants to elaborate in as much detail as possible until the point at which they indicate that they have no more to add. At this point, the researcher guides the participant through the next box in the same way until all four boxes have been explored. In this way, researcher interference with the data collection process is minimized and all data originate from the 'subjective stance of participants' (Joffe and Elsey, 2014: 178). Joffe and Elsey (2014: 181) also suggest that the use of the grid frees participants 'from the need to restrain their expression to a coherent, linear dialogue or detailed narrative'. Figure 8.1 illustrates a free association grid, as used in the GEM (Joffe and Elsey, 2014).

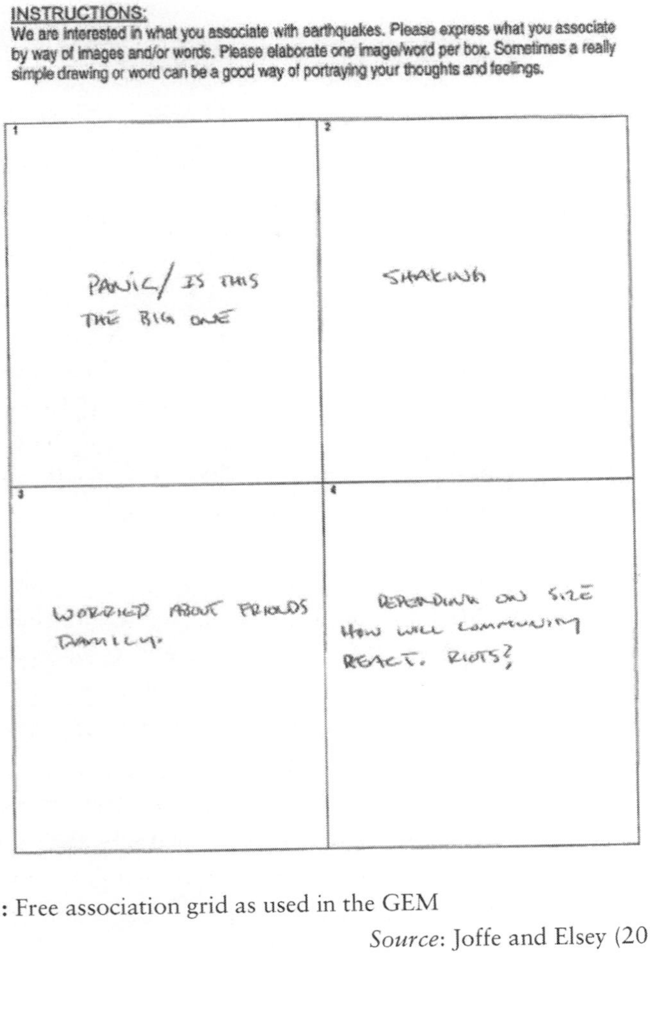

INSTRUCTIONS:
We are interested in what you associate with earthquakes. Please express what you associate by way of images and/or words. Please elaborate one image/word per box. Sometimes a really simple drawing or word can be a good way of portraying your thoughts and feelings.

1	2
PANIC/ IS THIS THE BIG ONE	SHAKING
3	4
WORRIED ABOUT FRIENDS FAMILY.	DEPENDING ON SIZE HOW WILL COMMUNITY REACT. RIOTS?

Figure 8.1: Free association grid as used in the GEM

Source: Joffe and Elsey (2014)

The GEM process

I provided my participants with a blank GEM grid containing the following written instructions:

> I am interested in what you associate with experiences of transition. Please express what you associate by using images and/or words. Please put one image/word/phrase in each box. Sometimes a really simple drawing or word can be a good way of portraying your thoughts and feelings. (Instructions adapted from Joffe and Elsey, 2014)

Interviews took place on a one-to-one basis. It was important to establish with each participant that there were no right or wrong answers, and that there was space for each participant to respond to the GEM grid in whatever ways felt important and appropriate for them. There was some variation in the way each participant responded to the GEM grid; some chose to write a few words or a phrase while another drew sketches. Rather than see this as an obstacle to the collection of useful data I was encouraged by it, viewing it as a demonstration of how flexible and responsive an information-gathering tool the GEM could be in relation to gaining the views of each unique individual.

The next step in the GEM was to support my participants to elaborate on their associations. Once they had filled in the four boxes, I asked participants to say a little more about each box in sequence, following the order in which they completed each box, so as to trace the order of their associations. This approach ensured that the material to be explored was deeply connected to the unique and personal experience of each participant. Participants were encouraged to take up the freedom to say whatever came to their mind in an attempt to elicit narratives that were structured and defined by implicit and emotive motivations. Rather than applying a set of pre-defined questions, as in many forms of semi-structured interview, I guided my participants through their initial four associations to the subject of 'transitions' in order to encourage a fuller exploration of their unique experiences. I drew upon techniques espoused by Hollway and Jefferson (2008, 2013) and Joffe and Elsey (2014) such as encouragement, parroting (using the participant's own words to encourage further detail) and asking participants to 'tell me more about … ' until the point at which they indicated to me that they had no more to say about their association. These principles were adopted in order to empower my participants and to facilitate exploration of constructs that were personally meaningful to each participant. This also enabled me to clarify the participants' understanding of the questions being asked and clarify their thinking, for example through summarizing and reflecting back my understanding of what I thought they were telling me.

The GEM offered a means of collecting data through visually structuring individual interviews in which the material to be explored was generated by each participant's unique and personal associations to 'experiences of transition'. The GEM grid itself functioned as a visual tool, which prior research suggested could be helpful when interviewing young people with autism; for example Hill (2014) and Shepherd (2015) argue that visually mediated methods may strengthen the communication abilities of young people with autism.

Pen portraits and data extracts

To aid the reader in appreciating the individual context and background of each participant, brief pen portraits are described below. I have also outlined examples of their unique responses to being given the GEM grid to complete. By presenting information in this way, I hope to encourage reflection from the reader about the kinds of knowledge that may be gained through using the GEM and how its use may empower voices to be heard.

'Stephen'

> The next stage in life is another door into a new world waiting to be explored. That is, basically, what transition means ... I think that entering into a new world of something that you're not sure about is scary, but if you think about it, if you think of that concept, that it's just another door going into a new world of your life, the next stage of your life, everybody has to go through it. (Stephen)

Stephen is a friendly 22-year-old male who was enrolled on an NVQ Level 3 in Health and Social Care. Having attended a mainstream primary school, Stephen transitioned into a specialist autism spectrum disorder (ASD) provision for secondary schooling where he stayed until aged 16. Stephen then briefly transitioned to a different FE college before settling at the college that he is now attending. Here he enrolled on the Health and Social Care programme. As well as studying, Stephen has a part-time job and often contributes to staff and student development by giving presentations on autism awareness at the college, for which he was nominated and received an award. He reports looking forward to developing a career in the 'helping professions'. Stephen wrote lengthy aphoristic-style statements in the boxes of the GEM grid. Initially he wrote straight across the four boxes and ended up writing three statements.

'Ben'

> My new school is a new start ... I make new friends, stuff like that really ... it's ... it's exciting, kind of exciting ... you know, working with new people, a new classroom, and like learning your way around ... it's a bit scary to start off with but you tend to get used to it and you get less and less scared. (Ben)

Ben is a shy 21-year-old male in his fourth year of attending an FE college. Ben went to a mainstream primary school then attended an autism specialist provision for a time, transitioning back into mainstream education in Year 8 until the end of Year 11. Having successfully completed the Skills for Work and Life training, Ben enrolled on a mainstream catering course and is part of a team who have won awards for their high standards of cookery. Ben enjoys sports and has a small but close group of friends at the college whom he has known since school. He is working towards his Level 2 qualification and following completion he plans to investigate developing his computing and IT skills with a view to having a future career in this field. Ben chose to write just a few words in each box. He began with emotions or feeling states ('happy and scared') and moved around the grid to name the experience ('new start').

'Samantha'

> Happy. Cos you're making new friends, meeting new people, new experiences ... On the first day I was a little bit scared but I knew a few people who, that started the course so that helped a bit. (Samantha)

Samantha is a trendy 18-year-old female in her third year of attending the local FE college. Samantha attended mainstream schools until the end of Year 11, at which point she transitioned to college. She has always been interested in working with children and is currently studying for her NVQ Level 2 in Childcare, which she loves, and hopes to develop a career in this area. Samantha drew sketches of stick people in her boxes, each representing a feeling or emotion. During the interview she expressed the view that the stick people represented her.

'Jamie'

> I've learnt things from all this high school experience and primary school experience. So it's all good. Like I say, it's been a journey and there have been positives and negatives as always ... but anyway, it's all good and now I look up to the stars and I don't think about it anymore. (Jamie)

Jamie is an outgoing 18-year-old male in his second year of attending an FE college. Jamie attended mainstream schools until achieving his GCSE results in Year 11, when he moved to college and enrolled on a Music Technology course. He is a talented performer and already works as a freelance guitarist, music producer, sound technician and sound engineer. Jamie plans to go to university to further his skills and develop a career in music. Jamie wrote about his different life stages in the four boxes, starting from early years through primary to high school and finally college. He then selected what he saw as the most salient points and elaborated on them in the interview.

Key points for EP practice

The research question this study addressed was: 'What are the transition experiences of young people on the autism spectrum?' A number of key protective factors that contributed to the facilitation of a positive transition into FE emerged from the process of data analysis using Thematic Analysis (Braun and Clarke, 2006). These included the value of having healthy relationships with peers and with teaching and support staff, having a positive outlook and a resilient mindset, accessing appropriate tailored support, learning practical and emotional life skills, and for individuals with autism being understood in terms of their skills and strengths. In summary, though there was significant variation between individual participants in terms of their unique transition experiences, six discrete (though related) themes emerged from the data:

- Resilience in terms of building the necessary skills to help them successfully navigate through life. Participants commonly alluded to overcoming challenges and demonstrating a positive attitude to transition.
- The young people's experiences, while not always comfortable, led to growth and development through learning from experience, acquiring

academic and life skills, making plans for the future and making a positive contribution to the community.

- This links to the theme of relationships, in which my participants described the importance of supportive staff and peer relations and some of the challenges in forming new friendships.
- Mental well-being, in which participants described the impact of anxiety, depression, confusion and stress on their transition experiences, also recounting painful incidents of bullying and of not being understood by teachers and college staff.
- Agency, whereby my participants spoke of how having access to appropriate tailored support enabled them to develop greater independence and autonomy; frustrations at external constraints on agency in some respects such as access to appropriate or desired college places and aspects of their training; and how knowing yourself, knowing what works for each individual and tailoring support accordingly, could enable the young people to manage the challenges of college life with increasing independence and autonomy.
- Understanding difference, in which participants described the impact of their experiences of being judged or misunderstood in their lives, and the value of being accepted and understood.

Participant experiences of the GEM

At the end of each interview I asked my participants to let me know what the experience of taking part in this piece of research had been like for them. Having already established rapport and a comfortable working relationship, it is my view that my participants would have felt able to give frank and honest feedback in the one-to-one context. All four reported having had a positive experience, each reflecting on their own response to the research process. Samantha in particular appreciated the chance to represent her 'feelings' pictorially instead of being asked directly, expressing the view that 'it was good to show people's, like, feelings, if you get them to draw stuff instead of just asking them'. Ben came to the interview with the aim of 'getting his point across', which he reported having achieved. For Stephen, the research experience lent him a chance to be characteristically altruistic, while Jamie reported what I understood to be a sense of catharsis, of having gone on what he described as a 'memory tour'.

Extensions of the GEM into applied EP practice: Case studies

I would now like to illustrate two ways in which I have extended the GEM into applied EP practice when working with young adults in FE in my role as a link EP with a local college. Since completing my research I have begun to experiment with ways of using the GEM to elicit views, particularly (though not exclusively) with young adults on the autism spectrum. This was prompted by two pieces of work in which I was (a) requested to seek the views of young people with complex needs; and (b) in all honesty felt unsure about how best to proceed. I will outline these as case studies. All sensitive information has been anonymized and neither case study contains personally identifiable information.

'Ryan'

Ryan is an 18-year-old young man on the autism spectrum who was in the process of transitioning to an FE college when I worked with him for the first time. He had participated in some taster sessions and had met with key staff members. Background information and consultation with key family and school staff members helped me to understand that, previously, Ryan had struggled to manage the transition from primary to secondary school. His family background was complex. Managed moves between secondary schools were attempted, though placements quickly broke down, and Ryan experienced several fixed-term exclusions. Eventually this led Ryan to be home educated for Years 10 and 11. Plans were now being put in place to support him to transition into a part-time course at a college. As part of this process I was asked by the college to work with Ryan in order to gain his views and aspirations. Due to his past negative experiences of educational professionals it was felt that Ryan would struggle to engage with professionals. The defeatist narrative around him seemed to be 'you'll be lucky to get anything out of him'. I reflected for some time about how best to support Ryan to work with me. In order to gain insight into Ryan's perceptions of his prior and current educational experiences, his feelings about school/college and his future aspirations, I decided to try using the GEM to elicit Ryan's associations, which we then gently explored. Ryan engaged well with this visually oriented approach and benefited from plenty of time to process and formulate his responses.

School.

This school are kind and helpfull.	Every school is the same there is no Diffrence.
I didn't like my old school because they just threw you in to lessons.	This school isn't as boring as my other schools.

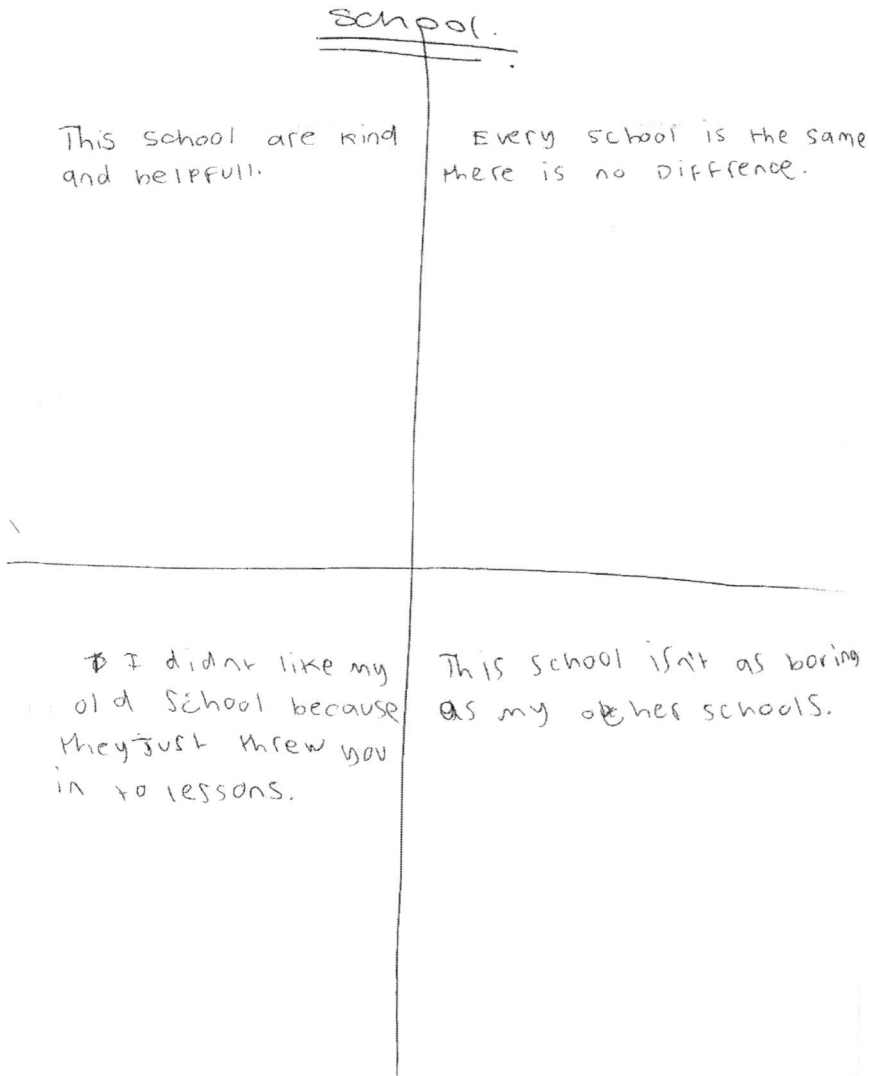

Figure 8.2: Ryan's completed GEM grid

'THIS COLLEGE IS KIND AND HELPFUL.'

Ryan was able to let me know that he felt college staff were 'all just nice people' and that he now feels thought about and supported. He felt that staff at the college offer to do things for him and help him out if needed. However, Ryan expressed the view that he dislikes being supported in his classes by a teaching assistant and that he never wanted this kind of support.

'EVERY SCHOOL IS THE SAME, THERE IS NO DIFFERENCE.'
Ryan let me know that his experience of school was that they are 'always crowded with too many people'. Ryan expressed feelings of school being hopeless and pointless, that 'a school's a school' and that they are all the same, though 'College is a bit different'.

'I DIDN'T LIKE MY OLD SCHOOL BECAUSE THEY JUST THREW YOU INTO LESSONS.'
Ryan let me know that, at his previous mainstream secondary settings, he often felt 'nervous', though he feels that he is now more confident and less nervous, which Ryan attributed to 'growing up'. Ryan felt that in the past he was 'just nervous all the time, I couldn't speak to anyone, couldn't go to the shop or speak to the shopkeeper'. He also felt that not many people would have known or noticed this, only himself and his mum.

'THIS PLACE ISN'T AS BORING AS MY OTHER SCHOOLS.'
Ryan felt that, in his previous experiences of secondary school, he 'just sat there non-stop' and that there were few opportunities for enrichment activities such as cooking and football, which were his favourites. I wondered aloud about how often he experienced feelings of academic competence and Ryan felt that he couldn't remember having such feelings. He seemed to be approaching the idea of moving to college with an emerging optimism. Ryan's response to the GEM exceeded even my hopeful expectations and certainly shifted the narrative that his views could not be accessed.

'Lucy'

Lucy is a 19-year-old young woman on the autism spectrum. Educational psychology involvement was requested by key college staff due to expressed concerns around Lucy's capacity to manage her emotions appropriately in social situations that she found challenging. Information shared by the college indicated that Lucy struggled with emotional self-regulation and could quickly become frustrated and irritable. Though she was able to reflect afterwards, at the time of an incident or a difficult situation occurring she was not yet able to respond appropriately. In the past this had resulted in suspension from her course. Lucy has a complex family background and, at the time of my involvement, was in the process of leaving care and moving into supported accommodation. This was a significant change for her and at times Lucy was struggling to manage, despite the provision of a high level of pastoral support. Lucy was keen to develop a set of coping strategies to help herself. College staff reported that Lucy had made excellent academic progress over the three years she had attended college. They also wished to support Lucy to develop her own capacity for managing her emotional responses to social situations that she found challenging, with increasing independence, in order to support her to make a successful transition into adulthood. It was agreed that I would offer some one-to-one sessions with Lucy.

When meeting Lucy for the first time I chose to use the GEM both as a means of rapport-building and of eliciting information from her about her hopes and aspirations for our work together. I was aware that this piece of EP work had been commissioned by the college and, with this in mind, I wanted to ensure as best I could that Lucy was giving fully informed consent to partake in individual work with me and to make sure she had ownership over what was discussed. I wished to establish what kind of support could be most useful to her and the type and extent of support desired. In her recommendations around ensuring fully informed consent, Loyd (2013) places particular emphasis both on using effective, often visually oriented, modes of communication and on giving opportunities to potential participants 'to say "no" in different ways, different contexts and to different people on different occasions' (Loyd, 2013: 41). As Joffe and Elsey (2014: 181) explain, the GEM 'provides a means of eliciting material that is subjectively relevant to respondents, without presuppositions as to what they should think or even concerning the lines they should be thinking along'. In research, the use of free association in the GEM is intended to ensure that the material to be explored in the interview that follows directly stems from each participant's unique experiences and adequately reflects the 'emotional underpinning of participants' remembered experiences' (Hollway, 2015: 44). Using the GEM provided a means of eliciting information from Lucy that was led by her, thus supporting her to set the agenda for discussion and to take the lead in discussing issues of importance to herself.

It can be seen from Figure 8.3 that Lucy's primary preoccupation on this occasion was with her family. It transpired that she had very recently received information about her early background and history that had been unsettling to read. Lucy let me know that her boyfriend of two years, who she had met at college, was a significant source of support and comfort. Following exploration of the two other boxes on the GEM grid, 'Coping with my friends and managing to stay calm when needed' and 'Make my behaviour better than a couple of years ago' became the founding basis of our individual work together.

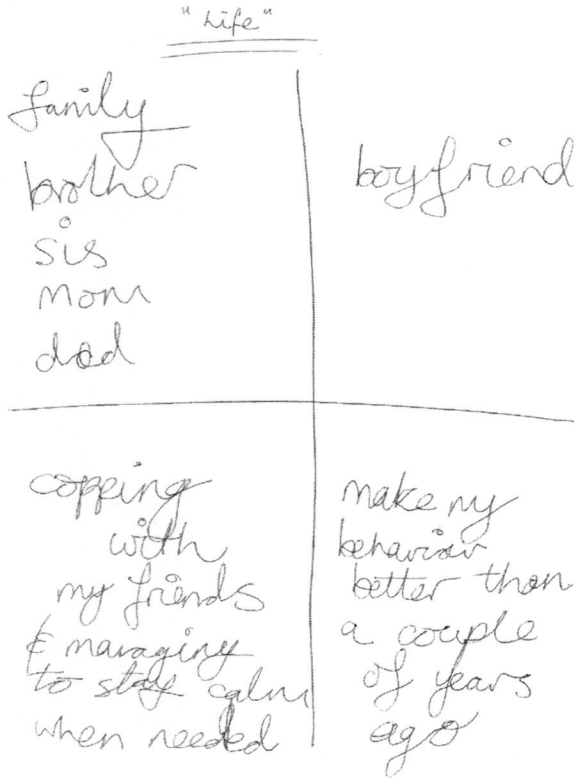

Figure 8.3: Lucy's completed GEM grid

Encouraging further application of the GEM

Both in my research and in subsequent applied practice making tentative and exploratory use of the GEM, I have wondered to myself how else I would have been able to access the rich and valuable information that was made available to me by the young people with whom I was fortunate to work. I hope the examples in this chapter provide an apt demonstration of ways in which EPs can take up an advocacy role when working with young adults on the autism spectrum and ensure that their voices are heard in relation to decisions that have an impact on their future and on their well-being. The use of the free association GEM with its integrated visual element shows how using 'light-touch' visual support can be helpful in enabling the views and voices of young people with autism to be expressed. Further to this, as advocated by Billington (2006), it is hoped that this study may helpfully empower EPs to draw upon existing skills in order to develop the EP role and engage with young people with autism in the 18 to 25 age range, particularly in relation to gaining insight into their experiences and their views. Ultimately, the message I hope to convey is that, whatever tools we use, EPs are well positioned to have a key role in facilitating and representing the views of young people at the heart of decision-making about their futures. It remains vital to hear from these young people's perspectives and to establish both the kind of support that is most useful to them and the type and extent of support they desire.

Acknowledgements

This chapter and the subsequent experiences I have had working in FE colleges would not have been possible without the contributions of the four young people who agreed to spend time with me sharing their unique experiences. I am indebted to them for their time and their trust in me to relate their stories.

References

Ambitious about Autism (2011) *Finished at School: Where next for young people with autism?* London: Ambitious about Autism. Online. www. ambitiousaboutautism.org.uk/sites/default/files/AAA_Finished_at_School_ Report_0_0.pdf (accessed 25 September 2018).

Beardon, L., Martin, N. and Woolsey, I. (2009) 'What do students with Asperger syndrome or high-functioning autism want at college and university? (in their own words)'. *Good Autism Practice*, 10 (2), 35–43.

Billington, T. (2006) 'Working with autistic children and young people: Sense, experience and the challenges for services, policies and practices'. *Disability and Society*, 21 (1), 1–13.

Braun, V. and Clarke, V. (2006) 'Using thematic analysis in psychology'. *Qualitative Research in Psychology*, 3 (2), 77–101.

Browning, J., Osborne, L.A. and Reed, P. (2009) 'A qualitative comparison of perceived stress and coping in adolescents with and without autistic spectrum disorders as they approach leaving school'. *British Journal of Special Education*, 36 (1), 36–43.

de Mijolla, A. (ed.) (2005) *International Dictionary of Psychoanalysis*. Detroit: Macmillan Reference.

DfE (Department for Education) and DoH (Department of Health) (2015) *Special Educational Needs and Disability Code of Practice: 0 to 25 years: Statutory guidance for organisations which work with and support children and young people who have special educational needs or disabilities.* London: Department for Education. Online. https://assets.publishing.service.gov.uk/government/ uploads/system/uploads/attachment_data/file/398815/SEND_Code_of_Practice_ January_2015.pdf (accessed 23 August 2018).

Hill, L. (2014) '"Some of it I haven't told anybody else": Using photo elicitation to explore the experiences of secondary school education from the perspective of young people with a diagnosis of autistic spectrum disorder'. *Educational and Child Psychology*, 31 (1), 79–89.

Hollway, W. (2015) *Knowing Mothers: Researching Maternal Identity Change.* Basingstoke: Palgrave Macmillan.

Hollway, W. and Jefferson, T. (2008) 'The free association narrative interview method'. In Given, L.M. (ed.) *The SAGE Encyclopedia of Qualitative Research Methods.* Thousand Oaks, CA: SAGE Publications, 296–315.

Hollway, W. and Jefferson, T. (2013) *Doing Qualitative Research Differently: A psychosocial approach.* 2nd ed. London: SAGE Publications.

Joffe, H. and Elsey, J.W.B. (2014) 'Free association in psychology and the grid elaboration method'. *Review of General Psychology*, 18 (3), 173–85.

Loyd, D. (2013) 'Obtaining consent from young people with autism to participate in research'. *British Journal of Learning Disabilities*, 41 (2), 133–40.

Milton, D., Mills, R. and Pellicano, E. (2014) 'Ethics and autism: Where is the autistic voice? Commentary on Post et al'. *Journal of Autism and Developmental Disorders*, 44 (10), 2650–1.

Mitchell, W. and Beresford, B. (2014) 'Young people with high-functioning autism and Asperger's syndrome planning for and anticipating the move to college: What supports a positive transition?'. *British Journal of Special Education*, 41 (2), 151–71.

Shepherd, J. (2015) '"Interrupted interviews": Listening to young people with autism in transition to college'. *Exchanges: The Warwick Research Journal*, 2 (2), 249–62.

UK Parliament (2014) 'Children and Families Act 2014'. Online. www.legislation. gov.uk/ukpga/2014/6/contents/enacted (accessed 25 August 2018).

Wehman, P., Schall, C., Carr, S., Targett, P., West, M. and Cifu, G. (2014) 'Transition from school to adulthood for youth with autism spectrum disorder: What we know and what we need to know'. *Journal of Disability Policy Studies*, 25 (1), 30–40.

Chapter 9

Listening to the voices of young adults with autism and severe learning difficulties: The transition to adulthood

Rai Fayette and Caroline Bond

Introduction

There are many challenges for young people making the transition to adulthood; these challenges relate to broad issues of identity and autonomy as well as more practical tasks such as acquiring key life skills. This transition can be particularly difficult for young people with severe learning difficulties and autism who may struggle to communicate their views and may be at an early stage in developing their life skills and independence. In this chapter we focus on how educational psychologists (EPs) can work with schools and colleges to enable young people with autism and severe learning difficulties to play a central role in planning their transition to adulthood. Given that a focus of this chapter is upon young people's voice, the terms 'autism' and 'on the autistic spectrum' are used as they are terms preferred by members of the autism community (Kenny *et al.*, 2016). The chapter begins by considering the specific needs of young adults with autism and learning difficulties within the broader legislative context. This is followed by a consideration of the role of schools in transition planning and approaches to listening to the voice of this group of young people. A framework for supporting the transition to adulthood process is outlined followed by a good practice example focusing on one school in one local authority.

Autism and severe learning difficulties

Autism is a broad spectrum that is characterized by core difficulties in social communication and social interaction and restricted or repetitive behaviour or interests (American Psychiatric Association (APA), 2013) that may or may not be accompanied by learning difficulties. In the United Kingdom the terms 'learning disability' and 'learning difficulty' are often used interchangeably, for instance in the *Special Educational Needs and Disability Code of Practice* (Department for Education (DfE) and Department of Health (DoH), 2015). Learning difficulties are also on a continuum with severe learning difficulties being characterized by significant cognitive difficulties, which may also be accompanied by difficulties with communication, life skills, mobility or medical needs (Holland, 2011).

Autism is the second-largest form of special educational need (DfE, 2017). In 2016, 25.9 per cent of the children and young people in England who had an Education and Health Care Plan (EHCP) issued identified their primary need as autism whereas only 14 per cent had an EHCP issued for severe learning difficulties (DfE, 2017).

Although the majority of young people on the autism spectrum are educated in mainstream schools, currently there are approximately 21,600 children and young people on the autism spectrum being educated in special schools (Moore, 2016). Not all young people with an autism diagnosis attending specialist settings have severe learning difficulties, but there may be quite a number of pupils in special schools who do have both of these needs and could be recorded as having either autism or severe learning difficulties as their primary need. This chapter focuses specifically on pupils with autism and severe learning difficulties, although given the spectral nature of both these difficulties some of the strategies discussed may also be useful for other pupils with autism or learning difficulties.

Transition planning policy and legislation

Transition is 'the process or a period of changing from one state or condition to another' (Oxford English Dictionary). This usually involves coping with new environments and adapting to new demands that can often be a challenge for young people on the autism spectrum and their families (Strnadová *et al.*, 2016). Wittemeyer *et al.* (2011) found a dearth in policy and guidance regarding effective transition planning to achieve good adult outcomes. More recently, though, the *Special Educational Needs and Disability Code of Practice* (DfE and DoH, 2015) has recognized the complexity of the transition to adulthood and states that planning for students' transitions to adulthood should begin when pupils are in Year 9 and the process should involve collaboration between school staff, the young person, parents and professionals. The Mental Capacity Act 2005 (see Social Care Institute for Excellence (SCIE), 2016) and Preparing for Adulthood guidance documents (Mott MacDonald, 2015) have helped to broaden the focus of transition practices.

Mental Capacity Act 2005

The Mental Capacity Act 2005 is based on the premise that those aged over 16 are able to make decisions for themselves. The Act applies to anyone caring for people aged 16 and over who are unable to make all or some decisions for themselves. It is underpinned by the following five key principles:

- A presumption of capacity, so it cannot be assumed that someone is not able to make a decision because they have a particular disability.
- Individuals should be supported to make their own decisions and be involved as much as possible in the decision-making process.
- The right to make unwise decisions.
- If someone does lack mental capacity the decisions made for them should be done in their best interests.
- The decisions made should be the least restrictive intervention for each individual.

Lack of capacity should not be assumed to be permanent and assessment of mental capacity should be specific to that time and decision. Someone may be assessed as not being able to make their own decisions if: they cannot understand the information given; retain the information; evaluate the information or communicate their decision (SCIE, 2016). It is expected that carers will use alternative methods of communication and supports for decision-making as required.

Preparing for Adulthood

In the United Kingdom the Preparing for Adulthood (PfA) guidance includes the four key dimensions of higher education/employment; independent living; participation in society; and being healthy (DfE and DoH, 2015). These are underpinned by five key good practice elements: developing a shared vision across agencies; planning services together; a personalized approach; raising aspirations; and improving post-16 options (Mott MacDonald, 2015). The process should begin early and centre on the young person's aspirations and interests. This is a complex task and there are currently limited empirical research evaluating tools or strategies in individual PfA dimensions or across dimensions or focusing on strategies for specific special educational needs and/or disabilities (SEND) groups. A survey of employment providers by Moon *et al.* (2011) found that for students attending special education an integrated transition approach over time was perceived as significant and, rather than purely academic instruction, needed to include: self-management skills such as hygiene and dressing; functional skills such as using public transport or a mobile phone; and self-advocacy such as communicating preferences and reporting abuse. They also identified that previous work experience and information about individual preferences of the student were important for employment providers when matching the student to suitable supported employment. There is also emerging evidence of the importance of transition planners being knowledgeable about local employment options, modelling and shaping vocationally related skills and providing programmes to address social skills needs (Westbrook *et al.*, 2015). McAnaney and Wynne (2016) evaluated 15 transition to education and work programmes from the perspective of school leavers with a range of difficulties including severe learning difficulties and autism. Highly rated projects were characterized by:

- a person-facing process that included self-advocacy, informal learning, mentoring, and individualized supports and interventions such as autism-specific stress management plans
- environment-facing processes including supporting families and staff training, e.g. in relation to managing challenging behaviour
- systems-facing processes such as data collection, monitoring and review.

McAnaney and Wynne (2016) concluded that personalization was important to success when working with such a diverse client group. The limited research in this area highlights the complexity of ensuring a successful transition to adulthood for young people with SEND.

The role of schools in the transition planning

Poor adult outcomes, particularly relating to employment and independence, have been linked with poor transition experiences (Knapp *et al.*, 2009; Strnadová *et al.*, 2016; Wittemeyer *et al.*, 2011). Strnadová *et al.* (2016) surveyed parents and teachers in Australia regarding secondary school to post-school transition for students with intellectual disability and/or autism and found limited educational and post-school living options and a lack of information for parents and school staff about options. Teachers were involved in preparing pupils for post-school life and used students' interests as part of this process. However, the process often began later than Year 9 and students were often not involved in the planning process, with some teachers perceiving the young person's learning disability being a reason to exclude them. On the other hand, participation in transition meetings has been found to increase the likelihood of enrolment in higher education (Chiang *et al.*, 2012) and students' self-esteem and advocacy are increased when they lead transition meetings themselves (Mason *et al.*, 2002). In the United Kingdom, parents and practitioners who participated in Wittemeyer *et al.*'s (2011) survey also identified that transition planning practices should improve. Given the complexity of transition planning for young people with autism and severe learning difficulties, there is evidence of a need for teacher training and support for schools in developing effective practice.

Listening to the voice of young adults with autism and severe learning difficulties

Listening to the voice of children and young people is enshrined in the United Nations Convention on the Rights of Child (United Nations, 1989), which states that children and young people should be involved in decisions that affect their lives. For young adults this also fits with the requirements of the Mental Capacity Act.

Research to date that has looked at eliciting the views of young people with autism and learning difficulties about their educational experiences is limited. Researchers have tended to focus primarily on eliciting the views of young people who are able to engage in verbal discussion or eliciting the views of young people with special educational needs generally (Fayette and Bond, 2018a). This means that there is limited research for schools and practitioners to draw on in relation to best practice for eliciting the views of young people with autism and severe learning difficulties.

However, young people with autism and learning needs may have specific individual needs that require careful consideration when eliciting their views as part of transition planning. For instance, they may experience specific difficulties with identifying emotions, abstract thinking or future questions, which are all important concepts underpinning transition (Beresford *et al.*, 2004). In addition, they may have other difficulties related to their learning difficulties in areas such as cognition and communication. These difficulties can make it hard to know how much someone has understood, particularly in a single interaction. Strategies such as Talking Mats have proved useful in supporting young people with learning and communication difficulties.

When students are able to participate in transition meetings this can enable them to develop their self-determination skills and identify their strengths and future goals (Wehmeyer *et al.*, 2007). However, there continue to be barriers to active participation such as students preferring their parents to attend and relay information to them (Beresford *et al.*, 2013) and young people with autism perceiving themselves as less autonomous and having greater difficulties in social situations than young people with other disabilities (Wagner *et al.*, 2007). McNeish and Newman (2002) suggest that for all young people meaningful participation is underpinned by a process of eliciting young people's views over time and enhancing their motivation to participate in the process.

The literature to date has illustrated that it is crucial for young people to participate in decisions about all aspects of their future lives, but this can be particularly challenging when working with young people who have severe learning difficulties and autism. Some of the key tasks for practitioners and families are:

- understanding the young person's aspirations
- developing key skills required to fulfil those aspirations
- being able to provide relevant and appropriate information about opportunities available
- providing ways of learning about these options and ensuring meaningful participation in decisions.

A framework for post-16 transition
Introduction
Focusing on pupils' transition during their secondary education prepares them for life after school (Wehman *et al.*, 2014). The framework described below was informed by the authors' research (Fayette and Bond, 2018a, 2018b). It is intended to illustrate the potential contributions of EPs at different levels to ensure that transition practices are active and collaborative.

The framework illustrated in Figure 9.1 conceptualizes transition as having three distinct yet interconnected phases. The framework also takes into consideration the influence of policies in both the local authority and each individual education provision towards the success of each individual's transition to adulthood. It can be seen that phases build upon and complement each other over time. While it may not always be possible that pupils, their parents/carers and relevant professionals are familiar with the whole framework, EPs may act as a link between phases to increase the continuity of practice across all phases.

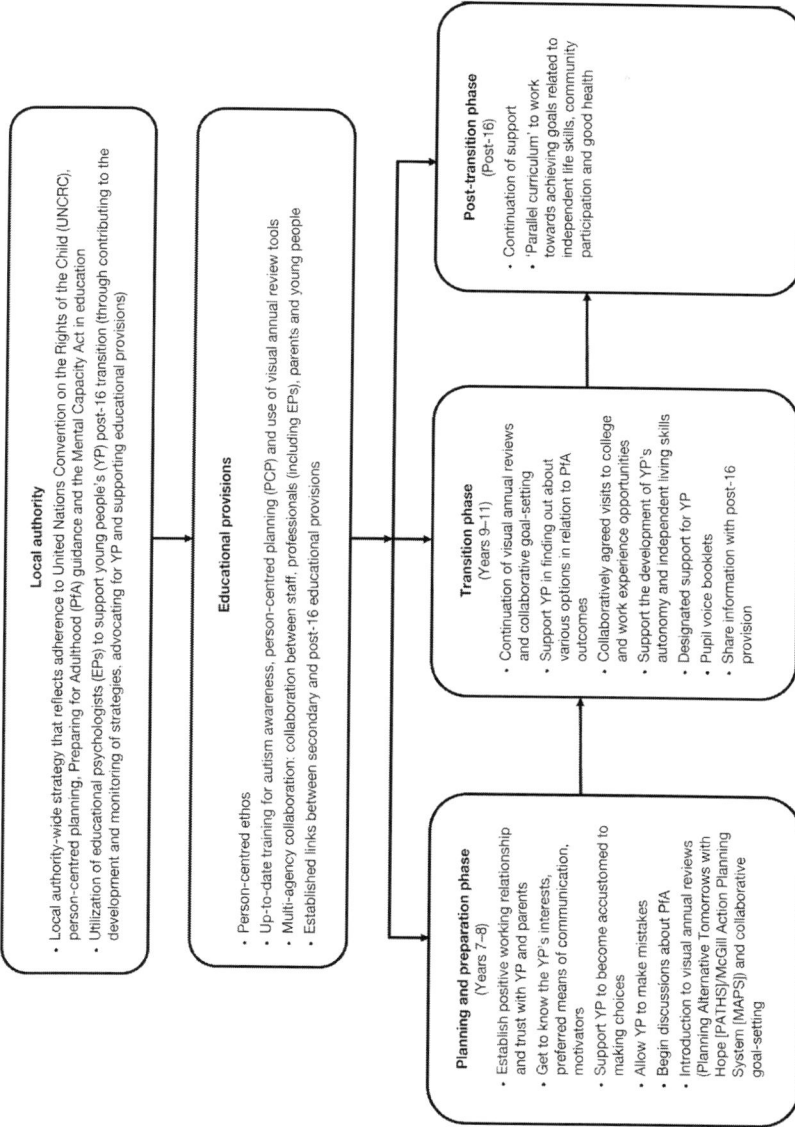

Figure 9.1: Framework for post-16 transition of pupils with autism

Local authority

Local authorities should expect that everyone involved in the transition of young people, including those with autism, engages fully to support them to achieve the best possible outcomes. Doing so would require an in-depth understanding of the difficulties and limitations that individuals on the autism spectrum face. It is therefore important to utilize the knowledge and experiences of professionals such as EPs, social care workers and teaching staff to inform policy.

One way of doing so is by establishing a steering group that comprises such professionals, which aims to enable different professionals to review and develop local authority-wide policies in the light of existing good practices in schools and colleges, up-to-date research evidence and government legislation. Previous research also found that a steering group can enable school staff to access support from other members of the network that help them improve their practice as well as provide a platform for them to share their school's good practice (Bond and Hebron, 2016). It would also help raise awareness of other resources and organizations that may be able to offer support to young people and their families during the time of transition.

Educational provisions

Fayette and Bond (2018b) found that effective transition processes are underpinned by a school-wide person-centred ethos and a positive view of individuals with autism. In addition, while educational provisions aim to adhere to the local authority-wide transition policy, each of them present with contextual factors such as staff's confidence and competence in implementing approaches that may influence the success of a young person's transition. As such, link EPs have a role to play in providing support on a systemic level. For instance, they can provide training on topics such as autism awareness, person-centred planning (PCP) and the use of specific tools that can be used to support pupils' goal-setting and annual reviews such as Talking Mats (Murphy and Cameron, 2008), Planning Alternative Tomorrows with Hope (PATHS; Pearpoint *et al.*, 1993) and the McGill Action Planning System (MAPS; Forest *et al.*, 1996), to build on the knowledge of the staff in both secondary and post-16 educational provisions. All of these factors influence the success with which aspects of each phase of young people's transition to adulthood are implemented. While EPs may not be involved in all of the activities described for each of the phases of transition, they have an important role in making sure that schools, colleges, parents and relevant professionals understand that these activities are significant. EPs can also provide support in monitoring these activities, and guide the schools if changes are needed.

Three phases of transition to adulthood
1. Planning and preparation

The *Special Educational Needs and Disability Code of Practice* (DfE and DoH, 2015) states that planning for pupils' transition to adulthood should begin when they are in Year 9. Toor *et al.* (2016) found that the likelihood of pupils with autism having a positive transition experience can increase if transition processes are tailored in a way that values their voice. Therefore, it is important to make sure that the necessary skills such as decision-making, communicating and evaluating their choices are taught to pupils with autism and learning difficulties in order for them to be able to participate meaningfully in the planning stages of their transition. As highlighted in Fayette and Bond's (2018b) paper, the process should ideally start as early as Year 7 for young people on the autism spectrum.

Secondary school staff should therefore dedicate time in Years 7 and 8 to build positive working relationships with each pupil and their parents, to get to know the pupils' interests, hobbies, strengths, and preferred method of communication, among other things. School staff should also ensure that pupils with autism are given plenty of opportunities to make decisions on a daily basis. These could include choices of activities in lessons and unstructured times, food at lunch, or who they sit with in lessons. Choices should be presented multiple times using each pupil's preferred method of communication (Loyd, 2015). It is also essential for staff to allow pupils to make mistakes, as long as they and others around them are safe. Staff and parents should support the pupils to understand the link between their choices and their consequences, to support the development of their ability to make informed choices in the future.

During this phase, parents, staff and relevant professionals should explicitly teach the concept of adulthood to pupils. Since most individuals with autism experience difficulties in understanding abstract concepts, such as adulthood, concrete representations should be used as well as tools such as social stories (Gray, 1998). In addition, parents, pupils, staff and relevant professionals should ensure that annual reviews include dedicated time to collaboratively develop post-16 goals and the relevant steps to achieve them. As the adults get to know the pupils, it is hoped that the agreed goals will not be based on their perceived limitations of the young people, but rather on their strengths, ambitions and potential (Hendricks and Wehman, 2009).

2. *Transition phase*

Years 9–11 should be spent strengthening the pupils' autonomy by continuing the activities and routines established in the first phase. In addition, the goals and strategies that were collaboratively agreed during the past annual reviews should be explicitly discussed by staff, parents and pupils to ensure that the pupils understand the link between the annual review meeting itself – an activity that they do once a year – and their day-to-day lives.

Pupils should also be supported in reflecting on the aspects of their educational lives that they find useful, and would like to continue to experience in post-16 education. Previous research such as that of Barnhill (2016) and Toor *et al.* (2016) found that pupils with autism perceived having additional time in exams, structured learning, and support for time management and planning helped make their educational experiences positive. Environmental factors such as the level of noise, visual stimuli, frequency with which the pupil needs to navigate through a crowd on a daily basis, as well as opportunities to engage in social interactions, should all be given equal consideration as academic factors (Toor *et al.*, 2016). However, it is important to elicit the views of each pupil to find out the exact type of support that they find useful.

Pupils with autism should be given a variety of work experiences based on their interests and strengths. In addition, they should be given the opportunity to visit different post-16 educational settings to provide them with a concrete reference to further inform their decision. Staff should support the pupils in evaluating these options, for instance by supporting them in developing a tick list that includes five to ten things that they are looking for. Pupils and staff should then discuss their 'findings' after each work experience or college visit (see Fayette and Bond, 2018b).

This phase should also be spent introducing other aspects of adulthood such as good health, independent living and community participation. It should be noted that explicit teaching and opportunities to practise activities relating to these aspects of adulthood may not be practically possible due to the nature of the secondary school curriculum, particularly in mainstream schools. However, being aware of the pupils' strengths and areas of needs should still enable parents, staff and pupils themselves to develop specific outcomes that can be worked on in post-16 educational settings.

In order to ensure that the appropriate support is carried through beyond secondary education, a partnership between schools and colleges should be fostered. In addition, detailed records of each pupil's academic, social and sensory abilities, and their goals and strategies to achieve them, should be shared with the agreed post-16 educational provision destination.

3. Post-transition

It is essential for post-16 educational provisions to carry out the agreed level and type of support after transition. It is also ideal for a key adult to remain in contact with young people for at least a year after their move to post-16 provisions (McConkey, 2010).

As discussed above, most pupils with autism and learning difficulties will have Preparing for Adulthood goals that may be practically challenging to work on during their secondary education, such as those that relate to good health, community participation and independent life skills. It is therefore ideal that their post-16 education should develop – in partnership with EPs – and incorporate a 'parallel curriculum' aimed to explicitly teach these skills. Since the timetables of pupils in post-16 educational provisions typically include independent study periods where pupils are not required to attend classes, some of these periods could be used for this 'parallel curriculum'.

The following case example illustrates how some of the processes outlined in the transition framework supported one young person's transition into college over time.

Case example: Preparing for post-16 transition

Please note that the names of the pupil, schools and local authority have been anonymized through the use of pseudonyms.

Background information

This case example focuses on a Year 11 pupil called Ian who was diagnosed with autism when he was 4 years old. He had an EHCP that stated he experiences difficulties in the areas of communication and interaction and cognition and learning. Although he was able to communicate verbally, his receptive and expressive language abilities were under-developed. In addition, his cognitive profile indicated that he had severe learning difficulties.

Ian was educated at Questel Specialist School (QSS) where he spent all of his secondary education. QSS is one of three specialist provisions at Marthorpe local authority (MLA) – a large city in the North West of England. QSS has more than 100 pupils aged 11–19 with moderate, severe and profound learning difficulties. A fifth of the student population in QSS have a diagnosis of autism.

Local authority and school contexts

In response to the publication of the *Special Educational Needs and Disability Code of Practice* (DfE and DoH, 2015), MLA developed a policy that requires schools to conduct person-centred annual review meetings including discussions about young people with EHCPs' Preparing for Adulthood (PfA) outcomes. As such, from the end of Year 7, pupils, their parents/carers, school staff and relevant professionals in mainstream and specialist secondary schools discuss and agree short- and long-term outcomes in the areas of education and employment, good health, community participation and independent living.

Annual person-centred planning and review meetings have been a part of QSS's practice even before the introduction of the *Special Educational Needs and Disability Code of Practice* (DfE and DoH, 2015). However, the PfA guidance helped refine the outcomes and strategies discussed in such meetings. In addition, staff in the school collectively believed that young people with SEND, including those with autism and severe learning difficulties can achieve meaningful outcomes. A person-centred ethos and positive attitude towards individuals with autism and severe learning difficulties are shared by all the staff at QSS. This meant that their good practice was not dependent on a few individuals, and was therefore not susceptible to change if members of staff chose to leave the school. There was also a shared understanding between all staff that plenty of time and effort should be spent to enable the meaningful participation of individuals with autism and severe learning difficulties.

Key Stage 3

At QSS, most of Key Stage 3 is spent getting to know the pupils and helping them become accustomed to making choices. After Ian joined the school, the staff who worked with him spent time engaging him in one-to-one, problem-free communication activities every day and joining in his favourite activity, which was searching the internet for and colouring in images of trucks. Not only did these interactions foster positive working relationships between Ian and the teaching staff, but they also helped the staff develop an understanding of Ian's likes, dislikes and preferred communication medium.

In addition, Ian's daily timetable included plenty of opportunities to practise making choices, such as break-time play activities and food to have during lunch times. It is important to note that, in accordance with the Mental Capacity Act, staff allowed Ian to make choices that may be deemed unwise as long as his safety was not at risk. This enabled Ian to understand and reflect upon the link between his choices and their consequences. The link between choices and consequences was explicitly discussed with Ian during PSHE lessons and one-to-one discussions.

Working collaboratively

Collaborative working between relevant professionals, school staff, individual pupils and their parents was fostered as pupils join the school. For instance, the staff engaged in regular communication with Ian's parents through a home-school diary, emails, and through face-to-face interactions during coffee mornings. Annual review meetings were attended by the school's EP, Dr Hamilton, whose role was to provide advice on PfA outcomes and strategies to achieve them.

Key Stage 4

Having known Ian for two years, the staff knew that he needed plenty of time to prepare for his transition to post-16 education. As such, informal conversations between them and Ian about post-16 education and employment options were held once a fortnight from the beginning of Year 9. Having this time built into Ian's timetable enabled the staff to explain each aspect of the transition to him. It also enabled him to ask staff questions.

During one of these conversations Ian expressed an interest in working for a truck delivery service but he was unsure of what exact role he preferred. The staff then presented him with three choices: driving, cleaning or loading the trucks. Despite this, Ian was still unable to make a decision. Ian's class teacher and Mrs Shane (the school's deputy head teacher) then arranged for Ian to undertake work experience in a small local delivery service, supported by a school teaching assistant. While he was not able to join the employees during their delivery trips, they explained the routes and the procedures to him. He spent a few weeks cleaning the vehicles, then a few weeks loading them. Once the work experience placement concluded, Ian was able to let his teacher know that he still wanted to work for a similar company and that he wanted to just clean the vehicles.

This experience enabled the school staff to understand that Ian requires concrete representations and actual experiences of different choices before being able to make decisions. As such, during his annual review at the end of his Year 10, he, his parents and the school staff arranged for him to visit four post-16 educational provisions at least twice to take pictures, experience being in their lessons and have food in their dining rooms, as well as having the opportunity to meet some of the teachers. After each visit, Ian and the class teaching assistant (Miss Jenkins) discussed what he liked and did not like about each provision, prompted by the pictures he took. Records of these discussions were shared with Ian's parents so they could have the same discussions with Ian at home. After visiting all four provisions, Ian still decided to remain at QSS.

Eliciting Ian's views

In preparation for Ian's person-centred transition planning meeting, Miss Jenkins spent four 20-minute one-to-one sessions with Ian to fill in his 'pupil voice booklet'. This booklet contains pupil-friendly questions about young people's likes, dislikes and preferences with regard to the four PfA areas. Filling in this booklet in advance provided Ian with the opportunity to express and record his views in case he was not able to attend the actual meeting, for instance, due to anxiety. Having four sessions to collect Ian's views enabled Miss Jenkins to ask the questions multiple times, which checked for consistency in Ian's responses. It also allowed her to ask clarifying questions.

Transition planning meeting

Ian's person-centred Year 11 transition planning and review meeting was attended by Ian, his mother and father, Miss Jenkins, Mrs Jerry (Ian's Year 11 class teacher), Mrs Shane (chair of the meeting), Mrs Booth (education caseworker) and Dr Hamilton. Throughout the meeting Ian was given plenty of opportunities to agree or disagree with the accounts of the attendees. He and his parents were also given opportunities to ask questions if they were unsure of anything. However, it was evident that due to all of the work completed by staff with Ian and his parents since the start of Ian's secondary schooling to prepare him for his transition to adulthood, everyone in the meeting had a shared understanding of Ian's strengths, needs and interests. This enabled everyone collaboratively to develop longer-term outcomes for Ian, as well as to plan for his transition to the school's sixth form provision.

Conclusion

As illustrated by Ian's case study, transition planning for young people with autism and learning difficulties is an important process that requires considerable time and planning. However, to date there has been little research to support the development of good practice in this area (Wittemeyer *et al.*, 2011).

The proposed framework has sought to integrate research, policy and good practice in transition planning for young people with autism and learning difficulties. It emphasizes the importance of strategic interagency collaboration and joint planning of services (Mott MacDonald, 2015). Education settings also need to ensure that the transition planning process is valued and begins early (Fayette and Bond, 2018b). Transition processes also need to take place over time (McNeish and Newman, 2002) to be accessible (Loyd, 2015), collaborative and person-centred (Fayette and Bond, 2018b). These processes also need to focus on facilitating the development of young people's decision-making (Toor *et al.*, 2016) and autonomy (Wehmeyer *et al.*, 2007). The framework is anticipated to provide a starting point for EPs and other professionals in developing and researching systems to support young people with autism and learning difficulties making the transition to higher education.

EPs can potentially play an important role in transition at local authority, educational provision and individual levels within this framework. They can bring a holistic view of individual development to local policy and resource development and work with other professionals, school networks, local authority officers and charities to facilitate the development of good practice. EPs are also well placed to support individual education settings to develop transition planning processes that ensure pupil views are central to decision-making. As in Ian's case EPs can help to ensure that annual reviews go beyond educational outcomes to focus on a range of PfA outcomes. As EPs work across settings and at different levels they can also have an important role to play in helping to identify gaps in systems and ensuring continuity for young people during transition.

However, as highlighted by employers in the study by Moon *et al.* (2011), there continue to be significant challenges in meeting the wider PfA outcomes of employment, independent living, participation in society and being healthy. These are potentially innovative areas for EP practice and research in order to enable young people to lead healthy and fulfilling adult lives.

References

APA (American Psychiatric Association) (2013) *Diagnostic and Statistical Manual of Mental Disorders: DSM-5.* 5th ed. Arlington, VA: American Psychiatric Association.

Barnhill, G.P. (2016) 'Supporting students with Asperger syndrome on college campuses: current practices'. *Focus on Autism and Other Developmental Disabilities*, 31 (1), 3–15.

Beresford, B., Moran, N., Sloper, T., Cusworth, L., Mitchell, W., Spiers, G., Weston, K. and Beecham, J. (2013) *Transition to Adult Services and Adulthood for Young People with Autistic Spectrum Conditions: Final report* (Working Paper DH 2525). York: Social Policy Research Unit. Online. www.york.ac.uk/inst/spru/pubs/pdf/TransASC.pdf (accessed 5 February 2018).

Beresford, B., Tozer, R., Rabiee, P. and Sloper, P. (2004) 'Developing an approach to involving children with autistic spectrum disorders in a social care research project'. *British Journal of Learning Disabilities*, 32 (4), 180–5.

Bond, C. and Hebron, J. (2016) 'Developing mainstream resource provision for pupils with autism spectrum disorder: Staff perceptions and satisfaction'. *European Journal of Special Needs Education*, 31 (2), 250–63.

Chiang, H.-M., Cheung, Y.K., Hickson, L., Xiang, R. and Tsai, L.Y. (2012) 'Predictive factors of participation in postsecondary education for high school leavers with autism'. *Journal of Autism and Developmental Disorders*, 42 (5), 685–96.

DfE (Department for Education) (2017) *Special Educational Needs: An analysis and summary of data sources*. London: Department for Education.

DfE (Department for Education) and DoH (Department of Health) (2015) *Special Educational Needs and Disability Code of Practice: 0 to 25 years: Statutory guidance for organisations which work with and support children and young people who have special educational needs or disabilities*. London: Department for Education. Online. https://assets.publishing.service.gov.uk/government/uploads/system/uploads/attachment_data/file/398815/SEND_Code_of_Practice_January_2015.pdf (accessed 23 August 2018).

Fayette, R. and Bond, C. (2018a) 'A systematic literature review of qualitative research methods for eliciting the views of young people with ASD about their educational experiences'. *European Journal of Special Needs Education*, 33 (3), 349–65.

Fayette, R. and Bond, C. (2018b) 'A qualitative study of specialist schools' processes of eliciting the views of young people with autism spectrum disorders in planning their transition to adulthood'. *British Journal of Special Education*, 45 (1), 5–25.

Forest, M., Pearpoint, J. and O'Brien, J. (1996) '"MAPS": Educators, parents, young people and their friends planning together'. *Educational Psychology in Practice*, 11 (4), 35–40.

Gray, C.A. (1998) 'Social stories and comic strip conversations with students with Asperger syndrome and high-functioning autism'. In Schopler, E., Mesibov, G.B. and Kunce, L.J. (eds) *Asperger Syndrome or High-Functioning Autism?* New York: Plenum Press, 167–98.

Hendricks, D.R. and Wehman, P. (2009) 'Transition from school to adulthood for youth with autism spectrum disorders: Review and recommendations'. *Focus on Autism and Other Developmental Disabilities*, 24 (2), 77–88.

Holland, K. (2011) *Factsheet: Learning disabilities*. Birmingham: British Institute of Learning Disabilities.

Kenny, L., Hattersley, C., Molins, B., Buckley, C., Povey, C. and Pellicano, E. (2016) 'Which terms should be used to describe autism? Perspectives from the UK autism community'. *Autism*, 20 (4), 442–62.

Knapp, M., Romeo, R. and Beecham, J. (2009) 'Economic cost of autism in the UK'. *Autism*, 13 (3), 317–36.

Loyd, D. (2015) 'Gaining views from pupils with autism about their participation in drama classes'. *British Journal of Learning Disabilities*, 43 (1), 8–15.

Mason, C.Y., McGahee-Kovac, M., Johnson, L. and Stillerman, S. (2002) 'Implementing student-led IEPs: Student participation and student and teacher reactions'. *Career Development for Exceptional Individuals*, 25 (2), 171–92.

McAnaney, D.F. and Wynne, R.F. (2016) 'Linking user and staff perspectives in the evaluation of innovative transition projects for youth with disabilities'. *Journal of Intellectual Disabilities*, 20 (2), 165–82.

McConkey, R. (2010) *Transitions and Young People with Autism Spectrum Disorders*. Belfast: Eastern Health and Social Services Board.

McNeish, D. and Newman, T. (2002) 'Involving children and young people in decision making'. In McNeish, D., Newman, T. and Roberts, H. (eds) *What Works for Children? Effective services for children and families*. Buckingham: Open University Press, 186–204.

Moon, S., Simonsen, M.L. and Neubert, D.A. (2011) 'Perceptions of supported employment providers: What students with developmental disabilities, families, and educators need to know for transition planning'. *Education and Training in Autism and Developmental Disabilities*, 46 (1), 94–105.

Moore, C. (2016) *School Report 2016: Two years on, how is the new Special Educational Needs and Disability (SEND) system meeting the needs of children and young people on the autism spectrum in England?* London: National Autistic Society.

Mott MacDonald (2015) 'SEND pathfinder information pack: Preparing for Adulthood: Version 5'. Online. www.sendpathfinder.co.uk/preparing-for-adulthood-information-pack (accessed 5 February 2018).

Murphy, J. and Cameron, L. (2008) 'The effectiveness of Talking Mats® with people with intellectual disability'. *British Journal of Learning Disabilities*, 36 (4), 232–41.

Pearpoint, J., O'Brien, J. and Forest, M. (1993) *PATH: A workbook for planning positive possible futures*. Toronto: Inclusion Press.

SCIE (Social Care Institute for Excellence) (2016) *Mental Capacity Act at a Glance*. www.scie.org.uk/mca/introduction/mental-capacity-act-2005-at-a-glance (accessed 5 February 2018).

Strnadová, I., Cumming, T.M. and Danker, J. (2016) 'Transitions for students with intellectual disability and/or autism spectrum disorder: Carer and teacher perspectives'. *Australasian Journal of Special Education*, 40 (2), 141–56.

Toor, N., Hanley, T. and Hebron, J. (2016) 'The facilitators, obstacles and needs of individuals with autism spectrum conditions accessing further and higher education: A systematic review'. *Journal of Psychologists and Counsellors in Schools*, 26 (2), 166–90.

United Nations (1989) *Convention on the Rights of the Child*. Online. https://www.ohchr.org/Documents/ProfessionalInterest/crc.pdf (accessed 27 August 2018).

Wagner, M., Newman, L., Cameto, R., Levine, P., Marder, C. and Malouf, D. (2007) *Perceptions and Expectations of Youth with Disabilities: A special topic report of findings from the National Longitudinal Transition Study-2 (NLTS2)* (NCSER 2007-3006). Washington, DC: US Department of Education. Online. http://files.eric.ed.gov/fulltext/ED498185.pdf (accessed 5 February 2018).

Wehman, P., Schall, C., Carr, S., Targett, P., West, M. and Cifu, G. (2014) 'Transition from school to adulthood for youth with autism spectrum disorder: What we know and what we need to know'. *Journal of Disability Policy Studies*, 25 (1), 30–40.

Wehmeyer, M.L., Agran, M., Hughes, C., Martin, J.E., Mithaug, D.E. and Palmer, S.B. (2007) *Promoting Self-Determination in Students with Developmental Disabilities*. New York: Guilford Press.

Westbrook, J.D., Fong, C.J., Nye, C., Williams, A., Wendt, O. and Cortopassi, T. (2015) 'Transition services for youth with autism: A systematic review'. *Research on Social Work Practice*, 25 (1), 10–20.

Wittemeyer, K., Charman, T., Cusack, J., Guldberg, K., Hastings, R., Howlin, P., Macnab, N., Parsons, S., Pellicano, L. and Slonims, V. (2011) *Educational Provision and Outcomes for People on the Autism Spectrum*. Online. https:// researchers.mq.edu.au/en/publications/educational-provision-and-outcomes-for-people-on-the-autism-spect/ (accessed 6 September 2018).

Chapter 10

Using personal construct psychology with young people aged 19–25 to help them make sense of their behaviour and the world in which they live

Michael Hymans

Introduction

If we wish to help young people understand how they *construe* their world, a useful starting point is the theory of personal construct psychology developed by George Kelly (1991) [Volume 1: Theory and personality; Volume 2: Clinical diagnosis and psychotherapy]. This theory is based on the philosophical background of *constructive alternativism*, which suggests that each young person invents or *constructs* their own way of interpreting the world they experience. Additionally, Kelly suggested that young people should always have some alternative way of dealing with their world rather than having their understanding determined by their circumstances or biography (Fransella *et al.*, 2004).

Kelly presented his theory in the form of a *fundamental postulate* and 11 *corollaries*: for a more detailed description of this, see Bannister and Fransella, 1986. A *postulate* is an idea that is suggested as or assumed to be the basis for a theory. The *fundamental postulate* states that 'a person's processes are psychologically channelized by the ways in which s/he anticipates events'. This means that young people's thoughts, feelings and behaviour follow on from the way in which they anticipate things. Essentially, Kelly is viewing the individual as striving for personal meaning.

A *corollary* is the reasoning involved in drawing a conclusion or making a logical judgement on the basis of circumstantial evidence and prior conclusions (i.e. postulating) rather than on the basis of direct observation. Kelly argues that individuals grapple to understand their world: they perceive similarities and themes in events before them, propose theories about such events, foster anticipations about the future and seek to continually test out how much sense has been made of their world through their behaviour. Teenagers, in particular, are often in a state of flux as they revise their *core constructs* about who they are and what they value, and test out whether the *construction* of their world is accurate and makes sense to them. Whether or not a young person changes their constructs will depend on the *permeability* of the construct and the extent of any such change will depend on the inter-relationships between constructs and their position within a young person's behaviour repertoire (i.e. ordinal hierarchical framework or *organizational corollary*). These formal aspects of the nature of constructs will affect both the content and structure of a young person's construct system such that seen as a whole each young person is likely to have a unique system.

So what is a *construct, and* why is it important for a young person to discover their constructs?

At its most basic level, a construct is the distinction a young person makes (e.g. *polite* versus *ill-mannered*) that has a particular range of usefulness for them: it cannot be applied to ice cream for instance and is probably grouped with other constructs, perhaps for example *considerate* versus *inconsiderate,* under a hierarchy such as *well-behaved* versus *uncouth.* Importantly, these words are merely labels used by the young person, based on their personal experiences, and psychologists should always avoid making assumptions about what each word means to the young person based on their own construct system. Kelly champions asking the young person if you want to know how they perceive their world.

A key assumption within Kelly's personal construct theory is the *individuality corollary:* 'People differ from each other in their construction of events.' This central theme runs throughout the theory as great stress is laid on the uniqueness of each young person's system. However, according to Kelly, unless young people have some understanding of another person's set of personal constructs about a topic under discussion and that person has some understanding of the young person's constructs, the process of communication between them will be inadequate. This is Kelly's *sociality corollary,* which implies the need to come to some understanding of the current conceptualization of the subject matter and is where a *repertory grid* can be useful.

The grid is therefore a way of having a structured conversation, as well as culling from a large amount of data a picture small enough to be useful to both psychologist and young person, without over-reductionism. A grid provides a space for listing and ranking or rating elicited constructs in connection with the topic under consideration. The repertory grid supports a credulous listening approach, allowing the psychologist faster access to a young person's world and allowing the young person to look at themselves in an organized way. Thus problem areas can be identified jointly and the results can be a starting point for a psychologist's dialogue and intervention with a young person.

By eliciting a young person's constructs, the psychologist is tapping into the personal dimensions the young person uses to anticipate events, and thus it is a means of finding out and sharing with a young person how they use their personal constructs. The process can be viewed as a first tentative sketch of how a young person might see their world and provide a focus for future interventions.

How can constructs be elicited?

In practice constructs can be elicited using the 'traditional' *triadic difference'* method, which would usually be along the following lines: *'Think of three people you know. You don't need to tell me who they are, but tell me in what way one of these three people is different from the other two. Tell me in terms of their behaviour and/or how they are as people and not in terms of whether they are male or female or in terms of eye/hair colour or their height.'* And typical responses might be: *he is smart* or *she completes all assignments and hands them in on time.* I would then say for example: *'What would you contrast being smart with?'* Note the use of the word *contrast* rather than *opposite*, because I do not want the young person to give me a dictionary definition of the opposite of smart. Care also has to be taken in case the respondent says that one is smart and the other two are stupid. We have to be sure that for the young person being *stupid*, for example, is the *bipolar contrast* of being *smart*. On the other hand, young people's contrasts often illuminate differences, so for one person the contrast to *smart* might be *thick*, whereas for another young person it might be *gets bullied*, due to the particular contexts or the triad of people chosen. To elicit further constructs, I would say to a young person: *'Either use the same three people or choose another three or any combination of these options (i.e. keep two of the people and add another one or keep one and add another two). And tell me in what way one of these three people is different from the other two ... Etc.'*

More recently, in undertaking a doctorate in applied psychology/ education at the University of Nottingham, 2003–7, I have chosen to use *dyadic elicitation*: in the present context this could include, for example, asking a young person to compare their *behaviour*, or any other aspect of their personality, when younger, say two to five years ago, with their behaviour now, and asking: *'Is your behaviour the same or different?'* and irrespective of the response, then asking *'In what way?'* Once a response (construct) is elicited, the young person is asked for the *contrast* to their *construct*. This form of questioning can be repeated in order to elicit more constructs and their contrasts. Another way of using *dyadic elicitation* is with the use of an initial question: *'Think of a person you know who is successful/happy/has lots of friends [or any other aspect of a young person's life under investigation] with another person who is not so successful/ happy or who does not have many friends'* and then ask: *'In what ways are they different?'* The contrast to the elicited construct is then obtained. It is important to note some contrasts may overlap with the elicited constructs, in which case the psychologist has to confirm which bipolar constructs are 'true' or accurate for that young person.

A further series of methods (which can be used singularly or in combination) for eliciting constructs from young people can be found in Butler and Green (2007), which I summarize below, noting that a *contrast* to the elicited *construct* is always obtained.

General description

- *Tell me three things [it could be any number] about the young people you know/hang around with.*
- *Give me three descriptions of what your brother/sister/best friend is like.*
  Who are you?
- *If I were to ask you to tell me three things that best describe you, what would you say?*
  Self-evaluation
- *If I were to ask (e.g. your mum, dad, best friend) to describe you, tell me the three most important things s/he could say about you.*
- *[Alternatively] Tell me three things about the sort of young person who worries a lot about going to school/work/completing assignments/ meeting people.*

The bipolar constructs can then be elaborated upon by asking a young person, for example: which end of the pole they would prefer to be; what is important or special about the chosen/preferred end of that pole; and asking that young person to describe the behaviours they would associate with a chosen construct, via *pyramiding* (see below), that is what a young person typically does when they are described by that construct.

Other alternative methods of construct elicitation with young people include:

Self-portraits or presenting a young person with a sketch of another person's (child or adult) face when they are looking angry or sad for example, and asking:

- *How do you guess this person is feeling?*
- *Do you ever feel like that?*
- *What might make the person feel this way?*
- *What thoughts might go through your mind whenever you feel this way?*

Portrait galleries, where young people are asked to draw faces showing different feelings, and they are then asked to say when and/or what makes them feel this way. **Drawings in context** (e.g. a newspaper or magazine picture) can be shown to young people, with accompanying questions such as:

- *What do you think is happening?*
- *What do you imagine the person or people in the drawing/picture might be thinking?*
- *Why do you think they are feeling this way?*
- *What do you guess would make a difference to the way the person/ people is/are thinking?*

The words/phrases used by the young person when using self-portraits, portrait galleries and drawings in context questions are in fact that person's constructs and therefore the contrast to each elicited construct is also sought.

Kelly (1991) developed *self-characterization* as an idiographic narrative assessment that involves a qualitative analysis by a psychologist to identify self-constructions of a young person. This additional tool for construct elicitation consists of a character sketch written in the third person in which the young person is asked to take a broad view of themselves rather than concentrate on the focal interests of the psychologist. The overall objective of this kind of enquiry is to see how a young person structures a world in relation to which s/he must maintain themselves in some kind of role. Therefore the young person's personal construct system is the primary focus of this assessment; with only a secondary focus being where that young person places themselves with respect to the personal categories and dimensions that make up their world (Winter, 1992). The characterization can be a valuable clinical tool in that the analysis of the protocol, providing the educational psychologist with a sense about the willingness of the young person to experiment with new outlooks and new approaches to their problems, as well as a sense of how that person will approach therapeutic change. The young person's objectives, purposes and feelings of progress may be explored as well as obstacles, difficulties and successful solutions or readjustments to past problems. This assessment also enables the young person the opportunity to introduce significant issues that might have been too intimidating to reveal directly to the psychologist.

Young people are instructed: *'Please write a character sketch of* [name of person], *just as if s/he were a major character in a book, movie or play. Write it as a friend, who knew her/him intimately and sympathetically, perhaps better than anyone could really know her/him, might write it. Be sure to write it in the third person. For example, start out by saying,* [name of person] *...'* The contextual area chosen by the young person indicates where s/he sees themselves as being distinguishable from other people and also where s/he feels secure enough to be able to elaborate their personal construct system. In making an analysis of a young person's sketch the psychologist can consider sequences and transformations, the topic and opening themes and the possible meaning of each statement both independently and in the context of the total protocol. The sequence of particular areas represents progression either from the well-structured to the more problematic or from the more general to the more specific. Particular attention should also be paid to the individuals who are mentioned because they are a sample of figures who populate the young person's world (Kelly, 1991; Winter, 1992).

Butler (2001) devised the *Self-Image Profiles* (SIP), which he says tap into a young person's theory of self and 'through inviting individuals to consider both "how I am" and "how I would like be", various measures of self-construing are obtained. Self-construing is, arguably, a core or fundamental aspect of psychological functioning' (page 1 in the Self-Image Profiles Manual). Interestingly, Kelly's (1991: 46) fundamental postulate states: 'A person's processes are psychologically channelized by the ways in which he anticipates events.'

Fundamentally the SIP is built on acknowledgement of both personal construct theory (Kelly, 1991; Bannister and Fransella, 1986; Butler and Green, 1998) and the developmental and organizational model of self as proposed by Harter (2000). The principles underpinning the SIP are: a differentiation between self-image and self-esteem; target population generated content in that the construction of the scales requires recognition of cognitive development, ability to understand certain concepts and language skills; a developmental notion of self in that there appears to be increasing discrimination and organization in how the self is constructed; the multi-dimensional structure of self, through verbalized self-representations across various domains, such as appearance and social behaviour; the self is unique; self-descriptions are contrasts and therefore bipolar; there is an implicit acceptance of a *fragmentation corollary* (Bannister and Fransella, 1986) in that a young person can hold apparently contrasting views about their self across different domains or aspects of self; and only items or self-descriptions of a psychological nature are included.

In the development of the Self-image Profile for Adolescents (SIP-A) three secondary schools in the Leeds area were selected to cover a range of socio-economic status: two classes from each year group were randomly selected giving a total of 892 pupils who participated. The pupils were asked: *'If you could describe yourself in three ways, what would they be?'* A balanced range of the most frequently elicited items across age and gender were selected, which resulted in 25 items: 12 positive, 12 negative and 1 item to reflect self as 'I,' that is the extent to which a young person *feels different from others.*

The 12 *positive (self-image)* constructs are: kind, happy, friendly, funny, helpful, hard working, talkative, confident, sporty, intelligent, fun to be with and good looking. The 12 *negative (self-image)* constructs are: lazy, annoying, moody, mess about, shy, cheeky, loud, sarcastic/bitchy, worry a lot, bossy, short-tempered and get bored. The constructs are given singularly and respondents are asked to rate how unlike (0) to very much like (6), which is akin to a *Likert Scale.*

Using the SIP-A with the 12–16 age group the examiner can extract a young person's positive and negative self-image and their self-esteem and see how the raw score compares with standardized scores. However, in using the SIP-A with a 16-plus age group I simply look at ratings for each construct and ask one or more of the supplementary questions provided in the SIP manual.

The supplementary questions are: *'How come you gave yourself a rating of* [the score] *on* [the self-description kind, which is positive, or worry a lot, which relates to a negative self-image]? *How do you know you are like that* [chosen self-description]? *How does being that way make you feel? How is it that you are like this/How did you get to be like this?*[1]

Laddering and pyramiding

Hinkle (1970) developed the method of *laddering* to test out Kelly's (1991) *organization corollary:* 'Each person characteristically evolves, for their convenience in anticipating events, a construction system embracing ordinal relationships between constructs.' This is a system that looks a bit like a computer folder tree, and Hinkle's hypothesis was that the more superordinate a construct (i.e. the more abstract and higher up the hierarchy of constructs), the more it will resist change. In the *laddering process*, the psychologist is often asking a young person to consider aspects of their way of understanding the world that they may never have thought about before. Laddering consists of asking the question 'Why?' The young person is first asked which pole of a given construct they would prefer to describe. 'Why' questions can be phrased in different ways, for example: 'What are the advantages for you of being someone who … ?' Or 'Why is it important for you to be … rather than … ?' It can be seen that the question of importance is making use of laddering in that by being repeatedly asked 'why,' a young person climbs the 'ladder' of their construct system towards areas of their most superordinate constructs, and basic system of values. The information obtained may be alarming and threating for the young person, as well as interesting. Furthermore, the number of steps up the ladder is variable and the psychologist will sometimes be unsure when a young person's values have been identified. There are six different ways of knowing that value-laden constructs have been obtained.

Abstraction means that the constructs offered deal less with matters of behaviour, operational activity and detail, in that escalating the ladder leads to encountering constructs that deal with the essence of existence and life: not *good timekeeper* versus *poor timekeeper,* but rather *predictability and order* versus *unpredictability and chaos* perhaps. One way of assisting in the laddering process is to gently nudge the young person into even greater abstraction by saying, for example: 'Why for you, is that the personal preference? What's the essence of it?'

By their very nature, personal constructs deal in generalities of life (i.e. *universality*). When psychologists delve into a young person's values they are dealing with grand themes of existence rather than the small change of everyday living e.g. *freedom and choice* versus *slavery and constraint,* and with *universality* a helpful prompt might include asking: 'What would life be like if you chose this end of the construct? What would your world look like this way, rather than the other way?' pointing to each pole in turn. As the psychologist helps a young person progress up the ladder s/he will be dealing with issues that are personal and increasingly private (or *intimate*) for that young person and success in helping young people might make the psychologist feel a little vulnerable themselves, wondering whether the interview is going through another iteration: a lot will be dependent upon the situation, the topic and how well the psychologist knows the young person. So, if a psychologist gets the feeling that s/he is intruding a simple choice has to be made: have the young person's personal values been arrived at or should one more iteration be attempted?

Kelly (1991) defined a *core construct* as one that people use in order to place themselves in relation to their experience *(self-reference)*. All core constructs can be related to personal values, though not all personal values are necessarily core constructs (Jankowicz, 2004). However, the more frequently a young person talks about her/himself, the stronger the self-reference and the closer the psychologist will be getting to that young person's personal values.

It is also entirely appropriate for a psychologist to ask a young person whether it is worth going further (i.e. going for a yet-more-superordinate construct) and thereby obtaining more *explicit information. 'Shall we try just one more step?'* becomes, with your interviewee's permission, a shared experiment (Jankowicz, 2004). Similarly, acknowledging absurdity *(self-evidence)* is a good way of admitting that it may seem strange to examine an apparently self-evident preference, by for example asking whether a young person thinks there is more to it, and emphasizing that while a preference may be obvious in general terms, you are concerned with the young person's own reasons for their choice in particular.

Landfield (1971) described *pyramiding,* which as with laddering is another technique that is related to Kelly's *organization corollary* and the hierarchy of constructs. It is used because there are times when a psychologist may want to identify a young person's constructs at a detailed level from a particular point of view. There are also other times when the *variety* of the range of constructs or points of view offered by the young person warrants further investigation.

For example, the elicited constructs may be about feelings towards people and whether a young person feels comfortable with other people can be just one thing a psychologist wants to learn about. Or the constructs may be about trusting people, where trust is the topic and the psychologist is seeking as many different aspects of that superordinate construct as possible.

Pyramiding involves asking the young person to successively 'climb down' their construct system, to more concrete or *subordinate* levels. The questioning asks for more specific details of a young person's constructs.

For example, a psychologist might ask: '*What kind of person is someone who is introverted?*' The answer may be '*hard to get to know*' as contrasted with someone who is '*easy to get to know*'. A follow-up question might be: '*What kind of person is someone who is hard to get to know?*' The same questioning then takes place with the contrast or other end of the pole, and a young person's responses can be reproduced in schematic form as shown in Figure 10.1 below.

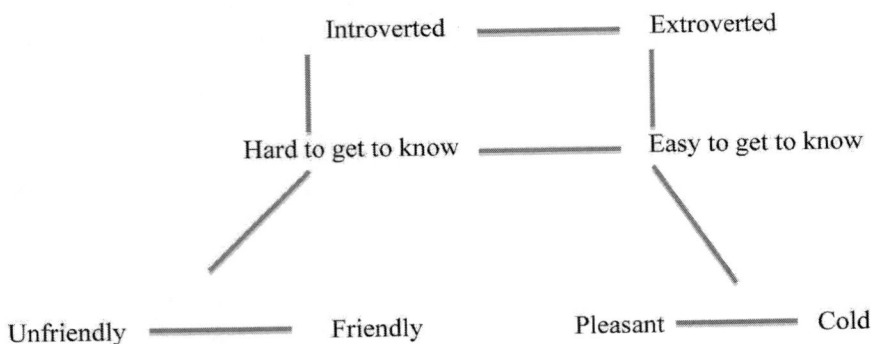

Introverted ———— Extroverted

Hard to get to know ———— Easy to get to know

Unfriendly ———— Friendly   Pleasant ———— Cold

Figure 10.1: An example of the pyramiding process

To get to specific behaviours, the psychologist can ask: '*How do you know when another person is cold? What do they actually do that makes you think they are cold?* One such answer might be: '*They look at you without blinking!*'

Some case study examples

In my capacity as a psychologist in private practice (PiPP)/expert witness I was asked to undertake a *capacity assessment* for the Royal Courts of Justice, and in completing the assessment I used a modified version of *self-characterization*, where the young person dictated her sketch. For background information, A was born in the early 1990s. She has learning difficulties/disabilities. She is reported to have had delayed expressive and receptive language and behavioural problems in childhood. A was born at 37 weeks, only weighing 3lbs and with cataracts in both eyes, which were removed when she was 3 years old. At birth she was kept in the special care unit at hospital for two weeks in order to monitor her weight. She received ongoing laser treatment to clear her vision when she was 9. She was described as presenting with immature behaviour that was reported to be aggressive and defensive at times. She was teased at primary school and did not have many friends. She was assessed and monitored by the local speech and language therapy service, and received blocks of speech and language therapy interventions. When she was 14 her mother reported to the local mental health trust that she had been found going off in a stranger's car after she had wandered off from home.

Mother also expressed concerns about A's lack of interest in completing homework and that she found literacy and numeracy difficult. Nevertheless during a second session at the Child and Family Consultation Service mother reported improvements in A's behaviour since she started secondary school and that she was behaving a little more maturely.

When A was 15 she made allegations of physical abuse against her father, which were investigated by the police. She attended a special needs school throughout most of secondary education. At age 19 she attended college where she studied childcare, and was provided with additional support. The January following her attendance at the college she moved out of her family home as she was having difficulties with her parents, and went to live with a friend, her father and grandmother, where she stayed for a couple of months after which she moved into a hostel.

A converted to Islam when she was 20 and obtained a visa to visit Pakistan at the end of that month. A got married in Pakistan, and later on returned to England, where she alleged that it was a forced marriage; she also said that the marriage was never consummated. She returned to England shortly after. During that winter A was evicted from her hostel and moved in with friends. Shortly afterwards A travelled to Romania with her friends, where they stayed in a hotel. A and one of her friends had an argument following A's interview with the police about the marriage.

It was reported that A could no longer handle the pressure and was physically violent towards her friend; in July she moved out of her friend's home and became homeless. A was then placed in a shelter where she has her support worker. She now wishes for her marriage to be annulled, as she did not validly give her consent. A has gone into hiding because she is scared and fearful that pressure will be put on her to make an immigration application on behalf of the man she married. A continues to be vulnerable and is assisted/supported by a social worker from a learning disability team.

A's *self-characterization* sketch revealed several constructs:

- Being bullied < > Having friends
- Getting angry < > Staying calm
- Put down by others < > Understood by others
- Treated as an adult < > Treated as a child
- Trusting < > Cautious
- Unable to deal with sarcasm < > Able to deal with sarcasm
- Scares others < > Helps others

- Not getting along with mother < > having fun with mother [who had a drink problem]
- Being grounded [by father for bad behaviour at school] < > Allowed to go out
- Finding college work difficult < > Finding college work fun

I then decided to draw up the following grid for selected constructs < > contrasts for A to rate, where a rating of '1' relates to the left hand (or *emergent*) end of the pole, and rating of '7' is at the right hand (*implicit*) end and which was elicited as the contrast to the emergent construct. A rating of '4' can be considered as 'neutral' or behaviour that occurs sometimes, and is neither at one end nor at the other end of the pole. Note too that the *elements* chosen for the grid relate simply to how A sees herself now and how she would like to be.

Table 10.1: A's grid

Constructs	Me now	How I would like to be	Contrasts
Being bullied	3	6	Having friends
Getting angry	4	7	Staying calm
Put down by others	1	7	Understood by others
Treated as an adult	4	1	Treated as a child
Unable to deal with sarcasm	1	5	Able to deal with sarcasm
Scares others	5	6	Helps others

I used the content of this grid to provide additional information for the court and more importantly for A's support worker that A has expressed a desire/need for help with: having friends; learning how to stay calm more often; what being understood by others would look like; being treated as an adult more often; and learning how to deal with sarcasm more effectively than at present.

The support worker would of course need to explore with A how she might make small steps towards these aspirations: e.g. how she might move from 1 to 2 in the grid above in terms of being understood by others; who needs to help her; what being understood by others would be or look like for A. The same approach can be used for each of the constructs in the grid.

M (male) was referred to me by his parents, in my capacity as an educational psychologist in private practice. M was in Year 14 of mainstream school with an additionally resourced autistic provision, and was at risk of exclusion. His parents were going to apply for a residential 19-plus specialist residential provision, and they wanted his special educational needs and/or disabilities (SEND) to be assessed with advice on the strategies/provision that should be put in place in his present provision to meet his identified needs.

M lives at home with his parents and younger siblings, F (male, 17 years) and H (female, 13 years). M received his autism spectrum disorder (ASD) diagnosis in 2012. M received occupational therapy interventions between 2012 and 2015, and in April 2017 he received a diagnosis of attention deficit hyperactivity disorder (ADHD) from child and adolescent mental health services (CAMHS).

M has had difficulties with sleeping and did not sleep through the night until 3 years of age; he now uses melatonin to help with sleeping. He was not completely toilet trained until 3 to 4 years of age. He had feeding problems during the first two months after birth as a consequence of severe reflux and failed to thrive. Otherwise all other developmental milestones were age-appropriate.

His parents described M as anxious, disorganized, distractible, impulsive, overactive and withdrawn: he daydreams, has temper tantrums and prefers to play alone. He lacks confidence and has a low self-esteem. He is argumentative, cries easily and doesn't understand social hierarchies in that he speaks to everyone as his peers. He finds the school day stressful, that is in coping with the demands and in behaving in socially appropriate ways. M's behaviour is '*controlled*' at home by his parents having very clear and consistent rules and expectations. In contrast, school report to parents increasing problems in managing his behaviour.

M takes no responsibility for his behaviour at home by letting others do or organize things for him and so he is not learning to manage himself either at home or school. M reacts to every request or demand, especially at school, with a panic reaction, and he will cry constantly saying: '*I can't do it; it's too difficult,*' etc. He will try various strategies to delay starting a task, including disrupting others. He particularly gets upset when given a time limit for completing a task, by saying: '*I can't bear the pressure, stop!*'

M is reluctant to put anything onto paper at school or even to type. He gets very anxious and emotional at the start of every task and often cries and says things like, '*It's too difficult/I can't do it.*'

Parents reported that M was becoming increasingly disruptive in class and often made inappropriate noises. '*He is inappropriately loud and struggles with maintaining attention and concentration. He sees a mentor twice a week at school and has some LSA [learning support assistant] support in class: he also attends a weekly spelling club. School have informed parents that the additional support in some lessons is not working and that the behaviour reward chart is ineffective, although parents say that the chart is not completed consistently and he is not engaged with it.'*

Parents were also of the opinion that support at school was not addressing the issues, which were escalating. Parents believed the problems centred on M's anxiety, lack of social skills and poor social understanding. M likes to control all play activities especially with his siblings, and says he hates his brother F, although in reality their relationship has improved. He listens to close friends, who are tolerant and will prompt M appropriately. He enjoys construction activities such as Lego and computer games, especially Minecraft. M attends Scouts and STEM (science, technology, engineering and mathematics) after-school clubs. Parents describe M's strengths as being creative, clever and agile.

I introduced M to the 25 single (*emergent*) constructs on the SIP-A and asked him for the bipolar 'contrasts' or *implicit* constructs: whenever he used an emergent construct as a contrast I discarded that single construct. So for example he used lazy as a contrast to hard working and therefore I only used hard working-v-lazy rather than ask for another contrast to lazy.

This meant that I had the following bipolar constructs for M:

1. Kind-v-Unkind
2. Happy-v-Unhappy
3. Friendly-v-Unfriendly
4. Funny-v-Serious
5. Helpful-v-Unhelpful
6. Hard working-v-Lazy
7. Talkative-v-Shy
8. Confident-v-Unsure
9. Intelligent-v-Stupid
10. Fun to be with-v-Sarcastic
11. Good looking-v-Ugly
12. Feel different from others-v-Feel the same as others
13. Annoying-v-Pleasant
14. Moody-v-Relaxed
15. Mess about-v-Well behaved
16. Cheeky-v-Polite
17. Loud-v-Quiet
18. Worry a lot-v-Carefree

19. Short-tempered-v-Calm
20. Bored-v-Interested

I used the following statements as elements: me now (or self-image); how I'd like to be (ideal self); what school thinks about me; what my parents think about me; and what my brother (F) thinks about me. I then asked M to rate each bipolar construct from -3 to +3, where -3 is most like the implicit construct and +3 is most like the emergent construct, and where a rating of 0 can be considered as neutral or sometimes like M.

I obtained the following grid shown in Figure 10.2.

	ele_1 Me now	ele_2 How I'd like to be	ele_3 What school thinks about me	ele_4 What my parents think about me	ele_5 What my brother thinks about me	
con_1 Kind	1	2	0	-3	-3	(-)con_1 Unkind
con_2 Happy	-3	2	0	-3	0	(-)con_2 Unhappy
con_3 Friendly	3	3	-3	-3	-1	(-)con_3 Unfriendly
con_4 Funny	-3	0	0	0	0	(-)con_4 Serious
con_5 Helpful	-3	1	1	-3	0	(-)con_5 Unhelpful
con_6 Hard working	0	2	-3	-3	0	(-)con_6 Lazy
con_7 Talkative	2	2	3	-1	3	(-)con_7 Shy
con_8 Confident	0	3	1	-2	1	(-)con_8 Unsure
con_9 Intelligent	3	3	0	3	3	(-)con_9 Stupid
con_10 Fun to be with	3	3	0	0	-2	(-)con_10 Sarcastic
con_11 Good looking	-3	0	0	0	-1	(-)con_11 Ugly
con_12 Feel different from others	3	3	-1	2	3	(-)con_12 Feel the same as others
con_13 Annoying	0	-3	1	3	3	(-)con_13 Pleasant
con_14 Moody	0	-3	1	2	3	(-)con_14 Relaxed
con_15 Mess about	2	-2	0	2	1	(-)con_15 Well behaved
con_16 Cheeky	0	-1	0	0	1	(-)con_16 Polite
con_17 Loud	2	-2	0	0	2	(-)con_17 Quiet
con_18 Worry a lot	3	-3	0	3	0	(-)con_18 Care free
con_19 Short tempered	3	-3	0	1	1	(-)con_19 Calm
con_20 Bored	0	-2	-1	3	0	(-)con_20 Interested

Figure 10.2: Grid ratings for each construct and element

Notes: Number of constructs: 20. Number of elements: 5. Grid type: rating. Scale range: -3.00 to 3.00.

I then used the *Idiogrid software* package: Idiogrid (Version 2.4) is software for administering, managing and analysing different types of self-report data. It was originally designed around George Kelly's repertory grid technique but has been developed to include person-centred and questionnaire methodologies employed by researchers from a wide variety of domains (e.g. personality psychologists, self-concept researchers, educational/clinical psychologists, market researchers and sociologists). Idiogrid is currently in use by hundreds of psychologists, psychological researchers and marketing/ business consultants in dozens of countries from around the world. I applied principal component analysis (PCA) to the above grid and obtained a bi-plot graph (see Figure 10.3), where the two principal components (PC) account for just over 75 per cent of the variance in the data.

The key constructs from PC1 relate to how M sees himself now (his self-image) and what he thinks his parents might say about him, whereas with PC2 the key constructs are connected with how he would like to be (his ideal self), as well as his self-image. So this means that it is significant that M construes himself as being: unhappy, serious, unhelpful, ugly, different from others, worrying a lot, and short tempered, as well as by way of contrast being friendly, intelligent and fun to be with. The key constructs in relation to what his parents might say about M are: unkind, unhappy, unfriendly (although this relates to his brother), unhelpful, lazy, annoying, worrying a lot, and getting bored. Ideally, M wants to be calmer, happier and better behaved, as well as more: confident, pleasant, relaxed, interested (in school work), and to worry a lot less.

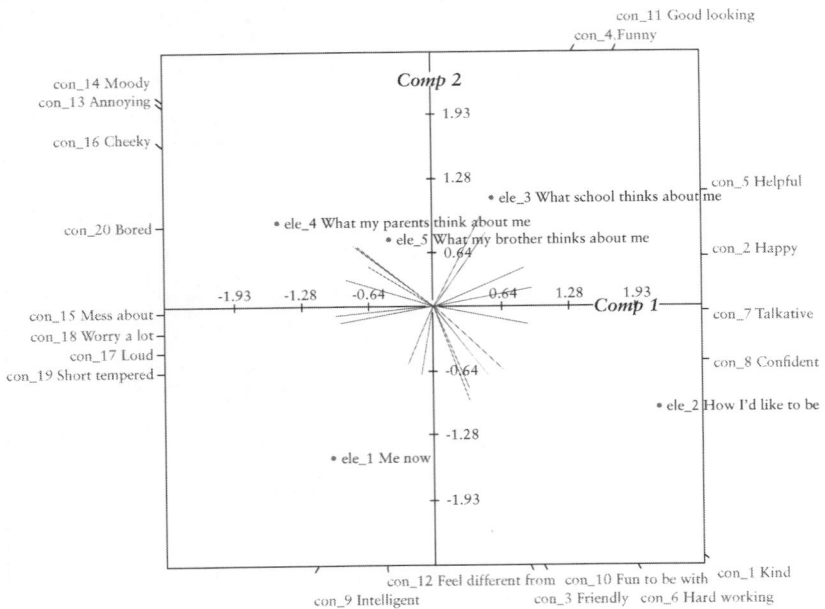

Figure 10.3: M's bi-plot graph for the PCA (Idiogrid)

Following a discussion at school with parents and the special educational needs co-ordinator (SENCo) and M, the prioritized constructs for change were agreed as being less *short tempered* and *worrying a lot* less (x5), as well as being *happier* and more *helpful*. We talked about a range of anger management and anxiety techniques and I suggested the use of cognitive behavioural therapy (CBT) resources for schools in these areas that included resources from Jessica Kingsley Publishers (www.jkp.com), as well as my book, *Whole-School Strategies for Anger Management* (Hymans, 2009). We then discussed what would need to happen for M to feel happier; what would he need to do; who could help him (staff and students, as well as his parents); how would he know he was happier, and how would others know. A similar approach was taken to being more helpful.

However, we agreed to prioritize anger and anxiety management, mainly as I suspect that if these mental health issues are better managed by M then he is likely to feel happier. Finally I suggested that once M's anger and anxiety are better under his control the constructs with a difference of 4 between self-image (SI) and ideal self (IS) should be targeted for change in order of agreed priority between M and school in conjunction with his parents.

A final consideration for school intervention is that M construes himself as feeling very different from others and he wants to stay like this in the future. Such an ideal might derive from a failure to develop 'an experiencing self' (Jordon and Powell, 2007) as he may have difficulties developing a personal memory for events; it was already evident from my cognitive assessment that he has a poor visual memory and has problems retrieving information from his long-term memory.

The implications for school staff are that M will need a visual and verbal structure that cues him into salient points; this could be by using photographs, videos and prompt scripts (e.g. social stories), especially as Jordon and Powell (2007) point to the inter-relatedness of emotions and thinking that leads to the attachment of 'meaning' to events. Without a personally experienced meaningfulness of events M will learn 'from the outside in', as it were, by rote and mechanistically. The challenge to staff is that of explicit teaching of meaning and therefore M's attention must be drawn to how new information affects the way in which he understands the world. In this sense, transferability of knowledge becomes a process that needs to be directly taught rather than assumed.

Note

[1] This may provide an understanding of the young person's theory of cause, either in terms of internal attributions, such as effort or ability, which that person perceives as having some control over, or as external attributions, such as parental expectations, which the young person considers less controllable.

References

Bannister, D. and Fransella, F. (1986) *Inquiring Man: The psychology of personal constructs*. 3rd ed. London: Croom Helm.

Butler, R.J. (2001) *The Self Image Profiles: For children (SIP-C) and adolescents (SIP-A)*. London: Psychological Corporation.

Butler, R.J. and Green, D. (1998) *The Child Within: Taking the young person's perspective by applying personal construct psychology*. Chichester: Wiley.

Fransella, F., Bell, R. and Bannister, D. (2004) *A Manual for Repertory Grid Technique*. 2nd ed. Chichester: Wiley.

Grice, J.W. (2002) 'Idiogrid: Software for the management and analysis of repertory grids'. *Behavior Research Methods, Instruments, and Computers*, 34 (3), 338–41.

Harter, S.L. (2000) 'Quantitative measures of construing in child abuse survivors'. *Journal of Constructivist Psychology*, 13 (2), 103–16.

Hinkle, D.N. (1970) 'The game of personal constructs'. In Bannister, D. (ed.) *Perspectives in Personal Construct Theory*. London: Academic Press, 91–110.

Hymans, M. (2009) *Whole-School Strategies for Anger Management: Practical materials for senior managers, teachers and support staff*. London: Optimus Education.

Jankowicz, D. (2004) *The Easy Guide to Repertory Grids*. Chichester: Wiley.

Jordon, R. and Powell, S. (2007) *Understanding and Teaching Children with Autism*. New Jersey: Wiley and Sons.

Kelly, G.A. (1991) *The Psychology of Personal Constructs*. Originally 1955. 2 vols. [Volume 1: Theory and personality; Volume 2: Clinical diagnosis and psychotherapy] London: Routledge.

Landfield, A.W. (1971) *Personal Construct Systems in Psychotherapy*. Chicago: Rand McNally.

Winter, D.A. (1992) *Personal Construct Psychology in Clinical Practice: Theory, research and applications*. London: Routledge.

Chapter 11

Narrative therapy and 16–25 year olds: Exploring what matters

Charmian Hobbs

This chapter shares ideas about using a narrative therapy approach when working with young adults. I start by considering therapeutic practice within educational psychologist (EP) work and where narrative therapy might sit. I go on to give an overview of narrative therapy for readers who are less familiar with this way of working. I consider this approach as my preferred way of working with young adults. I then offer a framework for how narrative therapy practice might look for this group of people. I conclude by asking readers who are interested in this approach to investigate it further.

Therapeutic practice in EP work

Therapeutic practice is part and parcel of the everyday work of EPs. Many people, children and adults come to us frustrated, distressed, tired, angry, harassed and much more, and through careful listening we offer them a space to talk and be heard. This conversation can be recuperative for them. For some people, a more formalized approach, including one that is manualized, might be offered by some EPs. This might be described as delivering an evidence-based psychological therapy, usually provided over a number of sessions with an evaluation of the outcome. Alongside these approaches are others that are drawing on practice-based evidence. In this latter case 'what matters in an individual case is whether change takes place or not as a result of an intervention' (Dunsmuir and Hardy, 2016: 14). So where does narrative therapy fit in? Certainly close to practice-based evidence, but my response is that for me narrative therapy is a way of thinking and working and would be present in all areas of my practice.

What is narrative therapy?

Narrative therapy was developed by White and Epston (1990) and is now widely practised internationally (for example see the Dulwich Centre, https://dulwichcentre.com.au/about/). One of the fundamental principles of a narrative approach is to recognize that each person is an expert in their own lives and someone who is capable of change. In narrative therapy both problems and actions are spoken of as if outside the person and their identity. This is known as externalizing. Externalizing conversations are ways of talking that separate the person from the problem so challenging the assumption that this is part of their identity. They lead to rich descriptions of the effects of the concern and the discovery of skills and resources that can be employed in response. These conversations require a shift in the use of language to allow for reconsideration of everyday assumptions and expectations. Using language with an 'externalizing grammar' introduces a different perspective to the problem (see Freeman *et al.*, 1997: 57 for full description of externalizing grammar). Externalizing creates a space between a person and a concern; it introduces a sense of agency. A person is no longer defined by a particular description, for example autism, but can begin to ask about the presence of autism in their life:

> *What is autism like in your life? Can you describe it? What do you call it? Is it the same with your family and your friends? Is it around all the time? How does it make you feel? How does autism fit in with how you like to spend your time? How does autism fit in with the plans you have for your future?*

The narrative approach states that over time, stories shape lives and give meaning to everyday experience. People are selective about what meanings they give or what meanings are given to their own experiences and this comes to frame and reframe their understandings of themselves and how they present to others. This process of selection highlights some stories and obscures others. In narrative practice this is described as thin and thick stories where a thin story is one in which there is factual information but limited recognition of lived experience and a thick story is one rich in personal detail and context (Morgan, 2000; White, 2007). In conversation we frequently assume an understanding. We have ideas about anger, anxiety, depression, bipolar disorder and so on. A narrative therapy conversation steps aside from these ideas to genuinely find out about the world of the young person. Curiosity is the key to narrative therapy. 'Questions are asked from a position of genuine desire to learn about the meanings of the child's world' (Winslade and Monk, 2007: 37). In this way conversations that can give details of events people have often repeated many times move to talking about the meaning of these events, what intentions and purposes are shaping these events and what conclusions have been drawn from these understandings.

Through a narrative conversation people's preferred stories can be developed and sustained. This is a collaborative process both providing a space in which any stories of difficulty can be heard and an entry point to previously unspoken and unproblematic stories more in keeping with their preferred identity. Narrative therapy is then interested in seeking out the alternative stories that highlight possibilities for change (Freedman and Combs, 1996) and for sustaining hope. Alternative stories can be surprising to both the person and the therapist. Knowledge that was previously unspoken or even unknown can be expressed and explored. Importantly the history of this new understanding is discovered through talking about other times when similar actions have happened. In narrative therapy, stories are 'events, linked in sequence across time according to a plot' (Morgan, 2000: 5). When preferred stories are revealed similar events can be linked together and we can make sense of them through the meaning we give to our experience. So through a narrative conversation we might ask you about the work you undertake with children who have some difficulties. You say that it is important to you that all children are seen as equal and no one should be disadvantaged because of a particular concern. We then ask about where this sense of equality comes from? How come you hold on to this value? You might recall that as a student you spent time with a family who lived with almost nothing and you found that very difficult to deal with. To you, it was unfair, unfair that simply because of birth they had so little and others had so much. You decided that this was something you were committed to try and change. Was there anyone who might know this about you? Who would not be surprised about this commitment? You respond by saying your father might know as he had cared for others through very difficult circumstances and you had tried hard to understand this. Thinking about this you reflect that some ideas of equity and fairness have come from your father's actions. So gradually through this conversation together we explore the history of commitment to care and equality.

Why use this approach with young adults?

Working with young adults I hope to support them towards living a more independent life or a life in which they can exercise as much choice as possible. Narrative therapy provides a way of working that is focused on their agency and recognizes the impact of the broader context on young adults who may have experienced difficulties for many years.

Narrative therapy is informed by social constructionism. Adopting this worldview offers useful ideas about power and knowledge. Much of what we have come to take for granted as 'truths' are worthy of reconsideration, of deconstruction. How come we hold this view? How does this affect the way we work with young adults? To take a relevant example from the history of learning disability, we can perhaps recall that the 1944 Education Act described those with learning disabilities as 'ineducable' and it was not until the 1970 Education (Handicapped Children) Act that made education universal that those with learning disabilities began to receive an education. It is probably unnecessary to say any more about the impact of such views on those young people seen to have learning disabilities, but we could examine current labels and the impact they have on sustaining separateness, othering and oppression. Foucault discusses how language is an instrument of power and those with power come to direct the discourses that shape society (see e.g. Foucault, 1965). Bruner (1986) writes:

> The ability to tell one's story has a political component: indeed, one measure of the dominance of a narrative is the place allocated to it in the discourse. Alternative, competing stories are generally not allocated space in establishment channels and must seek expression in underground media and dissident groupings. (p. 19)

So the young people with whom we work are often viewed through the lens of need and difficulty and their stories are often told through and by others. Narrative therapy brings to the fore the possibility of considering the social and cultural impact of the way in which many young adults with difficulties are viewed both in a general and in a particular sense. By separating the young person from their described difficulty, it enables the young adult to consider their relationship with the difficulty, its presence in their life and how this does or does not fit with what is important to them. A narrative therapy conversation through its genuine curiosity can provide a challenge to marginalization and provide a foundation for personal action and agency.

A framework

The young people we are likely to work with are those who have been identified with a difficulty or several difficulties. These difficulties may have been present throughout their lives, for example those seen as having learning difficulties or for others the difficulty may have raised its head at a later date, for example anxiety. It is probable that whatever the difficulty it is seen as something that is persistent or likely to regularly recur. Occasionally we may be involved with a limited concern, but this is rare. The focus of our work is then towards management. What provision can be put in place to try to address or minimize the effect of the difficulty? We may seek the views of the young adult about what they would like for their future, where they would like to live, how they would like to spend their time, what work they might be thinking of. All these ideas are linked with those around them to plan for the best provision. Then there is a search for the best provision match. This is essentially an assessment and review process; however, does this capture the meaning and understanding the young person has of their experience? Are we curious about the neglected stories that have been overwhelmed by the weight of the difficulty story?

> How persons are labelled is not all there is to know about them. Self-identity is fostered in this type of therapy by going beyond labels, beyond stereotypes, beyond our biases and predetermined ideas about people. This frees and allows for multiple, contradicting and simultaneously existing selves. (Anderson and Levin, 1997: 260)

A narrative therapy conversation usually starts with some questions about what has brought the young person to meet with me today. This may lead to a statement about an explanation for the meeting: 'It's because it's difficult at school' or some uncertainty. The conversation continues by following the young person's lead giving prominence to their views, concerns and constructions of the problem. This opens up the opportunity to learn about the difficulty and ask questions about what the problem is like for them:

> *What's the problem like? What kind of thing does it do? What does it look like? Do you have a name for it? What does it have you doing? How does it get on with your family, your friends, your teachers? Does it get in the way of things you want to do? How does it make you see yourself?*

I then go on to ask the young person to make an evaluation about the problem:

> *Do you see this as a good thing, a bad thing or something else? Does it make your life better or worse? Do you want to change how it is in your life or keep it the same?*

I am curious to know about the view the young person has about the problem. It may be that others want to see changes or manage the problem but that the young person has different views. They may want to have less anger around but not an absence of anger. They may want to have attention deficit hyperactivity disorder (ADHD) around at home but less so at college.

I then go on to ask about why the young person holds this judgment:

Tell me why you'd like things to be different. What is this problem getting in the way of? What plans is this problem sabotaging?

These questions are asking about what is important to that young person. They are drawing out ideas about the values the young person holds, what they are committed to in their lives, what intentions they have for themselves.

The conversation is a collaboration. I cannot experience the problem as it is experienced by the young person. The description provides a rich picture of the problem that is particular to that young person since no difficulty is an exact duplicate of anyone else's problem. In narrative therapy this is described as 'experience-near' and enables the young person to gain a greater knowledge of how the problem works in their lives. Using this knowledge they can become aware of their own know-how and how this might help them to address the difficulties they are having.

While asking about the problem, I am beginning to have an awareness of what is going on, I am listening for any exceptions when the problem seems less evident or even absent. I do not ask about these 'unique outcomes' immediately as I want to ensure that we have as full a characterization of the problem as possible so the young person has more knowledge for themselves. Checking with the young person, I go on to ask about the 'exceptions' or to ask about any times when the problem was less present:

When you said anger isn't around when you're with Jason, what do you think is happening? What would you say you are doing? How does this affect your relationship with Jason? Have there been other times when anger isn't around? Can you tell me about those times? What is it like for you at these times? Does it seem better or worse for you? Would you say this is a good thing or not? Does it fit with your plans for yourself?

This conversation follows the same categories of enquiry as the one exploring the problem. The categories are can be listed as characterization, connection, evaluation and location:

- **Characterization**: externalizing and exploring the problem or the initiative. This covers naming, drawing or modelling the problem or initiative and explores the way the problem or initiative works.
- **Connection**: this talks about the effects on the person, their family, their friends and other relationships. It traces the history.

- **Evaluation** : this asks about whether the problem or initiative is a good thing or a bad thing. Whether it suits or not.
- **Location:** how does this fit with what is important to the person? With respect to their values, commitments and hopes?

The framework of the conversation described above captures the route of an enquiry about a person's lived experience. White (2007) called this route 'statement of position maps' as a way of providing a helpful guide for the development of externalizing conversations. Of course in any conversation this linear route is rarely followed as the collaboration moves through the different categories, but it gives the context to the consultation as it moves towards the person coming to define their own *position* on the problem or initiative in their life. This is usually something new for the person whose experience has given rise to other people, including professionals, giving their own interpretation of the problem and stating their position on what needs to be done about it. The narrative therapist takes a decentred approach that enables the person to give voice to his or her own evaluation of the problem, but it is: 'also an influential position, as it is through the introduction of these categories of inquiry that the therapist provides people with an opportunity to define their own position in relation to their problems and to give voice to what underpins this position' (White, 2007: 39).

As I explore exceptions and unique outcomes with the young person that have emerged from the conversation we are beginning to develop knowledge that does not fit with the dominant story, the story that has captured the majority of air time. This exception is initially fragile. It has been 'off air'. I ask questions to find out more about the exception; about events, how these are linked together over time to form a plot. We are then considering actions that have taken place and have come together to make a particular story. In narrative therapy this is known as 'the landscape of action' and consists of questions such as:

> *What was happening at that time? Was anyone with you? Have you done this before? What were the steps leading up to this?*

I would then invite the person to reflect on the meanings of the exceptions that they have described. This is an exploration of the person's preferences, beliefs, values and purposes. As the conversation continues we are collaborating in creating an alternative story or stories to the dominant one in their life. These are 'landscape of identity' questions through which the person can begin to consider whether this alternative story is one that fits more with their beliefs for themselves.

The dominant story is one that has gained considerable prominence in a young person's life over many years. It is a well-honed story that has developed and been shared on many occasions. It is very 'known and familiar' in narrative therapy terms. It may well be the reason many people who seek professional help become frustrated by having to tell 'their story' again. Through a narrative therapy conversation the experience of this story and its meaning in someone's life can be explored and the possibility of other stories, preferred stories, drawn into the limelight. This new story, however, has little presence in contrast to the familiar story, so how can this new story be sustained? There are a number of ways in which this can happen within narrative therapy.

A process familiar to many readers will be that of documentation. By establishing some form of recording of a conversation, this can be revisited in the future. A principle that underpins documentation within narrative therapy is that of being generative, that it supports further reflection and possibility of action. By recording a conversation we are rescuing the spoken word, but it is worth thinking about how we do this such that it fits with collaboration rather than direction. The document, in whatever form – written, audio, email, text, visual – needs to be with the agreement of the young person as to what might be included and who, if anyone, could have access. However, when a conversation is documented it is an act of translation and what is recorded is what we are paying attention to. I try to record expressions of vividness, of hope and of possibility. Using direct quotes and questions for consideration offers possibilities for reflection and supports feedback. Feedback about the document is helpful in further collaboration.

A way of sustaining the new story that is perhaps less well known is that of outsider witness practice. Many practitioners might be familiar with reflecting teams (Andersen, 1993) where a team listens to a therapeutic conversation between a therapist and clients and then offers further ideas and thoughts from their reflection on the conversation. There are many differing approaches to working within reflective teams. In general, comments tend to be of a tentative and non-evaluative nature, which allow the clients to make their own decision about whether and how to respond. Within narrative therapy these ideas have been developed into a definitional ceremony. A definitional ceremony 'provides people with the option of telling or performing the stories of their lives before an audience of carefully chosen outsider witnesses' (White 2007: 165). The role of the outsider witness is not to offer applause – that is, for example, praise for managing to come through difficulties; or to provide professional evaluation or interpretation – that the way I see this is that you are having difficulty accepting that your relationship needs to change. Rather the outsider witnesses are asked to listen to a conversation and notice the expressions they have been drawn to, the images that have come into their mind's eye, about anything in the expressions and images that resonated with their own experience, and to say where listening to this conversation has taken them. In this retelling the alternative story is thickened and acknowledged. Furthermore, people become aware of shared themes in their lives. The invitation to be an outsider witness is within the gift of the person whose story will be shared and careful preparation is needed to ensure that outsider witnesses understand how they will join with the person's story. It may be that the person invites a family member or a friend or it could be that people who have similar experiences join as outsider witnesses, for example others with autism.

A narrative therapy conversation is an exploration and collaboration in finding out about:

> ... the subordinate storylines of people's lives. It is the redevelopment of these subordinate storylines that provides people with a foundation to proceed to address their predicaments and problems in ways that are in harmony with the precious themes of their lives. (White, 2007: 128)

The role of the narrative therapist is to provide a scaffold through thoughtful and careful questioning to richer knowledge about what someone holds dear in their lives. The conversation is led by the person seeking help through regular checking that the questions and ideas are useful to them. As such the conversation acknowledges that this is a young person's space where their story will be given a hearing, perhaps for the first time. The collaboration offers safety as the conversation can only continue in directions in which the young person enables it to go. Questions can be changed or unanswered. If a person chooses to share their story with a witness then this again will be with their agreement and in a way that asks for resonance and linkage rather than evaluation or interpretation. In this way people can gain agency to make a difference for themselves in their own lives.

I hope I have succeeded in introducing the ideas and ways of working within narrative therapy practice. Although this chapter is directed towards working with young adults, the approach is for anyone. It is not easy to begin to work in this way, as the externalizing language does not sit comfortably within our usual conversations. We are much more fluent with the structuralist approaches looking for truths and norms. Yet it is because narrative therapy offers the opportunity for a different conversation, for a generative conversation, that for me it has been so enriching. Conversations have taken place that have given rise to new knowledge, new understandings, new linkages that had been previously hidden or submerged. It seems to me that the experience of many of the people we work with is submerged by modernist ideas of solving and fixing and sorting, and that narrative therapy offers a way of being 'interested people ... who are skilled at asking genuine questions to bring out the knowledge and experience carried in the stories of the people we work with' (Freedman and Combs, 1996: 18).

I am still on the journey and invite others to join me, as narrative therapy practice is about community, listening for resonance and making links with others.

References

Andersen, T. (1993) 'See and hear, and be seen and heard'. In Friedman, S. (ed.) *The New Language of Change: Constructive collaboration in psychotherapy.* New York: Guilford Press, 303–22.

Anderson, H. and Levin, S. (1997) 'Collaborative conversations with children: country clothes and city clothes'. In Smith, C. and Nyland, D. (eds) *Narrative Therapies with Children and Adolescents.* New York: Guilford.

Bruner, E.M. (1986) 'Experience and its expressions'. In Turner, V.W. and Bruner, E.M. (eds) *The Anthropology of Experience.* Urbana: University of Illinois Press, 3–30.

Dunsmuir, S. and Hardy, J. (2016) *Delivering Psychological Therapies in Schools and Communities.* Leicester: British Psychological Society.

Foucault, M. (1965) *Madness and Civilization: A history of insanity in the age of reason.* Trans. Howard, R. New York: Pantheon Books.

Freedman, J. and Combs, G. (1996) *Narrative Therapy: The social construction of preferred realities.* New York: W.W. Norton and Co.

Freeman, J., Epston, D. and Lobovits, D. (1997) *Playful Approaches to Serious Problems: Narrative therapy with children and their families.* New York: W.W. Norton and Co.

Morgan, A. (2000) *What is Narrative Therapy? An easy-to-read introduction.* Adelaide: Dulwich Centre Publications.

White, M. (2007) *Maps of Narrative Practice.* New York: W.W. Norton and Co.

White, M. and Epston, D. (1990) *Narrative Means to Therapeutic Ends.* New York: W.W. Norton and Co.

Winslade, J.M. and Monk, G.D. (2007) *Narrative Counseling in Schools: Powerful and brief.* 2nd ed. Thousand Oaks, CA: Corwin Press

Part Three

3

Systemic responses to the
extended young adult
client group

Chapter 12

Preventing young people becoming NEET: The importance of early intervention, transition from school and how educational psychologists can make a positive impact

Tim Cockerill and Christopher Arnold

Introduction

A recent Department for Education (DfE, 2018a) publication regarding the characteristics of the individuals described as not in education, employment or training (NEET) should serve as an important reminder that there is much more that needs to be done to support vulnerable young people transitioning from Year 11 onwards. Tracking all school leavers in the United Kingdom in 2010/11 for three years, the DfE (2018a) outlined that at age 18, 4.8 per cent were classified as long-term NEET (NEET for a year). Although only 4.8 per cent of young people were long-term NEET, 37 per cent of individuals who had been a child in care were in this category and other risk factors were also identified, for example being permanently excluded from secondary school and attending an alternative provision, with 20 per cent or higher of these groups being classified as long-term NEET. Many other characteristics of the NEET population were identified in this report and Public Health England (2014) has outlined that being NEET often occurs among those already experiencing other sources of disadvantage. Although the national data can provide a useful starting point in the identification and prevention of those most at risk, the first section of this chapter outlines how to combine this information alongside local data to fully establish the most meaningful approaches to identifying and supporting those at risk of becoming NEET. In this chapter we will also address the importance of the transition from school at the end of Year 11 and suggest it has an important role in reducing negative outcomes for vulnerable and disadvantaged individuals, including those at risk of becoming NEET. The final section will focus on several key areas of practice in relation to the post-16 transition, with a discussion regarding possible implications for schools, settings and educational psychologists (EPs).

Developing a local preventative strategy

Analysis undertaken by the Audit Commission (2010) suggests that there is a four-to-one financial advantage when measures to prevent young people entering the NEET category are adopted rather than engaging in reactive strategies for those young people who have already entered this group. At least one other institution (New Economics Foundation, 2009) suggests the ratio is nine-to-one and the European Union puts the figure at seven-to-one (Arnold and Baker, 2017). All agree that money spent on preventative work is very cost effective. However, in times of economic restraint preventative strategies are vulnerable to cuts. There are probably several reasons for this, but at least two are relevant to highlight here. First, preventative strategies tend not to be very newsworthy while services responding to desperate people in desperate situations attract more attention. Second, the effectiveness of preventative services is often not well evaluated and some are not evaluated at all. With these thoughts in mind we describe a rationale and method for local services to develop, evaluate and justify an effective early intervention service in this area.

In times of limited resources it is necessary to target the most vulnerable young people. We suggest that this can occur at least two years before a young person can leave statutory education. However, it is necessary to base the target group on evidence of risk.

There are national published risk factor models (Filmer-Sankey and McCrone, 2012) and there is research looking at pan-national data (Walther and Pohl, 2005), but the relevance of these at local levels is limited. The European study found no systemic factors at work across the EU except gender. Data from national research miss important local factors. An example can be seen from the original study on which this chapter is based. A hypothesis was tested in a small town in the Black Country in the West Midlands: Young people in households with no access to cars or motorbikes were more vulnerable than those in families with these facilities. This was tested and found to be insignificant; the area was well served by public transport. However, less than 30 kilometres away in a rural area, the opposite was true. Young people in households with no car or motorbikes were far more likely to enter the NEET category. There was a limited public transport network in that area. So we concluded that research into the factors that indicate risk in particular communities would be needed in order to find an effective way of screening young people to highlight risk.

The following method has been adopted in a number of local authorities in the United Kingdom and at least four areas in other EU states. A fuller description can be found in Arnold and Baker (2013).

The proposition that young people with different life circumstances are more likely to enter the NEET category is offered to a group of experienced workers in the field. We are looking for what differences in circumstance might exist between those young people who become NEET from those who do not. The workers are invited to suggest *possible* risk factors. Ideally this occurs in a group, but it can be done individually if needed. A useful set of propositions to support the research include:

- There are measurable factors.
- The factors are sufficiently discrete to discriminate effectively.
- These factors are robust across time.
- It is economically viable and socially acceptable to collect data.
- There exist interventions that, if executed early, promote better outcomes.
- There is a political will, reflecting public opinion that such exercises are legitimate. (Adapted from Arnold and Baker, 2012)

This last point may seem superfluous, but some concerns can be raised by some groups about the ethics of screening large populations without their consent. The authors have worked in many different areas and been invited to present the project to elected members of the relevant councils. To date, there has never been any opposition or concern raised. It is on this basis that the projects have been launched.

Each project has nine different stages:

1. List all the possible contextual risk factors.
2. Look at economics of collecting data.
3. Decide feasibility of data collection.
4. Decide on sampling method (possibly use a pilot).
5. Collect data.
6. Analyse data – build model.
7. Test model in volunteer school (Year 8 or Year 9).

8. Build interventions.
9. Evaluate. (Arnold and Baker, 2012)

Typically around 20–30 initial hypotheses are generated by the group. Stages 2 and 3 are undertaken by a smaller group who have access to the data held on young people by the schools and colleges. Some hypotheses may be too expensive or difficult to gain data for and are discarded at this point. A sample of around 40 young people who have entered the NEET category are matched by age and gender to the same number who have remained in education, employment or training and the data relating to the presence or absence of the hypothesized risk factor are collected.

A simple statistical analysis of difference in occurrence between the two groups quickly reveals those factors that are relevant from those that are not. The factors revealing significant difference form the basis of the screening tool. A weighting exercise can be undertaken at this point (for more detailed information see Arnold and Baker, 2017).

The resulting screening tool is applied to the given population and individual risk scores are calculated. An example of this can be seen in Figure 12.1.

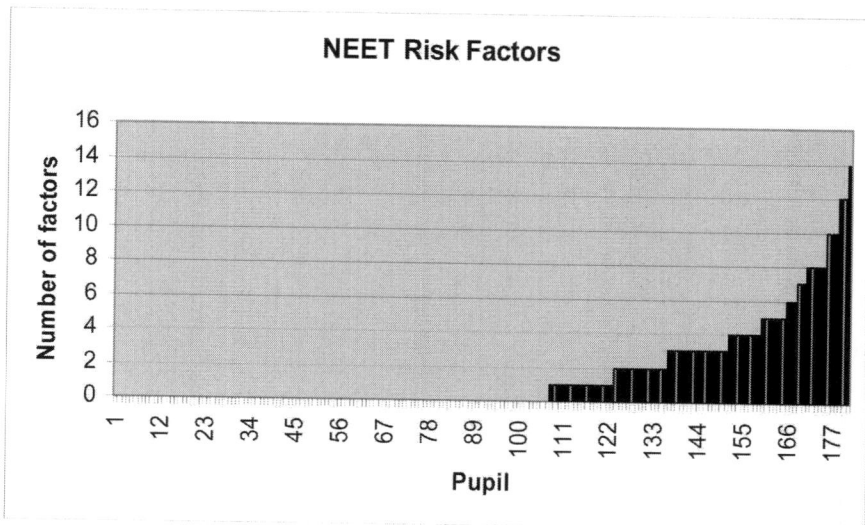

Figure 12.1: NEET risk factors

This demonstrates a Poissonian distribution indicating that the number of pupils with increasingly high risk gets smaller with the increasing risk.

Using these results it is possible to allocate young people into categories of risk. An example is:

- Highest 10 per cent – High risk
- Next 20 per cent – Medium risk
- Remaining 70 per cent – Low risk

These bands can be used to generate intervention programmes with the highest-risk students receiving the highest levels of intervention. An example of such banding interventions is:

- Highest risk – Allocated worker visits home to introduce themselves to parents/guardians, followed by monthly contact with student.
- Medium risk – Students are given preferential allocation of work/ study opportunities such as work experience, study visits and open evenings. Close to leaving school/college, personal contact is made with a named worker.
- Low risk – Students are offered the normal careers advice and guidance.

There follows an example from a Spanish further education college.
The hypotheses tested were:

- Drugs consumption
- Having friends who take drugs
- Bullying
- Ability to make friends
- Working or studying other things during the day
- Studying a course one did not choose
- Having children
- Living on your own
- Finding work
- Family matters: separated parents
- Family matters: parents ill or retired
- Lack of money to pay for courses
- Lack of intellectual capacity
- Problems with teachers or other students
- Taking too long a nap/siesta
- Alcohol
- Returning home late
- Being in a long-term relationship
- Technology addiction.

After the initial research was completed there were found to be statistical differences in only five of the possible factors:

- Drugs consumption
- Problems with teachers or other students
- Alcohol
- Taking too long a nap/siesta
- Being in a long-term relationship (protective factor).

This last element was a surprise. The staff thought that young men with stable girlfriends were more likely to want to spend time with them and would be more likely to drop out. The reverse was found to be the case. Some time after these findings were communicated with the college staff the principal contacted the author by Skype and told of a recent occasion in which a young man who was at risk of dropping out was marched into the principal's office by his girlfriend who said in front of the principal that if the young man wanted to have children with her, he was going to have to be able to earn enough money to keep the family. The girl pointed out that he needed to gain his qualifications to get a good job and that the college was the best place to help with this. The young man completed the course (we do not know whether the relationship survived though).

The data for 95 students from the first year showed that:

- 13 of them were classed as having a high risk of dropping out.
- 24 students were classed as having a medium risk of dropping out.
- The rest of the students (58) were classed as having a low risk of dropping out.

On the basis of the analysis of risk, the students were allocated to bands and more attention was paid to those with higher levels.

High-risk students received the following interventions:

- Reinforcement by classmates. In class, the aim was for students to develop. To help with this, those who were at high risk of dropping out were paired with an older student who could support them as a peer.
- Continued contact with parents. Teachers whose classes include a student who has a high risk level conduct an interview with a parent and then continue to keep in touch throughout the year.

In addition, some interventions were put in place for people at both medium and low risk of dropping out:

- Choosing the right tutor. Careful consideration was given to matching suitable tutors with individual students; these may be tutors who have more experience or who have a positive relationship with the student.
- A volunteer programme established to help students put their knowledge from class into practice and see how it is useful. It also helped them in the decision to continue in a specific area.
- Punctuality and uniform. This was a new idea to encourage people to arrive on time. It is a simple task of closing the school door after the school start time. A uniform was also introduced that has been shown to be a perfect tool for standardizing people in order to mask social differences.
- Evaluation through projects, with a principle of focusing on completing project tasks. The more projects you do, the more points you gain. This means that at whatever pace you work you can reach your points score if you work step by step. This promotes encouragement and a sense of achievement.

The results of the survey developed after the first year had been completed showed that, of 95 students in the first year:

- 13 were shown to have a high level of risk of dropping out; 8 of them left the centre before the end of the year.
- 24 students were shown to have a medium level of risk of dropping out; 5 of them left the centre before the end of the year.
- The other students (58) were deemed to have a low level of risk of dropping out; 4 of them left the centre before the end of the year.

So the overall drop-out rate was 17.9 per cent, a reduction from 32 per cent.

Similar reductions were found in other contexts (See Arnold and Baker, 2017).

Educational psychology offered many unique processes for this project. In summary they appeared to be:

- an understanding of the nature of risk in students
- a method of undertaking action research in the field
- experience of simple statistical analysis
- a model for creating graduated responses for different students
- the development of a credible evidence base to justify early intervention
- a method of evaluation that included written reports.

The transition from school to further education or training

The importance of educational transitions is widely acknowledged and the primary to secondary school transition in particular has been conceptualized as a very challenging time in the lives of children (Zeedyk *et al.*, 2003). This transition has been well researched from a theoretical and practical perspective and a wide range of interventions, guidance documents and policies have been developed to support a smooth transition for Year 6 children moving to secondary school. This additional focus is well justified and takes into account that transition can be a risk factor for long-term difficulties if not managed effectively, particularly for vulnerable groups (Qualter *et al.*, 2007). Educational psychologists have also promoted and supported a focus on this major transition point, through research projects, helping schools to develop their whole-school transition systems, designing group interventions as well as collaboratively developing bespoke packages of support for children where needed. The vast majority of schools seem to understand the importance of this transition and support arrangements are often effective, comprehensive and overseen by senior leaders.

For the transition at the end of Year 11, the current system seems to be appropriate for many young people and they are able to navigate the transition with some support, whether that comes from parents, friends, staff or careers guidance. These young people demonstrate resilience, a level of maturity and have the skills needed to do well on their course or apprenticeship and progress through to adulthood. There are also many examples of good practice for students transferring from school with an Education, Health and Care Plan (EHCP). The *Special Educational Needs and Disability Code of Practice* (DfE and Department of Health (DoH), 2015) advocates transition planning between schools and colleges for those with special educational needs and/or disabilities (SEND) and for those with an EHCP; there is a duty on all schools to focus on preparing for adulthood from Year 9 onwards. Transition planning must be built into the EHCP and there is an emphasis on the aspirations of the student and parental voice, alongside multi-agency planning. The EHCP therefore arguably acts as an important and protective tool for ensuring quality transition support and planning for post-16 provision. This support is informed by statutory guidance and influenced by nationally funded organizations such as Preparing for Adulthood, which seeks to promote positive outcomes for young people with SEND transitioning to adulthood.

Although there are examples of good practice with the post-16 transition, transition arrangements for students leaving secondary school are variable (Craig, 2009; House of Commons Education Committee, 2011) and a lack of communication and support for some students can increase the likelihood of negative outcomes, including drop-out (Mallinson, 2009). There are several practical factors that can act as barriers to effectively supporting young people as they leave school. These can include the location and size of the colleges or training providers, which can reduce the ease of partnership working. There will also be a wide range of options and possibilities for post-16 provision and decisions are often made or changed at late notice due to exam results. Although many further education colleges start courses in September, they have substantial numbers enrolling outside the standard time frames and this can represent a big challenge for the transition. Not only is this later start a barrier to information sharing, planning and curriculum access, but it also adds a potential risk around the development of peer relationships that are very important in young people's experience of transition from school (Craig, 2009).

Although these practical barriers make transition planning between school and post-16 destinations more challenging, it is unlikely to fully explain the variability of practice. One factor influencing the focus on post-16 transition could be the accountability system, where schools have not been accountable for post-16 destinations. Interestingly, however, the inspection framework has been updated relatively recently and Ofsted is now able to consider destination data (including NEET data) when judging schools. The emphasis placed on this transition point may also partly reflect Ofsted guidance and priorities, for example, the *School Inspection Handbook* (Ofsted, 2017) states that inspectors will consider:

> how information at transition points between schools is used effectively so that teachers plan to meet pupils' needs in all lessons from the outset – this is particularly important between the early years and Key Stage 1 and between Key Stages 2 and 3. (Ofsted, 2017: 50)

In relation to post-16 transition, this is not specifically mentioned in the handbook, but the descriptors for an outstanding secondary school include:

> In secondary schools, high quality, impartial careers guidance helps pupils to make informed choices about which courses suit their academic needs and aspirations. They are prepared for the

next stage of their education, employment, self-employment or training. (Ofsted, 2017: 57)

Within the *Further Education and Skills Inspection Handbook* (Ofsted, 2018) there is no reference to transition with feeder secondary schools/settings or information sharing. This appears to conceptualize the end of school as having a clear end-point, focusing on ensuring the young person is prepared for the next stage and has received impartial guidance to help them. This formulation does not consider transition in a broader sense, which would recognize that educational transitions are often a longer process of significant change and work best when settings work in collaboration to actively share information and plan for young people where needed. Crafter and Maunder (2012), for example, consider transition within a sociocultural framework and outline how transitions are complex and multi-faceted, and involve changes in self-identity born out of uncertainty in the social and cultural worlds of the individual.

Students at risk of dropping out from further education appear to be particularly vulnerable to poor transition support, and high drop-out rates have been associated with reduced information sharing and poorer partnerships with schools when compared with providers with lower drop-out rates (Trotter and Roberts, 2006). This highlights a potential gap in support when considering the evidence regarding the characteristics of young people who drop out of college/training and the reasons for this drop-out. The Centre for Economic and Social Inclusion (2015) outlined that in the year 2012/13, 178,000 16–18 year olds withdrew from courses that they were taking, and this included 25 per cent of all apprenticeships not being completed. In further education, 15.7 per cent of all 'learning aims' taken by 16–18 year olds did not result in qualification, either through drop-out or non-achievement, estimated to cost £814 million. It is also worth noting that it has been suggested by *TES* (Belgutay, 2016) that these figures do not include individuals who withdrew from a course within the first six weeks, which in 2015/16 was reported to be 6 per cent of the total (33,000), although this was 10 per cent of those on a Level 1 course, suggesting particular retention difficulties for young people on lower-level courses (Belgutay, 2016).

It is necessary to treat the data with some caution as there are no destination data available for young people who withdraw and many may have entered employment, education or training at a different setting. Many of these, however, will enter the NEET category following their withdrawal and it is useful to consider some of the common reasons for withdrawal.

Although there are various potential reasons for withdrawal from further education or training, Mallinson (2009) obtained the views of young people in relation to drop-out from further education and various themes emerged including:

- Inaccurate or incomplete information about the course, in which the errors were attributed to both the school and also the college
- Limited systems and opportunities for induction, particularly for late applicants
- Attitudes from other students and staff, including perceived rejection and disrespect
- Disruption from other students in the class
- Work provided at the wrong level and not personalized, e.g. too difficult
- Financial reasons and lack of work experience opportunity.

These themes have been replicated in other research and following the study, Mallinson (2009) highlighted the importance of effective transition arrangements to reduce drop-out. Information from other sources also clearly indicates the importance of transition in reducing the NEET population and promoting positive destination outcomes. For example, the Work Foundation (Balaram and Crowley, 2012) outlines the strengthening of partnerships as a key priority, including connecting schools to local providers and employers. Similarly, Public Health England (2014) describes how young people are vulnerable to becoming NEET at age 16 and highlights that schools have a role to play in supporting this through collaboration with organizations and employers. In the publication *More Choices, More Chances* (Scottish Executive, 2006), the Scottish government outlines plans to reduce NEET and discusses the transition from school to post-school as a critical time where vulnerable young people are at risk of falling out of the system. It recommends effective information sharing prior to transition, partnership working between settings, one-on-one keyworker support, and commits to rolling out Post-School Psychological Services (PSPS) to NEET target areas. To our knowledge, the PSPS initiative is one of the clearest examples of integrated EP services working in the post-16 area. Mackay (2009) refers to this as a distinctive Scottish development and a 2009 (Vol. 26) edition of the BPS journal *Educational and Child Psychology* was dedicated to articles linked to PSPS.

Supporting effective transitions from school to further education and training

It has been suggested above that the transition support available for many young people as they finish school and progress to further education is not as effective as it could be and this is a contributory factor in young people becoming NEET. For many, high levels of support will not be necessary and most students seem to adjust to their new setting and make good progress. For others, particularly those with an EHCP and complex needs, the statutory framework supports positive and proactive multi-agency planning that can contribute to effective transition and support arrangements.

It is clear from the characteristics of those identified as long-term NEET that these young people are often vulnerable, with a complex and mixed set of needs. To maximize the chances of positive outcomes for this group, children's social care, education providers, employers, health services and other organizations need to work collaboratively to address the range of causes (Scottish Executive, 2006; Social Finance, 2016).

The role of EPs within the post-16 age range has been relatively minimal across the United Kingdom, with Scotland seeming to be an exception to this (MacKay, 2009). The changing context of the post-16 education and training sector alongside the reforms to the SEND system provides exciting and new ways for EPs to reconsider their role and how they can apply their unique skills and knowledge to support young people transitioning to adulthood. This section outlines some of the ways that EPs can make a positive contribution to vulnerable young people at the post-16 transition and beyond.

Personalized support and the psychological perspective

Crafter and Maunder (2012) argue that the needs of learners will vary over any transition and therefore 'one size fits all' approaches are unlikely to address individual requirements. For many young people approaching transition and at risk of becoming NEET, they can appear to have limited aspirations and interest in future careers. One of the key skills of an EP in this situation is to consider the young person within the context of their developmental history and environment and consider the possible underlying processes influencing the behaviours and attitudes presented. This individual approach is promoted by Hayton (2009) who suggests EPs are able to apply various skills, including from personal construct and coaching psychology. EPs' ability to elicit the voice and inner world of a young person may be useful at this stage in their lives and the application of psychological consultation could have many benefits when fully collaborative.

When looking at positive factors over the transition to college, good and clear course information was an important factor (Trotter and Roberts, 2006) and being on a course that does not meet the needs or expectations of a learner has been linked to drop-out (Mallinson, 2009). It is therefore important that stakeholders are aware that choosing the right course/training is essential and it is likely that a vulnerable young person will need regular support and mentoring as well as opportunities to gain accurate information about options. All young people need to have access to information about the full range of educational, employment and training opportunities that are available to them (DfE, 2018b). Mentoring from keyworkers can help a student to work through difficult questions about their transition and support them to develop goals, aspirations and confidence about the future. EPs are well placed to work with allocated keyworkers, to support the development of appropriate approaches and to act in a supervisory capacity.

The focus on characteristics of the NEET population can be very useful, but it is also important to remember that they often do not take into account influential psychological mechanisms. For example, being in care does not cause someone to become NEET, but there may be a range of co-existing vulnerabilities within this group, for example low resilience and self-efficacy, mental health and relational difficulties due to developmental trauma, low motivation, learning/literacy difficulties or financial difficulties. The majority of young people who are NEET have experienced mental health difficulties in childhood or adolescence (Goldman-Mellor *et al.*, 2016) and large-scale research projects focused on those who are NEET have highlighted the need for mental health support as well as support for transition and retaining young people in education (Rodwell *et al.*, 2018; Gutiérrez-García *et al.*, 2017).

EPs are uniquely placed to bring this psychological perspective to understanding and promoting the emotional and learning needs of these young people, drawing on a range of theory such as self-determination theory (Ryan and Deci, 2000), self-efficacy theory (Bandura, 1997) or theory linked to developmental trauma and attachment. The repeated finding of the importance of positive relationships for those at risk, including having a consistent allocated keyworker (Scottish Executive, 2006; Social Finance, 2016), is indicative of the relational needs of the population and EPs have a role in contributing towards greater understanding of these psychological factors within the post-16 sector.

EPs in Scotland have also demonstrated having a positive impact at a group level with the population of those who are NEET, for example Crichton and Hellier (2009) outline the impact of an intervention programme, which resulted in significant benefits for young people including in their aspirations and self-efficacy as well as having a positive impact on individuals entering further training and positive destinations. Similarly, Haughey (2009) reported a range of positive outcomes following an intervention aimed at disaffected young people, which led to an increase in attendance, a lower than expected NEET rate, and sustainability of post-16 destination. It was concluded that EPs can make a positive contribution to this vulnerable group when working in collaboration with other professionals.

Professional development and strategic influence

Ofsted's (2013) review of further education outlined the following in relation to learners from disadvantaged backgrounds:

> In schools, there is an increasing focus on the achievement of this group of children, influenced by national incentives such as the pupil premium. In the FE and skills sector, it is too often the case that managers and staff do not know who these young people are or what provision and support would be most appropriate for them. (Ofsted, 2013: 6)

EPs are well placed to apply their knowledge of adolescent development, psychology, learning and education to promote understanding and develop good practice. Although this can be done through consultation, wider training and staff support opportunities can have a broader impact. For example, drawing on the earlier theoretical frameworks mentioned, EPs would be well placed to offer professional development opportunities for staff, such as on aspects of mental health, self-efficacy or drawing on developmental trauma and adolescent attachment theory, particularly as applied to young adults at risk of becoming NEET.

The high drop-out rate for learners on low-level courses and the reasons provided regarding the work being at the wrong level suggest that EPs may have a role in supporting staff in developing best practice for teaching learners with additional needs. For example, EPs may be able to provide useful contributions to the use of evidence-based approaches, mediated learning and the effective deployment of support staff. In the South West of England, we have provided coaching to college staff, utilizing the EPs' solution-focused coaching skills and allowing staff to problem-solve areas of challenge within their practice and make positive steps forward.

Employers and training providers are also likely to benefit from professional development opportunities in relation to supporting vulnerable or disadvantaged young people, although access to these groups can be more challenging. In the context of traded services, some EP services are marketing and promoting their role in this sector, for example, in the South West, EPs have delivered training on the topic of SEND to staff overseeing young people completing apprenticeships and it was noticeable that this training was beneficial and well-received.

As suggested by Haughey (2009), there are also opportunities throughout the United Kingdom for EPs to influence transition policy and strategy, whether at a local authority level or more locally between a group of settings. This chapter has outlined one way of influencing local strategy, through involvement in the early identification of those at risk of becoming NEET, in which EPs have made a valuable contribution. EPs are also well placed to inform evidence-based practices at a broader level, for example drawing on their knowledge of good transition practice for vulnerable groups and relevant psychology as applied to NEET. Lastly, EPs' expertise in research could be utilized in what is still a relatively under-researched area, which requires a broader and stronger evidence base regarding what works.

Information sharing and partnership working

It seems obvious that good information sharing is critical to the accurate planning and providing of support for young people who require this. As discussed, there seem to be clear mechanisms for this within the statutory SEND system, but for those learners without an EHCP, practice is widely variable. There are a variety of barriers to information sharing and this can lead to various additional challenges being faced in the new learning environment. One such barrier links to the legalities and concerns regarding the sharing of confidential or sensitive information between settings, particularly when a young person has not yet been offered a place. In these situations, it is important that the secondary school has a clear policy in place regarding how and what information would be shared in the young person's best interests. This would be developed locally, considering relevant legislation and local authority data-sharing guidance, with the overriding aim of developing a system that allows for effective, confidential and safe sharing of information, which includes obtaining relevant consents to share. During the transition process, assurances regarding how information and data will be treated sensitively and confidentially will be important to ensure the young person feels comfortable in sharing the information. The use of a transition passport has proved to be particularly effective in Scotland, promoting person-centred approaches and supporting quality planning over transition.

A second barrier to effective information sharing is concern from the student and/or parents that information that indicates a learning difficulty, SEND, mental health problem or disability will reduce the chances of the young person being accepted onto a course. It is essential that all stakeholders involved are aware of the legal duties under the *Special Educational Needs and Disability Code of Practice* (DfE and DoH, 2015), which outlines that learners should not be refused access to opportunities based on whether or not they have SEND. Similarly, the Equality Act 2010 (UK Parliament, 2010) promotes equality of opportunity as follows:

> It is unlawful for a further or higher education institution to reject an applicant because of a protected characteristic ... If a person is refused a place on a course because they cannot comply with a condition of admission this could amount to indirect discrimination and also, in the case of a disabled applicant, discrimination arising from disability, unless this is a proportionate means of achieving a legitimate aim. (Equality and Human Rights Commission, 2014: 143)

We know from research and common sense that effective partnership working between a leaving and receiving setting is vital in promoting positive transitions. The call for schools to improve their partnerships with colleges, employers and training providers has followed much of the research that has been outlined. Although practical barriers to this have been discussed, EPs are well placed to utilize their expertise in transition support arrangements and apply this to the post-16 transition. This would be at various levels, including promoting good practice at secondary schools as well as in further education/training providers. EPs working across the secondary and post-16 sectors within a locality would be particularly well placed to make this contribution and should work with others to promote the development of effective systems for the identification and support of those requiring this, as well as promoting the importance of proactive and timely information sharing. This could be at a local level as well as influencing wider policy and procedures regarding post-16 transitions. Recent statutory reforms made to careers guidance (DfE, 2018b) outline a range of requirements, including the need for all secondary schools to name a trained 'careers leader' by September 2018. This provides a useful opportunity for EPs to shape this new role using their existing relationships with schools and promoting the importance of this role for supporting the population at risk of becoming NEET.

Conclusion

Over time, EPs should consider how they can replicate and adapt the wide and varied practice they offer at school age within the post-16 sector. One of the key mechanisms for this development will be to extend relationships between EP services and colleges/training providers. The role of EPs in further education is often limited and although there are barriers to the extension of EP services in this way, particularly with resourcing, it is clear that EPs have a valuable contribution to make. This chapter has suggested that EPs can have a strategic role in supporting early identification and intervention for young people at risk of becoming NEET. They have a wide range of applicable skills and relevant psychological knowledge that could facilitate improved transition planning and support for vulnerable young people at a challenging point in their lives. Working collaboratively with staff, settings and other organizations will be key to successful outcomes, and a focus on empowering staff and influencing policy appears to be a particularly powerful way EPs can make a valid contribution. To ensure psychological services are in line with the shifting education and training landscape at post-16, the EP profession needs to be proactive in shaping this role and confident in communicating and promoting all that it has to offer.

References

Arnold, C. and Baker, T. (2012) 'Transitions from school to work: Applying psychology to "NEET"'. *Educational and Child Psychology*, 29 (3), 67–80.

Arnold, C. and Baker, T. (2013) *Becoming NEET: Risks, rewards, and realities.* London: Trentham Books.

Arnold, C. and Baker, T. (2017) *Preventing Dropout: Lessons from Europe.* London: Trentham Books.

Audit Commission (2010) *Against the Odds: Re-engaging young people in education, employment and training: Technical paper – creating a predictive model of the characteristics of young people NEET.* London: Audit Commission.

Balaram, B. and Crowley, L. (2012) *Raising Aspirations and Smoothing Transitions: The role of careers education and careers guidance in tackling youth unemployment.* London: Work Foundation. Online. www.educationandemployers.org/wp-content/uploads/2014/06/Raising-Aspirations-and-Smoothing-Transitions.pdf (accessed 29 August 2018).

Bandura, A. (1997) *Self-efficacy: The exercise of control.* New York: Freeman and Co.

Belgutay, J. (2016) 'Falling through the cracks: More than 30,000 "invisible" learners quit college within six weeks of enrolling'. *TES*, 16 December. Online. www.tes.com/news/falling-through-cracks-more-30000-invisible-learners-quit-college-within-six-weeks-enrolling (accessed 29 August 2018).

Centre for Economic and Social Inclusion (2015) *Achievement and Retention in Post 16 Education: A report for the Local Government Association.* London: Centre for Economic and Social Inclusion. Online. https://feweek.co.uk/wp-content/uploads/2015/02/Achievement-and-retention-in-post-16-education-February-2015.pdf (accessed 29 August 2018).

Crafter, S. and Maunder, R. (2012) 'Understanding transitions using a sociocultural framework'. *Educational and Child Psychology*, 29 (1), 10–18.

Craig, L.J. (2009) 'Post-school transitions: Exploring practice in one local authority'. *Educational and Child Psychology*, 26 (1), 41–51.

Crichton, R. and Hellier, C. (2009) 'Supporting action research by partners: Evaluating outcomes for vulnerable young people in negative post-school destinations'. *Educational and Child Psychology*, 26 (1), 76–83.

DfE (Department for Education) (2018a) *Characteristics of Young People Who are Long-Term NEET.* London: Department for Education. Online. https://assets.publishing.service.gov.uk/government/uploads/system/uploads/attachment_data/file/679535/Characteristics_of_young_people_who_are_long_term_NEET.pdf (accessed 23 August 2018).

DfE (Department for Education) (2018b) *Careers Guidance and Access for Education and Training Providers: Statutory guidance for governing bodies, school leaders and school staff.* London: Department for Education. Online. https://assets.publishing.service.gov.uk/government/uploads/system/uploads/attachment_data/file/672418/_Careers_guidance_and_access_for_education_and_training_providers.pdf (accessed 29 August 2018).

DfE (Department for Education) and DoH (Department of Health) (2015) *Special Educational Needs and Disability Code of Practice: 0 to 25 years: Statutory guidance for organisations which work with and support children and young people who have special educational needs or disabilities.* London: Department for Education. Online. https://assets.publishing.service.gov.uk/government/uploads/system/uploads/attachment_data/file/398815/SEND_Code_of_Practice_January_2015.pdf (accessed 23 August 2018).

Equality and Human Rights Commission (2014) *Equality Act 2010 Technical Guidance on Further and Higher Education.* London: Equality and Human Rights Commission. Online. www.equalityhumanrights.com/sites/default/files/equalityact2010-technicalguidance-feandhe-2015.pdf (accessed 29 August 2018).

Filmer-Sankey, C. and McCrone, T. (2012) *Developing Indicators for Early Identification of Young People at Risk of Temporary Disconnection from Learning.* Slough: National Foundation for Educational Research.

Goldman-Mellor, S., Caspi, A., Arseneault, L., Ajala, N., Ambler, A., Danese, A., Fisher, H., Hucker, A., Odgers, C., Williams, T., Wong, C. and Moffitt, T.E. (2016) 'Committed to work but vulnerable: Self-perceptions and mental health in NEET 18-year olds from a contemporary British cohort'. *Journal of Child Psychology and Psychiatry*, 57 (2), 196–203.

Gutiérrez-García, R.A., Benjet, C., Borges, G., Méndez Ríos, E., Medina-Mora, M.E. (2017) 'NEET adolescents grown up: Eight-year longitudinal follow-up of education, employment and mental health from adolescence to early adulthood in Mexico City'. *European Child and Adolescent Psychiatry*, 26 (12), 1459–69.

Haughey, A. (2009) 'Pupils disengaged from school: Evaluation of an alternative vocational education programme'. *Educational and Child Psychology*, 26 (1), 52–9.

Hayton, R. (2009) 'Young people growing up in rural communities: Opportunities for educational psychologists to work with emerging adults'. *Educational and Child Psychology*, 26 (1), 60–6.

House of Commons Education Committee (2011) *Participation by 16–19 year olds in education and training*. Fourth Report of Session 2010-12. Volume II: Oral and written evidence. Online. https://publications.parliament.uk/pa/cm201012/cmselect/cmeduc/850/850ii.pdf (accessed 6 September 2018).

MacKay, T. (2009) 'Post-school educational psychology services: International perspectives on a distinctive Scottish development'. *Educational and Child Psychology*, 26 (1), 8–21.

Mallinson, A. (2009) 'From school to further education: Student and teacher views of transition, support and drop-out'. *Educational and Child Psychology*, 26 (1), 33–40.

New Economics Foundation (2009) 'Backing the future: Why investing in children is good for us all'. Online. http://neweconomics.org/2009/09/backing-the-future/?sf_action=get_results&_sf_s=preventative&_sft_latest=research (accessed 29 August 2018).

Ofsted (2013) *The Report of Her Majesty's Chief Inspector of Education, Children's Services and Skills 2012/13: Further education and skills*. Online. https://assets.publishing.service.gov.uk/government/uploads/system/uploads/attachment_data/file/386807/Ofsted_Annual_Report_201213_FE_and_Skills.pdf (accessed 6 September 2018).

Ofsted (2017) *School Inspection Handbook: Handbook for inspecting schools in England under section 5 of the Education Act 2005*. Manchester: Ofsted. Online. http://dera.ioe.ac.uk/30206/1/School_inspection_handbook_section_5.pdf (accessed 29 August 2018).

Ofsted (2018) *Further Education and Skills Inspection Handbook: Handbook for inspecting further education and skills providers under part 8 of the Education and Inspections Act 2006, for use from October 2018*. Manchester: Ofsted. Online. https://assets.publishing.service.gov.uk/government/uploads/system/uploads/attachment_data/file/667720/Further_education_and_skills_inspection_handbook_for_use_from_January_2018.pdf (accessed 29 August 2018).

Public Health England (2014) *Reducing the Number of Young People Not in Employment, Education or Training (NEET)*. Health Equity Evidence Review 3, September. Online. https://assets.publishing.service.gov.uk/government/uploads/system/uploads/attachment_data/file/356062/Review3_NEETs_health_inequalities.pdf (accessed 6 September 2018).

Qualter, P., Whiteley, H.E., Hutchinson, J.M. and Pope, D.J. (2007) 'Supporting the development of emotional intelligence competencies to ease the transition from primary to high school'. *Educational Psychology in Practice*, 23 (1), 79–95.

Rodwell, L., Romaniuk, H., Nilsen, W., Carlin, J.B., Lee, K.J. and Patton, G.C. (2018) 'Adolescent mental health and behavioural predictors of being NEET: A prospective study of young adults not in employment, education, or training'. *Psychological Medicine*, 48 (5), 861–71.

Ryan, R.M. and Deci, E.L. (2000) 'Self-determination theory and the facilitation of intrinsic motivation, social development, and well-being'. *American Psychologist*, 55 (1), 68–78.

Scottish Executive (2006) *More Choices, More Chances: A strategy to reduce the proportion of young people not in education, employment or training in Scotland*. Edinburgh: Scottish Executive. Online. www.gov.scot/Resource/Doc/129456/0030812.pdf (accessed 29 August 2018).

Social Finance (2016) *New Insights into Improving Outcomes for At-Risk Youth: The Newcastle experience*. London: Social Finance. Online. www.socialfinance.org.uk/sites/default/files/publications/insights_1_newcastle.pdf (accessed 29 August 2018).

Trotter, E. and Roberts, C.A. (2006) *Enhancing the Early Student Experience*. Salford: University of Salford. Online. http://usir.salford.ac.uk/1210/1/et1_04.pdf (accessed 29 August 2018).

UK Parliament (2010) 'Equality Act 2010'. Online. www.legislation.gov.uk/ukpga/2010/15/contents (accessed 25 August 2018).

Walther, A. and Pohl, A. (2005) *Thematic Study on Policy Measures concerning Disadvantaged Youth: Study commissioned by the European Commission, DG Employment and Social Affairs in the framework of the Community Action Programme to Combat Social Exclusion 2002–2006: Final report*. Tübingen: Institute for Regional Innovation and Social Research. Online. http://ec.europa.eu/employment_social/social_inclusion/docs/youth_study_en.pdf (accessed 29 August 2018).

Zeedyk, M.S., Gallacher, J., Henderson, M., Hope, G., Husband, B. and Lindsay, K. (2003) 'Negotiating the transition from primary to secondary school: Perceptions of pupils, parents and teachers'. *School Psychology International*, 24 (1), 67–79.

Chapter 13

Working with care leavers: A model for effective transition to adulthood

Cathy Atkinson, Rebekah Hyde and Catherine Kelly

Introduction

A child or young person is defined as 'looked after' by a local authority under the Children Act 1989 (Chapter 41) if he or she is:

i.   provided with accommodation for a continuous period for more than 24 hours
ii. subject to a care order
iii. subject to a placement order, or
iv. accommodated by a voluntary arrangement with their parents.

Previously, to support care leavers in their transition to adulthood, local authorities had a continuing obligation to offer support to any child over the age of 16 who was, or had been, a looked-after child, until they reached 21; or 24 if they were pursuing an educational or training programme (UK Parliament, 2000, 2008). However, recent changes under the Children and Social Work Act 2017 entitled all young people leaving care to personal adviser support up to the age of 25, irrespective of whether they are engaged in education or training (Department for Education (DfE), 2018a). Nevertheless, care leavers continue to be identified as a vulnerable group living in a problematic context. Forty per cent of 19–21-year-old care leavers (10,870) were not in education, employment or training (NEET), compared with 13 per cent of all 19 to 21 year olds (DfE, 2017) and in turn, low participation rates in higher education and post-16 training equated to less choice in entering an already overburdened youth labour market (Stein, 2006). Moreover, there is a shortage and inadequacy of independent living arrangements for care leavers (Hiles *et al.*, 2014; Centre for Social Justice, 2015) and the mental health needs of care leavers have been found to be neglected during transition from care to independence (Dixon *et al.*,

2006; House of Commons Education Committee, 2016). The process of support for care leavers, involving personal advisers and pathway planning, has also proved inadequate, with pathway plans not facilitating meaningful engagement with future goals (Driscoll, 2011), being left incomplete (Munro *et al.*, 2011) and in some cases leaving care leavers uncertain about whether they even have a plan (Dixon *et al.*, 2006).

Preparing for Adulthood and the four outcomes

Preparing for Adulthood (2013) identifies four outcomes, developed through consultation with young people, to be addressed in preparing for adulthood – paid employment, good health, independent living and community inclusion. These were predated by The Care Leavers (England) Regulations (DfE, 2010), which perpetuated a discourse of choice and participation, and came as a response to pressure placed on the government to take more seriously its duties as corporate parent to care leavers (Dixon *et al.*, 2006).

Highly relevant to the preparing for adulthood context was the Right2BeCared4 (Munro *et al.*, 2011) pilot report. The project began in 2007 and operated to support the following principles: young people having a greater say in the processes regarding their exit from care; fostering a culture where young people should not be expected to leave care until the age of 18; and ensuring that all young people should be properly prepared for independent living.

Despite its goals, the Right2BeCared4 evaluation report highlighted a system at variance with the aspirations set down in Preparing for Adulthood (2013) two years later. Professionals as well as young people shed light on a persistent lack of choice around placement availability and accommodation range for those leaving care (Munro *et al.*, 2011). Reports from those who had experienced abrupt exits from care were at odds with the emphasis on choice and control within Preparing for Adulthood (2013), with one-third of young people feeling they had little or no choice over the timing of their transition from care. In relation to community inclusion, the Right2BeCared4 report contained care leavers' accounts surrounding the 'emotional challenges' of living alone (Munro *et al.*, 2011), a finding reiterated in a more recent study incorporating the views of more than 100 care leavers (Centre for Social Justice, 2014).

More recently, the Staying Put arrangements (Children and Families Act, 2014) stipulated that those in foster care could reside with their foster carers until 21, as long as both carer(s) and young person were in agreement. Evaluation of the Staying Put pilot (Munro *et al.*, 2012) across eight UK local authorities found that those who remained with foster carers post-18 tended to experience smoother transitions to independence and were also more likely to be engaged in EET (education, employment or training) than those who did not. Young people were able to extend the attachments they had with carers and receive ongoing support in preparation for the transition to adulthood. Findings highlighted the positive correlation between Staying Put arrangements and care leavers' ability to realize Preparing for Adulthood (2013) goals.

Hard to comprehend, therefore, is that not all care leavers are currently eligible for the Staying Put arrangement. This includes some of the most vulnerable care leavers such as those who are NEET (Munro *et al.*, 2012), those in residential settings and late entrants to care (Lightfoot, 2013). This restriction has led the Centre for Social Justice (2015) to issue a parliamentary briefing paper for the Staying Put principle to be extended to residential settings. Nevertheless, there can be no doubt that the restrictions around the Staying Put duty, combined with the lack of accommodation choice for care leavers, underscores a striking paradox behind the current drive to 'prepare' looked-after children and young people (LAC/YP) for adulthood, which is that existing systems are not set up in such a way as to allow post-16 LAC/YP to exercise the degree of choice and control so strongly emphasized within Preparing for Adulthood (2013) and the Care Leavers (England) Regulations (DfE, 2010).

The role of the educational psychologist in supporting transition to adulthood

The extension of the educational psychologist (EP) statutory role to work with young people aged 16–25 potentially brings many more EPs into contact with care leavers, especially as previous figures have suggested that looked-after children are over-represented in figures detailing the number of children with special educational needs and disabilities (Department for Children, Schools and Families (DCSF), 2009).

Previously educational psychology literature has documented the role of the EP in working with young people in care (Bradbury, 2006; Cameron and Maginn, 2011; Francis *et al.*, 2017; Lightfoot, 2013; McParlin, 1996; Norwich *et al.*, 2010). Additionally, Atkinson *et al.* (2015) identified specific 16–25 transition competencies for EPs including supporting transition to adulthood, and multi-disciplinary liaison. However, perhaps due to the recency of the Children and Families Act 2014 and the 16–25 legislation, there has been limited attention given to how EPs can support the needs of care leavers (Hyde and Atkinson, forthcoming).

The aim of this chapter is therefore to propose a model, based on the findings of empirical research, to provide a starting point for EPs to consider, plan and develop their role in working with care leavers.

Theoretical underpinnings of effective practice

Previous research has discussed the 'poverty of theory' around supporting the needs of LAC/YP (Stein, 2006, 1). This section outlines the development of a model to guide practice, based on research exploring care leavers' perceptions of what factors enable and inhibit effective transition to adulthood (Hyde, 2018; Hyde and Atkinson, submitted, forthcoming). This body of research explored care leavers' perspectives about what was fundamentally important in preparing for adulthood, including perceived facilitators and barriers to effective practice. Based on findings that highlighted the need for flexible support, skills development, authentic and caring relationships and effective pathway planning, the proposed model is developed from three frameworks. First, it references the Preparing for Adulthood (2013) four outcomes. Second, it draws on self-determination theory (Ryan and Deci, 2000), an empirically based motivational theory receiving increasing prominence in educational psychology literature in relation to working with young people (Gabriel, 2015; Wilding, 2015). Finally, the model will draw on the principles of a framework of interdependence for care leavers, developed by Propp, Ortega and NewHeart (2003).

In the following sections, self-determination theory and the framework of interdependence will be first considered in turn, with direct reference to how they might help to support the effective transition of care leavers. Next, a framework for EP practice will be proposed, developed from all three frameworks. This will then be explored, using case studies involving LAC/YP. Finally, implications for the application of this model and possibilities for future development and refinement will be considered.

Self-determination theory

One proposed theoretical framework for elucidating the mechanisms behind care leavers' motivation to exercise choice and control around Preparing for Adulthood (2013) goals is self-determination theory (SDT) (Ryan and Deci, 2000). SDT names three psychological needs thought to be required for self-determination:

- Autonomy – the need for one's actions to be self-endorsed and congruent with one's own values and interests.

- Competence – the need to feel confident and effective in one's actions and able to achieve the goals set for oneself.
- Relatedness – the need to be connected to, and cared for by, significant others who support the individual's choices.

The ability to be self-determined enables individuals to engage in goal-directed behaviours and thus steer their own outcomes. SDT additionally proposes that the social context the individual inhabits influences the extent to which these three psychological needs are met, and has an impact on the individual's ability to be self-determined.

Previously, Gabriel (2015) used SDT to illuminate factors that aided those aged 16–25 to move out of NEET status. More recently, research highlighted its applicability in relation to the personal experiences of care leavers, and its relevance as a model for benchmarking optimal and sub-optimal practice (Hyde, 2018; Hyde and Atkinson, forthcoming).

Framework of interdependence

Within the context of the US child welfare system, (Propp *et al.*, 2003) recognized that young people transitioning out of foster care were expected to move from a family context to 'self-sufficiency' (p. 259). This can be contrasted against a generation of non-care leavers who are typically living with parents until much later in life, or return to the family home after university (Adley and Jupp Kina, 2017). A systematic literature review exploring care leavers' perspectives of transition to adulthood (Hyde and Atkinson, submitted) found that LAC/YP reported that opportunities for supported life skill development within an independent living context were limited, and untimely offers of support were often not repeated at more appropriate moments.

Propp *et al.* (2003) proposed that 'independence refers to the degree that one relies on external resources' while 'self-sufficiency refers to the ability for an individual to meet his or her own needs without external assistance' (p. 262). The authors question the extent to which self-sufficiency should be an ambition for care leavers, proposing instead the notion of 'interdependence' through which individuals leaving care are empowered by the support of others.

Within their paper Propp *et al.* (2003) defined a philosophical position, rather than an operational definition of what interdependence might look like. In this chapter we will try to offer specific indicators of what effective practice might look like, in the context of dependence (when in care) and interdependence (when leaving care), with self-sufficiency defined as a process-based outcome, rather than a point in time, for which care leavers might be unprepared.

A model for educational psychology practice

The following model (Figure 13.1) is proposed as a starting point for EPs working with care leavers. It proposes transition stages of dependence, interdependence and independence, acknowledging that progression through these may not be linear, and that revisiting previous transition phases may be necessary, particularly if circumstances (e.g. work, finances, mental health) become difficult. Relatedness is shown as a consistent factor, which should run through all stages of transition, although it is acknowledged the relationships will change over this period. The model also proposes promoting autonomy and competence throughout transition (including within the interdependence phase) to enable effective transition to adulthood. Hereafter, it will be referred to as the *SDT-interdependence* model.

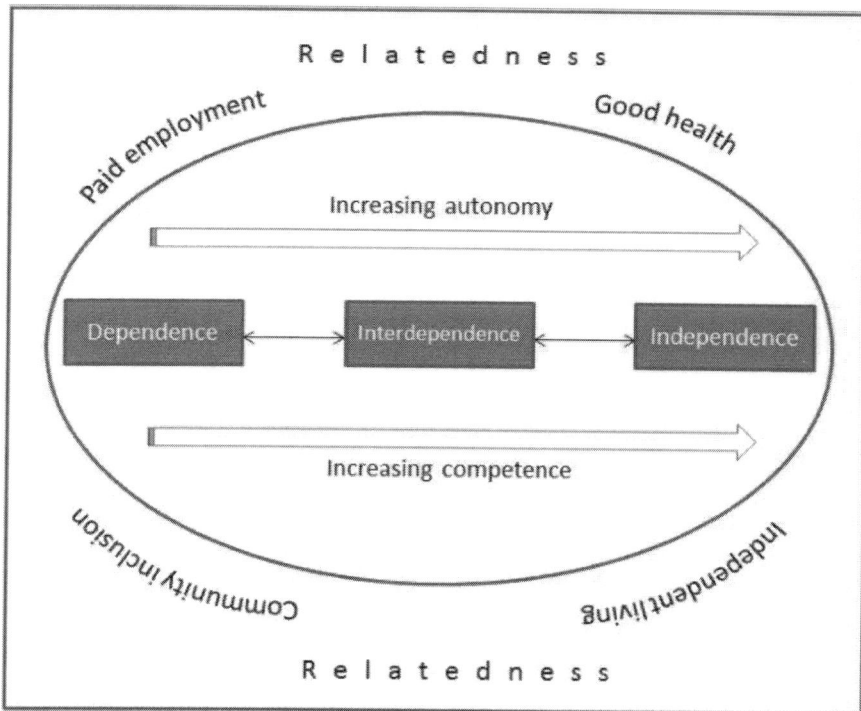

Figure 13.1: SDT-interdependence model for EPs supporting transition to adulthood

The chapter will now consider the model in relation to the four Preparing for Adulthood (2013) outcomes. Under each section, a brief literature review will set the context for a table, outlining how the concepts of autonomy, competence and relatedness can guide practice for each outcome. Finally, each session will offer a short case vignette illustrating the importance of considering these features.

Paid employment

In spite of the heightened emphasis on choice within the new *Special Educational Needs and Disability Code of Practice* (DfE and DoH, 2015a), the wider literature provides little evidence that post-16 looked-after young people are given the opportunity to make autonomous choices in relation to further education goals (Jackson and Cameron, 2012). Some care leavers lack knowledge about what higher education options are available to them (Who Cares? Trust, 2012). Further barriers include the tendency to steer care leavers down vocational routes without consideration of their interests (Jackson and Cameron, 2012; Wade and Dixon, 2006). The extent to which poor GCSE (General Certificate in Secondary Education) predictions and results can undermine the competence and autonomy of care leavers has also been acknowledged. A recent report incorporating statistical analysis of official data for England suggested that care leavers were around 11 per cent less likely to enter higher education than other young people with similar demographic profiles and qualification levels. However, even among those who gained entry to higher education, once entry qualifications were taken into account, care leavers were around 38 per cent more likely to withdraw from their course, suggesting that care leavers may face additional hurdles within higher education (Harrison, 2017).

The impact of personalized support on individual self-determination in relation to post-16 education/employment goals is particularly pertinent in the light of a recent Ofsted (2016) report. The report focused on how well high-need learners in the further education (FE) sector were being prepared for adulthood and found that many 16–19 year olds nationally were on programmes that did not fit with their personal aspirations, or lacked individualized support around their educational and support needs or employment goals. This may be even more problematic for older looked-after young people or care leavers, for whom adult support and guidance might be less available or consistent. This not only validates the Preparing for Adulthood (2013) emphasis on personalizing approaches to post-16 educational provision, but corroborates Wilding's (2015) hypothesis that person-centred thinking, which champions holistic, participatory, strengths-based approaches to planning, is likely to bolster self-determination (Preparing for Adulthood, 2015).

Table 13.1 indicates how, within the SDT-interdependence model, autonomy, competence and relatedness might inform practice around paid employment for care leavers at different stages of preparing for adulthood.

Table 13.1: Dimensions of the SDT-interdependence model, in relation to paid employment

	Dependence (in care)	Interdependence (leaving care)	Independence (adulthood and desirable outcomes)
Autonomy	Support to identify career preferences (Laverick, 2018) and to pursue self-set goals. Information about FE and higher education (HE) options.	Support to pursue chosen training and/or career goals. Access to information about relevant training and career choices. High expectations. Identifying and troubleshooting potential barriers with young person.	Employment within chosen career.
Competence	Educational grounding, including development of academic and vocational self-concept. Skills development related to career preferences.	Acquisition of educational, employment and training skills related to preferred employment pathway.	Transferable employment skills (relational and technical).
Relatedness	Meaningful adult role models. Sustained educational and career input from consistent, concerned adults.	Adult interest and support to be maintained through keyworker contact. As well as employment status, this should also consider social integration within the workplace.	Social connection through work; camaraderie; friendship.

Finally, within this section, a case study is used to identify some of these parameters within a real-life context.

CASE STUDY – ALICE

Alice is 18 years old. She spent several years in foster care before moving to a children's residential home, then moved to semi-independent living aged 16. Alice describes herself as self-reliant, but asserts this within the context of: 'social services, they don't care about you', suggesting that her self-dependence may relate to unmet relatedness needs.

In terms of paid employment, Alice describes having 'done loads of jobs, like … ridiculous amounts', due, in her own opinion, to a lack of motivation. At present, Alice is working in a call centre. The ability to earn money affords her a sense of autonomy.

Despite having 'yo-yo-ed' between jobs, Alice seems to enjoy her current job; however, as she is currently pregnant, she will soon go on maternity leave. Alice describes wanting to return to education once her baby gets older. Last year Alice attended night classes, achieving five GCSEs, something of which she is proud. Despite not having engaged in school and getting 'kicked out', Alice now thinks it is important for her to gain qualifications in order to have 'a career'.

Alice aspires to become a nurse, and has some knowledge of the avenues that might allow her to work towards this employment goal.

From an interdependence perspective, Alice's future opportunities to pursue paid employment will be dependent on those supporting her to: explore childcare options that could allow her return to training when and if the timing is right, and signposting to social welfare support (e.g. Job Centre, Citizen's Advice) in the interim periods between paid employment. In order to optimize Alice's openness to receiving good-quality advice with regard to paid employment, all support, where possible, should be delivered within the context of consistent, genuine relationships with relevant professionals.

Good health

Recent statutory guidance around supporting the health needs of post-16 LAC/YP specified that care leavers, including those preparing to leave care, should be 'equipped to manage their own health needs' (DfE and DoH, 2015b: 26), although this guidance did not provide any specific insight into how other care leavers might be enabled. Previous research findings have indicated that care leavers valued having choice and control around their health needs (Stanley, 2007).

However, implicit tensions in this self-management discourse become evident within the context of the wider literature, which has tended to stress the high level of mental health needs in this population (Stein, 2004; Centre for Social Justice, 2015). In doing so, however, it has contributed to portraying post-16 LAC/YP as passive agents whose health is determined by gaining access to overburdened systems (e.g. child and adolescent mental health services, CAMHS). A report by the Centre for Social Justice, for instance, gives weight to having 'CAMHS staff ... embedded in both children's services and leaving care services' (Centre for Social Justice, 2015). The problem with this approach, which is by no means to underplay the mental health of this population, is that it perpetuates the view that good mental health is CAMHS-determined. Ungar (2005) argued that, as young people have personal agency and make choices to engage with services, it is vital to ask them what services they need and how those services can be provided in ways that are meaningful to them. The pathologizing discourse that has come to be associated with the preparing for adulthood agenda must be viewed as a systemic barrier to self-determination (House of Commons Education Committee, 2016). A more empowering view embodied by the SDT-interdependence model would be that young people are capable of determining their own emotional and physical health when their needs for autonomy, competence and relatedness are met and when appropriate support is available.

Table 13.2: Dimensions of the SDT-interdependence model, in relation to good health

	Dependence (in care)	Interdependence (leaving care)	Independence (adulthood and desirable outcomes)
Autonomy	Increasing agency within health care through adolescence, including making appointments, monitoring physical and emotional well-being, taking increasing responsibility for own treatment.	Clear, accurate and jargon-free information about access to health care options. Support in making and attending appointments where required. Information about treatment options and diagnosis to be delivered in an accessible and young person-friendly manner.	Empowered in meeting physical and mental health needs. Appropriate services available.
Competence	Awareness of health support agencies and referral pathways. Basic skills development (e.g. making an appointment; seeking advice from a pharmacist).	Opportunities for modelled and supported health care access. Support to navigate the transition from child to adult mental health services.	Through understanding and skill development, health knowledge is generated that facilitates competence and empowers the individual, rather than their needs or circumstances being unnecessarily pathologized.
Relatedness	Help from supportive adults. Opportunities to talk openly about physical and mental health concerns.	Availability of flexible, responsive and empathic key adults, who help the individual to make sense of their health needs.	Physical and mental health that supports and is supported by a network of close and acquaintance relationships.

CASE STUDY – BYRON

Byron is 16 years old. He recently moved out of a youth offending unit and is currently living in a residential children's home. He anticipates moving to a 'trainer flat' next year. Byron is attending college and working towards an apprenticeship and thinks that he would like to become a personal trainer.

Relating to maintaining good health, Byron developed an interest in fitness when he was in the secure unit. Through regular gym attendance with a peer, whom Byron describes as having motivated him to attend, his fitness increased. Byron noticed his attendance decline once this friend left. Since leaving the unit, however, Byron has enrolled in a football club and regularly attends a gym.

By choice, Byron buys his own food and manages his own diet, which gives him a sense of ownership and autonomy over his health.

Byron is a regular smoker. Although this seems at odds with his pursuit of good health in other areas, smoking, for Byron, is associated with asserting choice and autonomy as he defines it within the context of the restrictions placed on smoking within the secure unit.

Byron has not explored apprenticeship routes as he anticipates moving across the country to be closer to family and friends. To maximize Byron's sense of autonomy around his post-16 life, it will be important for adults supporting him to maximize his opportunities to assert choice and control around decision-making. From an interdependence perspective, this might mean a key adult accompanying Byron to explore training routes that would allow him to qualify as a personal trainer; supporting him to develop his interest around diet in whatever way he chooses; and offering Byron choice around when he goes to the gym by assisting travel or supporting travel training. Increasing Bryon's sense of autonomy seems important given that he has recently left a placement where his ability to make choices was restricted.

Independent living

Munro *et al.* (2011) previously identified issues for LAC/YP in operationalizing choice around independent living, due to the lack of accommodation range and availability. Today shortcomings around accommodation arrangements continue to be problematic for some care leavers (DfE, 2017). Previous studies have additionally reported a lack of optimism among care leavers that views about living arrangements would be listened to and heard (Morgan, 2012; Munro *et al.*, 2011).

Reports by the Centre for Social Justice highlight the high degree of isolation experienced by care leavers who move to independence (Centre for Social Justice, 2013, 2014, 2015), with many care leavers suddenly finding themselves living alone without access to support networks (Centre for Social Justice, 2015). Within a self-determination framework, there are reports of emotional isolation leading to poor mental health, and foreground levels of unmet relatedness needs among care leavers. However, very little literature exists around how this might be redressed from the viewpoints of post-16 LAC/YP. This suggests the need for services to give precedence to the establishment of support networks and young people's access to those networks on their own terms; as well as for further research around how transition from differing care settings might influence the degree to which young people's needs are met, in relation to effective outcomes around independent living.

Table 13.3: Dimensions of the SDT-interdependence model, in relation to independent living

	Dependence (in care)	Interdependence (leaving care)	Independence (adulthood and desirable outcomes)
Autonomy	Pathway planning to ensure that care leavers have information about accommodation options; or signposting to where this is available.	Informed choice and control over living arrangements. Supported living arrangements, where appropriate.	Flexibility to make appropriate, independent judgements about living, as these emerge and develop in relation to changing financial, employment and relationship circumstances.

	Dependence (in care)	Interdependence (leaving care)	Independence (adulthood and desirable outcomes)
Competence	Development of skills for independent living (e.g. cooking, budgeting) while in care placement.	Support to develop 'emotional readiness' for independent living. Ongoing and repeated offers of life skill training (e.g. cooking, budgeting).	Independent living and household management skills – cooking, cleaning, repairs, budgeting. Safe and secure housing.
Relatedness	Modelling of skills by key adults. Mentoring from adults displaying genuine concern about future autonomy.	Consistency of care from genuine, empathic and interested adults. Someone to 'check in' on the young person.	Independent living that is embedded within a local community and a network of close and acquaintance relationships.

CASE STUDY – LEANNE

Leanne is 16 years old and in her final year at high school. She lives in a children's home, where she is being encouraged to develop skills of what she describes as 'semi-independence' and independence. At the stage of 'semi-independence' she was encouraged to prepare and cook her own food twice a week and to look after her own finances. She has progressed to what she describes as 'full independence, which is where you cook all of your meals and you take care of all of your own washing and bedding and finances and all that ... staff still help me obviously as I am technically still on semi-independence but usually I am pretty good about doing it all, everything myself'.

Leanne has been told that she will leave the setting between 17½ and 18. As she has just turned 16, these discussions have not yet begun, but Leanne is aware that there will be ongoing discussions with the social worker when the time arises. Leanne has plans to move out and would like to go to university.

From an interdependence perspective, it is useful that Leanne is developing independence skills within her care placement. University accommodation may represent a form of supported living that could very well enable effective transition to independent living. However, this should be reviewed as the time to move out of the care home draws closer.

Community inclusion

Previous literature has noted benefits of family contact during preparations for and transition to independence for post-16 LAC/YP (Wade, 2008) and highlighted care leavers' desire for (but lack of) consistent supportive relationships with professionals and others in their social network upon leaving care (Hiles *et al.*, 2014). This highlights a need to redress the social and emotional isolation experienced by care leavers upon transition to independence (Adley and Jupp Kina, 2017; Centre for Social Justice, 2015).

Also concerning were findings relating to the shortcomings of the personal advisory role specific to post-16 LAC/YP (Centre for Social Justice, 2015). This statutory role is intended to provide consistent support during preparations for adulthood, including help with widening a young person's social and emotional support network. However, problems with the role were noted, including high staff turnover in many local authorities and high caseloads leading to insufficient time for supporting each young person (Centre for Social Justice, 2015). The extent to which limitations of the personal advisory role, and the social isolation reported above, stand at variance with the value placed by post-16 LAC/YP on reliable support must be acknowledged as a systemic barrier to self-determination for this population (Hiles *et al.*, 2014). Revised statutory guidance offering enhanced personal adviser support in evenings and at weekends as well as greater flexibility around how young people engage with and request support may go some way to addressing some of these concerns (DfE, 2018b).

Table 13.4: Dimensions of the SDT-interdependence model, in relation to community inclusion

	Dependence (in care)	Interdependence (leaving care)	Independence (adulthood and desirable outcomes)
Autonomy	Support, where appropriate, to navigate real and virtual social worlds independently and safely. Access to and choice over community-based activities.	Ongoing support to raise awareness of community activities and resources. Inclusive ethos of community groups. Permission to try out groups and activities and make informed choice about preferences.	Choice about preferred activities, lifestyle and hobbies. Ability to make choices that reflect maturation and changing interests.
Competence	Development of skills for community engagement (e.g. independent travel; accessing local resources; social skills development).	Ongoing offers of skills support to enable engagement in community activities.	To have the skills and self-efficacy required to develop meaningful and lasting intimate relationships, friendships and acquaintances.
Relatedness	Support, where required, to develop lasting and meaningful friendships and relationships with members of the community.	Review with key person about how personal connections are developing and friendships and networks forming.	Healthy and appropriate development of friendships and intimate relationships. Experience of being part of a community or wider group. Informal support networks.

CASE STUDY – JOSH

Josh is 17 years old. He has been in a foster placement for the last seven years, having several placement moves prior to that. He is currently attending college and has a clear career plan in the field of animal care. Josh has benefited from support via a long-term relationship with his social worker. This is perhaps exemplified by the fact that, as a young child, when he requested placement moves, his social worker listened to his choices.

In terms of community inclusion, Josh is a member of his [foster] parents' church where he has a number of close friends who are important to him. He rides at the local stables and navigates the village on his bike. He has been in Scouts. Josh has been supported by an organization he describes as: 'for kids in care that gives them opportunities that they wouldn't necessarily have outside of being in foster care'. Being part of this organization has connected him with other young people in care and given him opportunities to try out activities such as canoeing. Josh is now a peer mentor for the organization. Josh has close relationships with his foster parents, members of his church and a number of close friends who are important to him.

While Josh is still living within a family unit, moving towards interdependence, his connections and standing within the community are likely to lead to better outcomes. It will be important for adults supporting his transition to ensure that his sense of community is maintained and has not been dependent on his foster carers and family context. This could be achieved by monitoring his friendships and community inclusion through ongoing contact and offering alternatives, if his peer group or interests change.

Conclusions

In the past, there has been something of a 'poverty of theory' surrounding the needs of the post-16 (Stein, 2006: 1). It is hoped through presenting the SDT-interdependence model for transition to adulthood, and through reconciling the two theoretical positions of SDT and the framework of interdependence, with the Preparing for Adulthood practice protocol, that practitioner EPs will be provided with a solid structure for considering the needs of UK care leavers. This conceptualization of the needs of this group also supports a comprehensive assessment of the services that are provided to meet those needs. This can be considered in terms of the extent to which services are available and accessible, and how well disparate services are co-ordinated to facilitate the interconnected outcomes of paid employment, good health, community inclusion and independent living. This is particularly important in the light of recent research (Hyde, 2018; Hyde and Atkinson, submitted, forthcoming) that suggested multiple systemic constraints to operationalizing choice and control around preparing for adulthood goals for care leavers, and a systems-led, rather than self-determined, preparing for adulthood landscape. A better understanding of a self-determined path to independence rests on the capacity of services to embrace a participatory approach to service design and delivery in order to be able to harness support for young people that is relevant to their context and culture and meaningful to the young people themselves. Such an approach is called for in promoting the participatory rights of care leavers under the United Nations Convention on the Rights of the Child (United Nations, 1989) and is enacted within person-centred thinking (Wilding, 2015). While there is evidence that these ideas are beginning to become more prominent within recent guidance, it remains unclear to what extent leaving care teams know how to promote participation, suggesting a potential role for EPs (DfE, 2018a).

Limitations and future directions

It should be noted that while the SDT-interdependence model has been driven by theory and research (Hyde, 2018; Hyde and Atkinson, submitted, forthcoming), and while discussions with specialist EP practitioners have suggested that it has face-validity, it has yet to be extensively practice-tested or empirically reviewed. It is hoped that practitioner and research feedback might enable greater development, refinement and embellishment of the model, thus further enhancing its potential utility.

Additionally, while the model has emerged through conversations with care leavers (Hyde, 2018; Hyde and Atkinson, submitted, forthcoming), to date, young people have not been consulted in its actual development. It would be useful to share the model with care leavers both in practice and in participatory research, providing opportunities for them to offer authentic and meaningful feedback, which can be acted upon. Young people's perspectives may also enable the model to be presented in a more accessible and user-friendly manner, potentially offering care leavers a structure through which both they, and supporting professionals, can advocate for their needs and choices. Additionally, there is the possibility that a more person-friendly version of the model could offer an educative or advisory function, in terms of guiding preparation for adulthood.

Wider applications of the SDT-interdependence model

Although this model has been developed through research with UK care leavers and has been designed to enable EPs to support their needs, implications for other young people are implicit. At a universal level, the principles of the SDT-interdependence model are applicable for all young people, even those who appear to be on positive trajectories, such as going to university or paid employment, or those who are likely to quickly become financially independent. For more vulnerable groups, for example, young people with special educational needs and disabilities, those who are NEET, or who have mental health difficulties, close attention to the SDT-interdependence model may be more imperative for enabling a planned, supported, flexible, monitored, and ultimately interdependent, transition to adulthood.

References

Adley, N. and Jupp Kina, V. (2017) 'Getting behind the closed door of care leavers: Understanding the role of emotional support for young people leaving care'. *Child and Family Social Work*, 22 (1), 97–105.

Atkinson, C., Dunsmuir, S., Lang, J. and Wright, S. (2015) 'Developing a competency framework for the initial training of educational psychologists working with young people aged 16–25'. *Educational Psychology in Practice*, 31 (2), 159–73.

Bradbury, S. (2006) 'Corporate parenting: A discussion of the educational psychologist's role'. *Educational Psychology in Practice*, 22 (2), 141–58.

Cameron, R.J. and Maginn, C. (2011) 'Living psychology: The "emotional warmth" dimension of professional childcare'. *Educational and Child Psychology*, 28 (3), 44–62.

Centre for Social Justice (2013) *"I Never Left Care, Care Left Me": Ensuring good corporate parenting into adulthood: A briefing paper for peers on proposed amendments to the Children and Families Bill 2013*. London: Centre for Social Justice.

Centre for Social Justice (2014) *Survival of the Fittest? Improving life chances for care leavers*. London: Centre for Social Justice.

Centre for Social Justice (2015) *Finding Their Feet: Equipping care leavers to reach their potential*. London: Centre for Social Justice. Online. www.centreforsocialjustice.org.uk/core/wp-content/uploads/2016/08/Finding.pdf (accessed 29 August 2018).

DCSF (Department for Children, Schools and Families) (2009) *Guidance on Looked After Children with Special Educational Needs Placed Out-of-Authority*. London: Department for Children, Schools and Families.

DfE (Department for Education) (2010) *The Children Act 1989 Guidance and Regulations: Volume 3: Planning transition to adulthood for care leavers.* London: Department for Education.

DfE (Department for Education) (2017) *Children Looked After in England (Including Adoption), Year Ending 31 March 2017.* London: Department for Education. Online. www.gov.uk/government/uploads/system/uploads/attachment_data/file/664995/SFR50_2017-Children_looked_after_in_England.pdf (accessed 29 August 2018).

DfE (Department for Education) (2018a) *Applying Corporate Parenting Principles to Looked-After Children and Care Leavers: Statutory guidance for local authorities.* London: Department for Education.

DfE (Department for Education) (2018b) *Extending Personal Adviser Support to All Care Leavers to Age 25: Statutory guidance for local authorities.* London: Department for Education.

DfE (Department for Education) and DoH (Department of Health) (2015a) *Special Educational Needs and Disability Code of Practice: 0 to 25 years: Statutory guidance for organisations which work with and support children and young people who have special educational needs or disabilities.* London: Department for Education. Online. https://assets.publishing.service.gov.uk/government/uploads/system/uploads/attachment_data/file/398815/SEND_Code_of_Practice_January_2015.pdf (accessed 23 August 2018).

DfE (Department for Education) and DoH (Department of Health) (2015b) *Promoting the Health and Well-Being of Looked-After Children: Statutory guidance for local authorities, clinical commissioning groups and NHS England.* London: Department for Education and Department of Health.

Dixon, J., Wade, J., Byford, S., Weatherly, H. and Lee, J. (2006) *Young People Leaving Care: A study of costs and outcomes.* York: Social Work Research and Development Unit.

Driscoll, J. (2011) 'Making up lost ground: Challenges in supporting the educational attainment of looked after children beyond Key Stage 4'. *Adoption and Fostering*, 35 (2), 18–31.

Francis, Y.J., Bennion, K. and Humrich, S. (2017) 'Evaluating the outcomes of a school based Theraplay® project for looked after children'. *Educational Psychology in Practice*, 33 (3), 308–22.

Gabriel, J. (2015) 'Young People's Experiences of Moving out of Being "Not in Education, Employment or Training" (NEET): An exploration of significant factors'. Unpublished doctoral thesis, University of Birmingham.

Harrison, N. (2017) *Moving on Up: Pathways of care leavers and care-experienced students into and through higher education.* Winchester: National Network for the Education of Care Leavers.

Hiles, D., Moss, D., Thorne, L., Wright, J. and Dallos, R. (2014) '"So what am I?": Multiple perspectives on young people's experience of leaving care'. *Children and Youth Services Review*, 41, 1–15.

House of Commons Education Committee (2016) *Mental Health and Well-Being of Looked-After Children: Fourth Report of Session 2015–16.* London: House of Commons.

Hyde, R. (2018) 'Care Leavers' Perspectives on Facilitators and Barriers to Effective Preparation for Adulthood'. Unpublished paper. University of Manchester.

Hyde, R. and Atkinson, C. (submitted) 'Care leavers' views about transition: A literature review'. Manuscript submitted for publication.

Hyde, R. and Atkinson, C. (forthcoming) 'Using self determination theory to explore care leavers' perspectives on corporate parenting'. *Educational and Child Psychology*, 36 (1).

Jackson, S. and Cameron, C. (2012) 'Leaving care: Looking ahead and aiming higher'. *Children and Youth Services Review*, 34 (6), 1107–14.

Laverick, T. (2018) 'Developing aspirations to inform interventions and support attendance and motivation'. Paper presented at the Division of Educational and Child Psychology Conference, Brighton, 11–12 January 2018. Online. www.kc-jones.co.uk/files/uploads/1516019775.pdf (accessed 29 August 2018).

Lightfoot, L.M. (2013) 'The Role of Practitioner Educational Psychologists in Supporting a Residential Setting to Meet the Needs of Looked After Children'. Unpublished doctoral thesis, University of Manchester.

McParlin, P. (1996) 'Children "looked after" (in care) – implications for educational psychologists: Relentless decades of prejudice, disadvantage and appalling educational outcomes'. *Educational Psychology in Practice*, 12 (2), 112–17.

Morgan, R. (2012) *After Care: Young people's views on leaving care: Reported by the Children's Rights Director for England*. Manchester: Ofsted. Online. http://hwb.warwickshire.gov.uk/files/2012/01/After_care1.pdf (accessed 6 September 2018).

Munro, E.R., Lushey, C. and Ward, H. (2011) *Evaluation of the Right2BCared4 Pilots: Final report*. London: Department for Education.

Munro, E.R., Lushey, C., National Care Advisory Service, Maskell-Graham, D. and Ward, H. (2012) *Evaluation of the Staying Put: 18 Plus Family Placement Programme Pilot: Final report*. London: Department for Education.

Norwich, B., Richards, A. and Nash, T. (2010) 'Educational psychologists and children in care: Practices and issues'. *Educational Psychology in Practice*, 26 (4), 375–90.

Ofsted (2016) *Moving Forward? How well the further education and skills sector is preparing young people with high needs for adult life*. Manchester: Ofsted.

Preparing for Adulthood (2013) *Delivering Support and Aspiration for Disabled Young People*. Bath: Preparing for Adulthood.

Preparing for Adulthood (2015) *Supporting Staff Working with Young People Preparing for Adult Life: A summary*. Bath: Preparing for Adulthood.

Propp, J., Ortega, D.M. and NewHeart, F. (2003) 'Independence or interdependence: Rethinking the transition from "ward of the court" to adulthood'. *Families in Society*, 84 (2), 259–66.

Ryan, R.M. and Deci, E.L. (2000) 'Intrinsic and extrinsic motivations: Classic definitions and new directions'. *Contemporary Educational Psychology*, 25 (1), 54–67.

Stanley, N. (2007) 'Young people's and carers' perspectives on the mental health needs of looked-after adolescents'. *Child and Family Social Work*, 12 (3), 258–67.

Stein, M. (2004) *What Works for Young People Leaving Care?* Ilford, Essex: Barnardo's.

Stein, M. (2006) 'Young people aging out of care: The poverty of theory'. *Children and Youth Services Review*, 28 (4), 422–34.

UK Parliament (1989) 'Children Act 1989'. Online. www.legislation.gov.uk/ukpga/1989/41/contents (accessed 25 August 2018).

UK Parliament (2000) 'Children (Leaving Care) Act 2000'. Online. www.legislation.gov.uk/ukpga/2000/35/contents (accessed 29 August 2018).

UK Parliament (2008) 'Children and Young Persons Act 2008'. Online. www.legislation.gov.uk/ukpga/2008/23/contents (accessed 29 August 2018).

United Nations (1989) *Convention on the Rights of the Child*. Online. www.ohchr.org/Documents/ProfessionalInterest/crc.pdf (accessed 27 August 2018).

Ungar, M. (2005) 'Pathways to resilience among children in child welfare, corrections, mental health and educational settings: Navigation and negotiation'. *Child and Youth Care Forum*, 34 (6), 423–44.

Wade, J. (2008) 'The ties that bind: Support from birth families and substitute families for young people leaving care'. *British Journal of Social Work*, 38 (1), 39–54.

Wade, J. and Dixon, J. (2006) 'Making a home, finding a job: Investigating early housing and employment outcomes for young people leaving care'. *Child and Family Social Work*, 11 (3), 199–208.

Who Cares? Trust (2012) *Open Doors, Open Minds: Is the care system helping looked-after children progress into further and higher education?* London: Who Cares? Trust.

Wilding, L. (2015) 'The application of self-determination theory to support students experiencing disaffection'. *Educational Psychology in Practice*, 31 (2), 137–49.

Chapter 14

What if there were a model of working with the 16–25 age group?

Enomwoyi Damali and Baruti Damali

Owing to the increased age range specified by the *Special Educational Needs and Disability Code of Practice* (DfE and DoH, 2015), a survey of working practices was conducted with Lewisham educational psychologists (EPs) and EPs from other London boroughs to build upon previous good practices with the 16–18 age group. Responses were categorized into seven themes with three additional factors. The case study presented is a culmination of our investigation up until the point of writing to initiate a model of working with 16–25 year olds in the London Borough of Lewisham.

Introduction

What questions did we have when we learnt that the age range for our work was increasing to 25 years? Possibly they were similar to those asked by other EP services. They included:

- What did that mean for our work?
- Would existing models of service delivery be appropriate for the increased age range? What did we know about stages of development for this age group?
- What additional assessments might be needed?
- Who gives consent for EP involvement and how?
- What would outcomes look like for this age group?
- What do we know about post-16 provision?

There were many questions, as this was a new area of work for us, creating some challenges, but also opportunities for developing new relationships, new ways of working and potential for new models of service delivery.

Our confidence in working with other groups such as early years, school-age and looked-after children has been gained over decades by developing clear, structured models of service delivery to guide our thinking and practice. Lewisham's Practice Framework (Figure 14.1) provides a structure to guide our work that we believe can be applied to the extended age range.

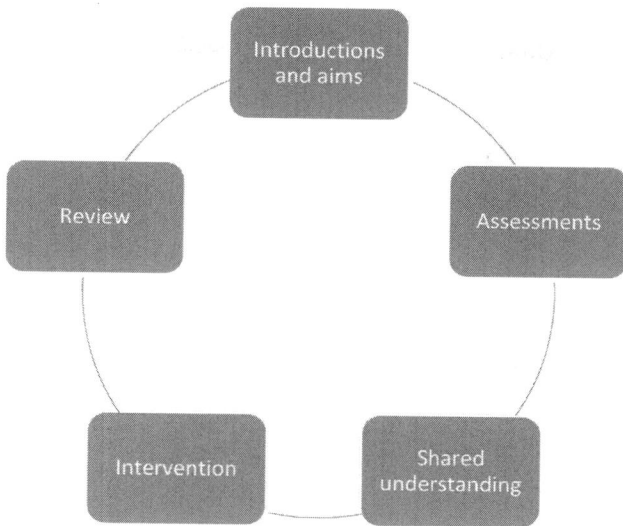

Figure 14.1: Practice framework

We already had experience of working with 16–18 year olds and had established much good practice, for example in terms of transition, liaison with other professionals and using person-centred approaches, but this really was new territory. We needed to develop a similar level of confidence in working with the extended age range by developing a model that would help us move from a sense of challenge to a sense of opportunity. As suggested by Clifford (2015), this required us to be clear about what knowledge and skills we already had that would be applicable to the extended age range, the knowledge and skills that we needed to further develop in our practice, and new knowledge and skills we would need to acquire.

In some ways it was felt that the principles guiding our work with younger age groups were similar to those that would shape our work with 16–25 year olds and therefore that elements of existing models of service delivery could be transferred to this enlarged age range. Person-centred and solution-focused approaches, needs-led assessments, multi-agency working and working within an 'assess, plan, do, review' framework all seemed wholly applicable and appropriate. However, it was also felt that there might be something unique and different about working with 16–25 year olds that warranted further exploration in order to be able to devise a coherent model appropriate to the needs of this age group.

Investigation

To explore models of service delivery we designed a 15-item questionnaire to elicit the views of colleagues about several details of their work with 16–25 year olds (see the appendix to this chapter). This questionnaire aimed to draw out key principles and practice that are important to us in the way we work with this age group. It included assessment tools, consent, rapport and eliciting views.

In addition, one of the authors attended a meeting of a post-16 special interest group in which EPs from several local authorities and independent practice shared their developments in terms of working with 16–25 year olds, features of their models of service delivery, and next steps for further development.

In this chapter we will summarize these and go on to make recommendations for further developments that other EP teams and services may wish to consider in their own model of working with 16–25 year olds.

Analysis

A person-centred approach

The Code of Practice (DfE and DoH, 2015) suggests that, whatever the prospective model might be, the overarching principle should be a person-centred approach, where the young person/adult's (YP/A's) views and aspirations are at the heart of our work and where our role facilitates them to be integral to the planning and decision process. Listening to the 'voice of the child' is a key principle in our work with all other age groups and we believe equally important as a foundation on which other elements of a service delivery model for working with 16–25 year olds lie. It applies whether the focus is on direct assessment models, consultation models, or a mixed model approach. Notwithstanding the issues of mental capacity, any model should encapsulate deliberate attempts to elicit, to incorporate and to elucidate their views, hopes, dreams and aspirations.

Sold services, traded services and time allocation to post-16 providers

Lewisham EP team offers a 'sold service' with schools buying in one to six visits per term. This offer was extended to one of our local colleges following their request for educational psychology assessment of YP/As. One EP with an interest in this area was assigned as the link EP to that setting, providing one three-and-a-half-hour visit per term with three-and-a-half hours for writing up consultation records. The work done in that time was negotiated following receipt of a referral form. The range of possibilities for work was written into our service level agreements, such as exam stress, study skills, motivation, and training for staff. In the main, the college wanted cognitive assessment, though the link EP also offered consultations to link her assessment to suggested interventions. Wilson (2015) described how her educational psychology service developed their traded model of service delivery, the offer made to local sixth form and further education colleges, and some of the challenges and practical considerations. She describes a range of creative pieces of work based on the needs of the young people and their settings, leading to subsequent development of the traded service that included a flexible delivery of their model.

Most of the EPs questioned in the post-16 interest group reported that they operated a free-time allocation model for post-16 work with anything from one day a week to two days a term. One or two EPs in each of these services have been designated as post-16 leads and are given protected time to carry out a wide range of activities including casework, liaison with relevant providers, attendance at and delivery of training, curriculum development, review, planning and transition meetings, and work as part of steering groups for post-16s. An important activity, especially initially, has been simply to 'find out what's out there', and to visit post-16 provision.

In terms of statutory work, some EPs in the post-16 interest group reported that this is allocated on a rota basis throughout the team, while in others, notably where there are few statutory requests, this is carried out by one or two EPs with post-16 specialism.

Consultation models

In Lewisham our existing consultation model of service delivery, which uses elements of Wagner's (2000) ideas, is felt to be applicable to working with 16–25 year olds with an added task of acquainting ourselves with an even wider range of providers – sixth form and further education colleges, and professionals from housing, health and mental health services, social workers and employment services. Our questionnaire indicated that the consultation model is useful to enquire about the YP/A, their family, educational provision (if they are in attendance) and any other professionals involved, to come to a shared understanding of that YP/A's strengths and needs. Following these we discuss and agree aspirations and outcomes and associated strategies and interventions to meet these.

One strength of the consultation model of service delivery is that it allows us to draw on the expertise of all those involved with caring for, supporting and teaching the YP/A while keeping their views and aspirations at the heart of the work. However, group consultation can be time consuming as opportunities for the full range of providers working with a 16–25 year old to be 'in the same room at the same time' is rare, and even if it were possible, may be overwhelming for some YP/As. Therefore there may need to be several 'conversations that make a difference' (Wagner, 2000) with the EP synthesizing all inter-related systems into a coherent whole.

The EPs questioned listed consultation with a number of post-16 providers as one of the features of their models, including job coaches, careers advisers, heads of learning departments at further education colleges, post-16 specialist advisers, managers of Preparing for Adulthood teams, case officers responsible for post-16s, and health professionals. Some of this consultation is around casework, but some is joint work at a strategic level, for example, curriculum development, resource management and provision development.

The consultation model has the potential risk of focusing energy on the systems around the child or young person (CYP) or YP/A at the expense of working directly with the CYP or YP/A themselves. Atkinson *et al.* (2015: 160) remind us of the intention that 'post-16 professionals should engage directly with the young person rather than via third parties so that those young people are integral to the planning process'.

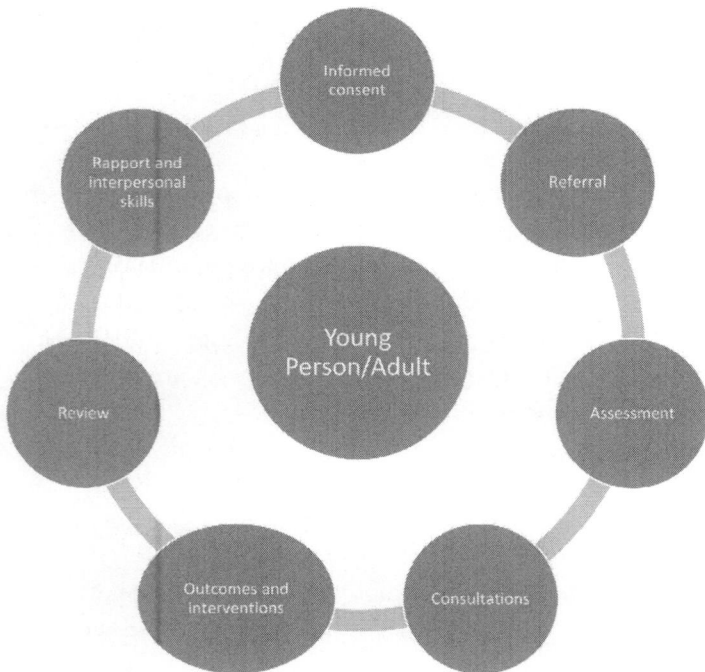

Figure 14.2: Seven themes

Themes in service delivery models

One theme running through the discussion about service delivery models was that EPs felt their services were at the beginning of their journey. Descriptions such as 'fluid', 'finding our feet', 'in a stage of exploration' were used by EPs when talking about their current 'models'. In fact their responses suggest that the term 'model' is used quite loosely, as the EPs felt their services are continuing to explore what is needed and negotiating pieces of work based on need rather than having a prescribed model.

We grouped the responses from the questionnaires and discussions into a number of categories that we call 'themes' (Figure 14.2). Other responses that did not fit easily into the themes are called 'additional factors'; these being:

- Age group related approach
- A person-centred approach
- EP satisfaction.

Informed consent

In Lewisham we gain written consent for our involvement using a Request for Involvement form signed by parent/carer of the YP/A, or in the case of looked-after children, their social worker. Some of the EPs in the post-16 interest group talked about redesigning their referral form with 16–25 year olds in mind. This is considered to be a useful a task, facilitating the explicit right of the YP/A to give consent themselves. The issue of informed consent is considered particularly important for the age range 16–25. In fact one EP responded to the question 'what is the single most important question you would ask a 16–25 year old (if you were limited to one question)?' with 'do you consent to taking part?' (indicating that she would ask this using different words). EPs believe that following the principle of a person-centred approach, the YP/A has the right, wherever possible, to consent to our involvement themselves.

A challenge may arise where the request has come directly from the special educational needs and disabilities (SEND) team as a statutory request. What if the YP/A does not give consent for our involvement even where the parent/carer has done so? Here we are guided by the Mental Capacity Act (UK Parliament, 2005), an area of legislation that for many of us is new and therefore requiring training. Some EPs have had training on the Act and others, having had this training, subsequently delivered training to their team. Where EPs have not had this training, consultation with relevant professionals is essential to help determine whether the YP/A has full legal capacity to make decisions for themselves. An interesting ethical question is, 'does the young person have the right to refuse a mental capacity assessment?'

For colleagues, establishing informed consent is essential. EP teams may wish to consider the following questions when thinking about informed consent:

- Has the YP/A given consent for EP involvement?
- To whom?
- How was this gained?
- If there is no consent, why is this?
- If the YP/A does not give consent, what are the grounds for the EP continuing with their involvement?

It is assumed that the majority of 16–25 year olds live at home with their parents. This can present a compounding situation if the YP/A refuses consent for part or all of an assessment process. While we believe it is holistic good practice to seek to engage in consultation with parents, we also acknowledge that the YP/A has the right to withdraw or withhold consent (Dunsmuir and Hardy, 2016). A controversy arises if the YP/A has 'mental capacity' and is assessed by all professionals as being in need of help, but that YP/A withdraws or withholds their consent, still leaving the local authority with a duty of care to act in the best interests of said YP/A. As controversial as it may appear, it is important for EPs to propose solutions to their local authority that are beneficial to the needs of the YP/A in cases such as these.

Building rapport and interpersonal skills

Another theme that emerged was the importance of building rapport and a relationship with the YP/A right from the very beginning with the welcome, introductions and sharing of role to the ending, and clarity about next steps.

Our questionnaire indicated a range of opening statements that we use to share and explain our remit, with EPs amending their statements depending on the needs of the YP/A. Statements included a greeting, 'who I am', 'why I'm here', 'what we are going to achieve together', with statements varying depending on the needs of the YP/A.

Using the term 'educational psychologist', checking whether this was familiar to the YP/A, and whether they had met an EP, were important to some EPs. EPs try to use very simple descriptions of their key tasks and reasons or purpose of their work (Education, Health and Care Plans or

EHCPs, helping them to be as happy as possible, doing well with their learning).

Though we did not ask specifically about this, rapport and interpersonal skills are also relevant to working with the adults who support the YP/A, particularly in terms of making connections, clarifying respective roles, and working collaboratively with post-16 education and vocational providers, careers services and other agencies. EPs felt that while they usually work one-to-one with the YP/A they include others of the YP/A's choosing to be present if that helps them to feel more comfortable and willing to work with the EP. In terms of the venue, EPs reported that they aim to meet with the YP/A in the venue that is most comfortable for them and that is usually the learning environment, because of familiarity, or the YP/A's home.

Assessments – what do we want to know and how can we find out?

'Assessment' here is viewed in terms of face-to-face work with the YP/A with the aim of eliciting their strengths and needs, using a variety of tools to offer recommendations for intervention. However, EPs acknowledge the importance of a triangulation of several sources of assessment information (Figure 14.3), including consultations, observations, reports from other professionals, etc.

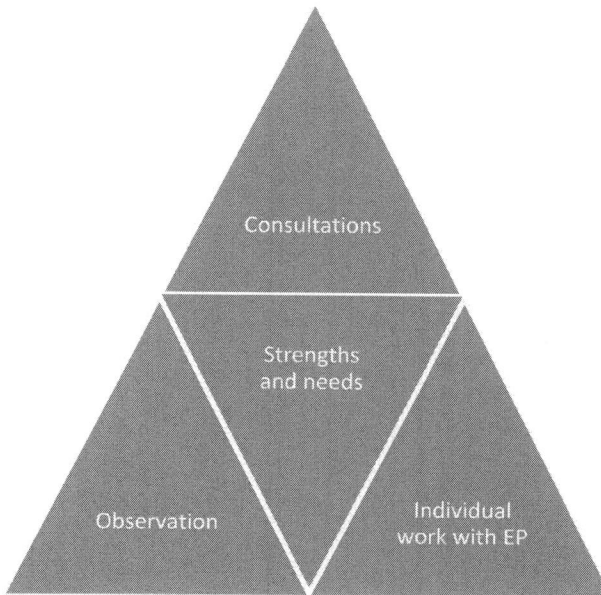

Figure 14.3: Sources of assessment information

In Lewisham we established existing assessment tools that would be appropriate in working with 16–25 year olds and we purchased additional materials to fill in the gaps. We purchased adult norms for the Weschler Adult Intelligence Scale (WAIS) and the Weschler Individual Achievement Test 11 (WIAT 11), and several resources to assess well-being – Resiliency Scales, Boxall Profile and Talking Mats.

Educational psychologists highlighted mental health and emotional well-being, language, relationships education and learning as areas of interest in assessments of 16–25 year olds, in addition to the four areas of need in the Code of Practice (employment, health, independence and community). There are continued discussions about which areas may be most relevant to EPs and which may sit more appropriately with other professionals.

The area of employment is one that EPs felt distinguished our work with 16–25 year olds compared with other age ranges. We are accustomed to exploring the aspirations of younger children and young people by asking questions such as 'what would you like to be when you are older?' and 'what work would you like to do when you finish your studying?' Stanley-Duke and Stringer (2017) describe the many levels of involvement of EPs in this area of employability, from assessing the YP/A's motivation to be employed, to the skills and experience needed to carry out the job (specific job-related skills as well as more generic skills applicable to many jobs). EPs need training on the range of employment pathways for YP/As and on the 'personal skills which they can carry beyond the classroom' (Hayton, 2009, cited in Wilson, 2015) such as self-awareness and sense of identity.

Preparing for Adulthood (2014) describes 'adult life outcomes' and considers the young person's transition into adulthood. It also suggests a focus on *paid* employment to help distinguish volunteering and other unpaid opportunities that may interest YP/As. Assessments therefore should include agreeing further aspirations with the YP/A. Do they want to continue with learning? Do they want to work? Given that there are a number of alternatives to learning and work (e.g. apprenticeships, work-related study, internships), discussion with the YP/A about their aspirations and goals forms an important and essential part of our assessment.

A model of working with 16–25 year olds should guide our thinking about the transition to adulthood, therefore it is important for us to have access to appropriate tools for measuring behaviours and skills that are directly relevant to this process such as problem solving, adaptability, resilience, motivation and self-direction. Clifford (2015) recommended the *Adaptive Behavior Assessment System*, Third Edition (Harrison and

Oakland, 2015), which looks at several domains covering 'self direction', 'functional academics' and social skills. BRIEF 2 (Behavior Rating Inventory of Executive Function; see Gioia *et al.*, 2015) is another resource, which, with training, may also be appropriate to assessing the relevant skills of YP/As, aged 16–18 years.

Assessments – cognition and learning

Our questionnaire showed that the British Ability Scales 3 (GL Assessment, n.d.), WISC-IV (Weschler, 2004) and WISC-V (Weschler, 2016) are the most commonly used standardized measures of cognitive skills of YP/A. Other standardized measures were the WRIT (Glutting *et al.*, 2000) and the WRAT (Robertson and Wilkinson, 2006). EPs are also using non-standardized measures such as dynamic assessments to assess learning skills, learning potential and to identify appropriate levels of support.

Assessments – listening to the voice of the YP/A

We believe that any model should uphold EPs' 'long standing interest in ascertaining the voice of the child' (Atkinson *et al.*, 2015: 159) and that we have a duty to ask about and listen to their views, hopes and aspirations and involve them in decisions about their future. In Lewisham we purchased new visual, kinaesthetic and digital resources to facilitate the voice of YP/As with severe and complex communication, learning and mental health needs.

We use a range of published and bespoke resources to elicit the views of 16–25 year olds, making these more or less visual and kinaesthetic depending on the complexity of the YP/A's needs. Strengths Cards, FINK Cards and Talking Mats are some of our frequently used resources as they are visual, tactile, kinaesthetic and therefore possibly more appealing and user friendly than pen and paper questionnaires. We also use questions from the MAP approach and personal construct approaches such as the Ideal Self and the Big Box of Little Questions (Gersch and Lipscomb, 2012). PATH is a visual and collaborative approach that several EPs have used to elicit the views of the YP/A and to determine the factors that facilitate that YP/A to achieve their dreams and aspirations.

In terms of more bespoke tools we use solution-focused scaling questions, again depending on the complexity of need (e.g. on a scale of 1–10, how important is living independently to you, where 10 is extremely important), drawings (e.g. Kinetic Family Drawings, miming, drawing a picture of doing their ideal job). We may suggest using the YP/A's own communication aids, such as a personalized set of symbols. EPs have also used spider diagrams, mind maps and photos to help elicit the YP/A's views and experiences, especially where verbal communication may be difficult.

Personalized questionnaires have also proved helpful, especially with those who are reluctant to or find it difficult to talk.

As many requests for involvement are for 16–25 year olds with complex communication and learning needs, EPs are being creative and eclectic, using visual, kinaesthetic, concrete and interactive resources to facilitate communication, understanding and motivation so that they can 'be the best they can be' within the limitations of an assessment context.

Assessments – social, emotional and mental health

The Vineland, Beck and Resiliency Scales were mentioned in responses as published measures of social, emotional and mental health development, but EPs also used a range of additional bespoke materials such as solution-focused and scaling questions, personal construct psychology tools (e.g. the Ideal Self).

Outcomes and interventions

The next theme is 'outcomes and (associated) interventions' and a key question for us is, 'what are the outcomes that link to the goal of Preparing for Adulthood?' Second, what are the 'skills or adaptations (that) will enable a person to function in real life settings' (Emerson, 1998, cited in Clifford, 2015). While these outcomes and associated skills will be determined in consultation with the YP/A, it may be useful for EPs to explore generic areas of importance for YP/As such as problem solving, confidence, self-esteem, time management, conflict resolution and resilience.

Through discussions and the questionnaires, EPs talked about outcomes for YP/As and also for the supporting adults. In Lewisham we have discussed how to make our outcomes SMART (specific, measurable, achievable, realistic, time-related) and have generated a bank of these outcomes in the four areas of need. This is recommended as a supportive sharing of practice across EP teams.

The range of involvement and intervention given in this relatively small sample was broad. EPs offered direct interventions to the YP/A themselves (study skills, planning and setting goals, stress management) and also offered advice and support for the adults who work to help those YP/As – reflective practice for tutors on managing behaviour; training on emotional aspects of transition; planning and supporting future placements.

Person-centred planning approaches were used to bridge the gap between where the YP/A is at present and where they want to be in future. In these approaches, outcomes are co-constructed with the young person and the key adults in their life, parents/carers and staff in their setting.

An additional question is what constitutes positive outcomes *for the EP*? What would a successful piece of work for the EP look like? Clearly supervision and peer support are opportunities for useful reflection about issues such as how the work with the YP/A made the EP feel, what went well and what they would do differently next time.

Review

This theme acknowledges the importance of evaluation being built into our work and scheduling time for review. This is often more difficult to achieve with statutory work where, having submitted advice, the EP may not be involved in the review process. In the discussion, local authorities had different models in terms of reviews. Some EPs were invited to all Year 9 reviews, planning ahead to post-16 transition. This was considered by all to be a key point for EP involvement with a suggestion of starting with a particular cohort to make the work more manageable, e.g. YP/As with autistic spectrum disorder (ASD) and anxiety.

Other EPs are alerted to annual reviews where EP involvement is considered to be important. One EP spoke of a principle of continuity so that EPs who have completed an assessment of a YP/A would, as far as possible, attend their annual review.

Referral

In Lewisham most referrals for our work with 16–25 year olds have been dictated by the request to contribute towards Education, Health and Care Needs Assessments (EHCNA) or conversion to an Education, Health and Care Plan. This makes the purpose of our involvement clear but still requires thinking about the details of what work we might do. The task is to share and negotiate with the YP/A, as far as possible, what work is to be done and why. This may also include who the YP/A does and does not want the final report or record to be shared with.

We asked EPs to tell us the age and gender of the last 16–25 year old referred to them and the reason for their involvement. We asked EPs for their last case in particular for the following three reasons. First, it is the most recent in their minds and therefore most likely to be memorable; second, we predicted that asking about their last case would make it more likely that EPs would respond; third, we have received relatively few requests for assessments and indeed some EPs will have received only one request in the last year.

Notwithstanding the potential limitations of asking EPs to reflect on their last case we found that six out of nine were male with three females and with the age range from 16 to 22, most being under 20. In four cases, the referral or request was for statutory work (three conversions, three updated EHCP advice and one each for advice for transition to college, assessment of 17-year-old girl with ASD, and assessment of a 17-year-old boy with learning needs).

Case study – Lewisham's journey so far

Lewisham's journey in working with 16–25 year olds and the development of a model of service delivery started before the Children and Families Act 2014 came into force (UK Parliament, 2014). This progress is supported by the good practice established in working with young people up to 18 years old prior to the changes brought about by the Act. We have made some progress in this journey with a number of tasks and activities to help us along the way:

- We have considered a number of questions, sharing our thoughts and ideas in several team meetings.
- Two EPs attended a day's training on working with 16–25 year olds organized by the Division of Educational and Child Psychology in 2015, and took the lead in this new area as part of our Service Development Plan.
- We looked at gaps in our assessment repertoire and purchased additional resources as a result.
- We carried out a scoping exercise to map out 16–25 provision and providers in our borough.
- We shared examples of statutory reports of 16–25 year olds, in particular the outcomes, and created an e-folder in which all reports are saved and therefore able to be shared with each other quickly and easily.
- We have participated in two 'market places' for parents/carers and YP/As, joining other providers in setting up stalls to promote our work with 16–25 year olds.
- The two EPs with a special interest in this area attended a conference organized by our Parent Carers Forum about supporting 16–25 year olds, gaining valuable information about employment pathways such as supported internships.
- We have sat on the Preparing for Adulthood group, working with parents and carers and other professionals to consider several issues related to this area, and to design a leaflet for YP/As about the range of services available to support them.

Case study: The present

Individually and as a team we have begun to develop some important, if not essential, elements of a model of service delivery. Like other teams, we feel we are at the beginning of our journey. Our work with 16–25 year olds is dictated to a large extent by the ongoing demands of requests for statutory assessments. This, by its very nature, has placed the emphasis on individual assessments and report writing. We continue to explore a flexible model of service delivery to include other additional bespoke and non-statutory pieces of work. This would allow more choice and flexibility based on the needs of post-16 provision in our area and the needs expressed by young adults living in our geographical area.

The seven themes

We have summarized the questionnaire responses and observations of practice in our team into seven themes. We feel that these themes identify good practice that can be built upon as part of a model of service delivery. We have also identified three additional factors and suggest that EP teams may also wish to consider these when developing their own models.

In Table 14.1 the seven themes are cross-referenced with the areas of need stipulated in the Code of Practice for this age group. Under the theme of 'assessment', we consider issues such as materials and resources under each of the four areas. Under the theme of 'consultation', we consider the key people service providers in the YP/A's life and the enquiries that we need to make in each of those areas. EPs in other services may wish to make their own cross-references to see how these apply to their approach to service delivery with 16–25 year olds.

Table 14.1: Seven themes – four areas of need

Themes	Employment	Health	Community	Independence
Referral				
Informed consent				
Assessment				
Consultation				
Outcomes				
Reviews				
Rapport and interpersonal skills				

Three additional factors
Age group related approach
Feedback from our questionnaire showed that most respondents felt that the 16–25 age group should not necessarily be treated as a homogenous group since, for example, the needs of a 16 year old might be very different from those of a 25 year old. Most respondents felt that there should be three separate groups. This is a factor that warrants further exploration, and the raising of awareness of the theories of adolescence and early adulthood learning.

A person-centred approach
Most EPs opted for using a person-centred approach and indeed selected assessments and planning resources that reflect this approach. We wish to pose the question, to what extent is a person-centred-approach the same as or different from an age-related approach? Is it possible to focus on the individual YP/A's hopes, dreams, aspirations, skills and abilities, without taking into account their age?

EP satisfaction
The authors suggest that an important, but relatively neglected, part of the work is 'EP satisfaction' and that this should be built into outcomes for the EP. How satisfied are we with the work that we did? How do we know that a session was successful? What would we do differently next time? Regular and supportive supervision will of course facilitate such discussions, but it is argued that the EP should bring this reflection into their practice on an ongoing basis. This is especially true at this stage in the development of service delivery models when many of us are debating, 'what does good practice actually look like when working with 16–25 year olds?'

Summary and conclusions
The authors designed a questionnaire to ascertain important elements that could be used to create a model of service delivery for working with 16–25 year olds. Discussion also took place with EPs from other services who shared that they, like us, are at the beginning of the development of our respective models. This initial investigation highlights a range of approaches to the work and highlights that EP teams are at the beginning of their journey in developing coherent models.

    The seven themes and three additional factors are presented as possible elements for consideration. It is suggested that these are cross-referenced with the four areas of need stated in the Code of Practice. Further work is recommended in terms of eliciting more detailed information from items in the questionnaire. This can then be used as a stimulus for team discussion about models of service delivery.

The years '16–25' are a gradual movement to becoming an independent adult and any model of service delivery needs to reflect that process of transition. The skills needed to work with this age group are not necessarily unique to those who are post-16 and our questionnaire and discussions suggest that many practices and approaches are similar to those used with younger age groups. Furthermore, there is a strong view that transition work should begin when young people are in Year 9 and that EPs have a key role in this respect.

Some key areas that EPs may wish to explore further are:

- the skills needed for successful transition from child (school age) to post-16 and then adulthood
- informed consent and mental capacity
- post-16 educational provision and employment pathways
- theories of adolescent development and adult learning.

Items for consideration

A number of items are now presented as warranting further consideration in EP teams.

The numbers in Table 14.2 refer to the areas for further development listed below:

1. Do we need to adapt our referral form?
2. Do we need training?
3. Who are the 16–25 service providers in our area?
4. How do we introduce yourself and your role?
5. Do we have a contract with providers, referrers and the YP/A – written or verbal?
6. Have we done an audit of assessments and resources? Do we need to buy additional resources?
7. Is there a measure of EP personal satisfaction and outcomes for rapport and engagement?
8. What is the overall purpose of working with the 16–25 age group?
9. What constitutes a 'good' referral or request for involvement?
10. What are positive outcomes for the YP/A?
11. What would constitute successful pieces of work for the EP?
12. Has the YP/A given consent for EP involvement?

Table 14.2: Areas for further development

Item no.	Informed consent	Referral	Assessment	Consultation	Outcomes and recommendations	Review	Rapport and interpersonal skills
1	√	√					√
2	√		√		√		
3		√					
4							√
5							√
6			√				
7			√				√
8		√					
9		√					
10					√		
11							
12							
13					√		
14							
15	√						
16	√						
17	√						

√ = Further work needed

• = Achieved

13. In what way is consent presented to the child?
14. How is that power given to them?
15. Does the YP/A have mental capacity? How do you know?
16. Who gives consent and how?
17. What happens if the YP/A with 'mental capacity' does not give consent but the parent does?

There is much potential in terms of the various ways EPs can be involved in working with YP/As, and EP teams and services will have scope to explore different models according to local need and expertise within the team. This paper has considered a number of approaches to the work that fit well within the four areas of need.

The authors suggest that any model of service delivery needs to be flexible and responsive to changing needs and demands and that there should be a built-in review mechanism. This will ensure that it adapts and changes in a professional culture of continuous development and improvement. With more than three years since the implementation of the Children and Families Act (UK Parliament, 2014), the authors also recommend a review of new or adapted service delivery models for 16–25 year olds across the United Kingdom.

References

Atkinson, C., Dunsmuir, S., Lang, J. and Wright, S. (2015) 'Developing a competency framework for the initial training of educational psychologists working with young people aged 16–25'. *Educational Psychology in Practice*, 31 (2), 159–73.

Clifford, V. (2015) 'Educational psychology: Working post 16'. Training session presented at the DECP event, 'Working with 16–25 year olds', London, 5 October 2015.

DfE (Department for Education) and DoH (Department of Health) (2015) *Special Educational Needs and Disability Code of Practice: 0 to 25 years: Statutory guidance for organisations which work with and support children and young people who have special educational needs or disabilities*. London: Department for Education. Online. https://assets.publishing.service.gov.uk/government/uploads/system/uploads/attachment_data/file/398815/SEND_Code_of_Practice_January_2015.pdf (accessed 23 August 2018).

Dunsmuir, S. and Hardy J. (2016) *Delivering Psychological Therapies in Schools and Communities*. Leicester: British Psychological Society.

Emerson E. (1998) 'Working with people with challenging behaviour'. In Emerson, E., Hatton, C., Bromley, J. and Caine, A. (eds) *Clinical Psychology and People with Intellectual Disabilities*. Chichester: Wiley, 127–53.

Gersch, I. and Lipscomb, A. (2012) *Little Box of Big Questions: Philosophical conversations with children and young people*. Syresham: Small World, Big Imaginations.

Gioia, G.A., Isquith, P.K., Guy, S.C. and Kenworthy, L. (2015) *BRIEF®2: Behavior Rating Inventory of Executive Function*. 2nd ed. Lutz, FL: Psychological Assessment Resources.

GL Assessment (n.d.) *British Ability Scales (BAS3)*. Online. https://www.gl-assessment.co.uk/products/british-ability-scales-bas3/ (accessed 6 September 2018).

Glutting, J., Adams, W. and Sheslow, D. (2000) *WRIT: Wide Range Intelligence Test*. Wilmington, DE: Wide Range.

Harrison, P.L. and Oakland, T. (2015) *ABAS-3: Adaptive Behavior Assessment System*. 3rd ed. Torrance, CA: Western Psychological Services.

Hayton, R. (2009) 'Young people growing up in rural communities: Opportunities for educational psychologists to work with emerging adults'. *Educational and Child Psychology*, 26 (1), 60–6.

Preparing for Adulthood (2014) 'Factsheet: The Mental Capacity Act and supported decision making'. Online. www.preparingforadulthood.org.uk/downloads/young-people-and-family-participation/factsheet-the-mental-capacity-act-2005-and-supported-decision-making.htm (accessed 29 August 2018).

Robertson, G.J. and Wilkinson, G.S. (2006) *WRAT4: Wide Range Achievement Test*. 4th ed. Lutz, FL: Psychological Assessment Resources.

Stanley-Duke, M. and Stringer, P. (2017) 'What is the meaning of "employability" and how can educational psychologists' involvement at post 16 embrace it?'. *DECP Debate*, 164.

UK Parliament (2005) 'Mental Capacity Act 2005'. Online. www.legislation.gov.uk/ukpga/2005/9/contents (accessed 25 August 2018).

UK Parliament (2014) 'Children and Families Act 2014'. Online. www.legislation.gov.uk/ukpga/2014/6/contents/enacted (accessed 25 August 2018).

Wagner, P. (2000) 'Consultation: Developing a comprehensive approach to service delivery'. *Educational Psychology in Practice*, 16 (1), 9–18.

Wechsler, D. (2004) *WISC-IV UK: Wechsler Intelligence Scale for Children*. 4th UK ed. London: Pearson.

Wechsler, D. (2016) *WISC-V UK: Wechsler Intelligence Scale for Children*. 5th UK ed. London: Pearson.

Wilson, J. (2015) 'Trading educational psychology services with post 16 provides: Issues and opportunities'. Presentation at the DECP event, 'Working with 16–25 year olds', London, 5 October 2015.

Appendix: Lewisham educational psychology questionnaire on working with the 16–25 age group

1. The 16–25 age group is often stated as a discrete grouping – please circle (a, b or c) where you feel it's more helpful as working sub groups:
    a) Work with the 16–25 as one homogenous group
    b) Split into 2 sub-groups: 16–20 21–25
    c) Split into 3 sub-groups: 16–18 19–21 22–25
2. The Code of Practice requires that we consider the four areas of Employment, Health, Independence and Community in our assessments. What other areas do you think are important?
3. What published tools, if any, do you use most often to elicit the views of 16–25 year olds?
4. What informal (i.e. not published or standardized) tools, if any, do you use to elicit the views of 16–25 year olds?
5. What tools do you use most frequently to assess the needs (personal and/or learning) of 16–25 year olds?
6. What opening statement(s) do you use when meeting with a 16–25?
7. What statement(s) do you use to end your meeting with a 16–25 year old?
8. What was the age and gender of the last 16–25 year old that you worked with and what was the reason for your involvement?
9. What do you feel is the key difference between working with 16–25 year olds compared with the younger age range?
10. What is the single most important question you would ask a 16–25 year old (if you were limited to one question)?
11. What is the main difference in eliciting the CYP's view between the old statementing process and that of the EHCP?
12. Do you believe that the CYP's view should be elicited aurally, visually or by tactile means?
13. Do you believe it's best to conduct these interviews at the CYP's home, educational setting or council premises?
14. Do you believe that the interview should be conducted in a therapeutic setting (private and one-to-one) or with selected persons present?
15. How do you introduce yourself and what do you say you are there to do?

Many thanks for helping me with this questionnaire!

Chapter 15

Multi-agency collaborations for the 16–25 age group: Strengths, obstacles and confusions

Amy Selfe, Gabrielle Pelter and Sarah Relton

Multi-agency collaboration refers to the activity of practitioners from a range of services and organizations working together 'sharing a common agreed vision, aims, objectives, goals, information, planning, tasks and responsibilities ...' (Cheminais, 2009: 45). The need for multi-agency work has relevance to support offered to young people aged 16–25 years, as they transition into adulthood.

Educational psychologists (EPs) have been identified as having a key role in collaborating with other services, schools, colleges, young people and their families, when supporting adolescents into adulthood (Atkinson *et al.*, 2015; Morris and Atkinson, 2018). The Preparing for Adulthood (2013) programme, funded by the Department for Education (DfE), considered the key elements to improving outcomes for disabled young people, which were reported to include:

- developing a shared vision
- raising aspirations
- personalizing your approach
- improving post-16 options and support
- planning services together.

These outcomes point to an integrated, multi-agency and collaborative effort, and importantly, one that includes the young person. A person-centred approach is embedded within the 2015 *Special Educational Needs and Disability Code of Practice* (DfE and Department of Health (DoH), 2015) and is pertinent for EPs, since empowering and enabling the voice of the child and young person is a key issue for practice (Atkinson *et al.*, 2015; Morris and Atkinson, 2018).

In response to changes to legislation in the Children and Families Act 2014 (UK Parliament, 2014), research was conducted to identify key competencies for EPs working with 16–25s (Atkinson *et al.*, 2015). The aim of the research was to develop a curriculum for EP training. The authors suggest that the framework should extend beyond initial training to be used by EPs to plan service delivery. The competencies that emerged from research contain three elements: new knowledge required for working with 16–25 year olds; process skills required to deliver psychological services in relation to 16–25 year olds; and existing knowledge that needs extension to work with 16–25 year olds.

Research developing the role of post-school psychological services in Scotland had previously highlighted the importance of multi-agency working (Hellier, 2009). This was also identified as a source of potential difficulty, whereby it is necessary for psychologists to become familiar with courses, pathways and to understand the role of professionals within adult services. With regard to the process skills required to deliver psychological services to 16–25 year olds, the competency framework developed by Atkinson *et al.* (2015) also identifies the need for professional collaboration. Section 6 of the framework states that professionals need two competencies:

- (6.2a) works collaboratively with others to support transitions made by young people aged 16–25
- (6.2b) within multi-disciplinary settings can work with other professionals to incorporate psychological knowledge into transition planning and monitoring.

These competencies raise the profile of collaborative working practices across education, health and social care when supporting those aged 16–25. To develop this practice, it is useful to consider opportunities and avenues for multi-agency collaboration, and to clarify some examples of the psychological skills and approaches that can be employed by EPs during multi-agency work.

Multi-agency collaboration supporting 16–25s

Section 19 of the Children and Families Act 2014 states the principles underpinning the legislation and the guidance that relates to children and young people with special educational needs and disabilities (SEND).

These principles underpinning the *Special Educational Needs and Disability Code of Practice* (DfE and DoH, 2015) make it clear that local authorities (LAs) must have regard to:

- the views, wishes and feelings of the child or young person and the child's parents
- the importance of the child or young person, and the child's parents, participating as fully as possible in decisions
- providing the information and support necessary to enable participation in those decisions
- the need to support the child or young person, and the child's parents, in order to facilitate the development of the child or young person and to help them achieve the best possible educational and other outcomes, preparing them effectively for adulthood.

A focus of work with 16–25s, therefore, is *supporting transitions*, which can include from child to adult health services; from child to adult social care; from school to further education (FE); and from education into employment.

Knox (2011) has suggested that young people with disabilities and learning difficulties have key needs during transition that should be addressed by professionals – including the social and relationship needs of the individual; physical and personal care needs; needs of the family in supporting the young person; and a need for autonomy – so that the young person is involved in making decisions. Knox (2011) in a sample of those with severe learning difficulties (SLD) identified that loss of old friendships and relationships can present a challenge for those during transition from school into college. Similarly, Carroll (2015) has highlighted that transition can present a period of stress and psychological disruption, particularly for those with learning difficulties. Careful and structured planning that aims to reduce stress is, therefore, essential. Research regarding post-16 transition has clarified processes involved, including planning, as well as providing important experiences for the young person, such as visits to new settings and meeting with key adults. However, Knox (2011) suggests that frequently there is an emphasis on the process at the expense of the immediate experiences of the young person during their transition from school into college. Further, much of the research regarding the post-16 transition of young adults with learning difficulties has reinforced a deficit model (Carroll, 2015). Consequently, research has often failed to fully capture the complexity of the transition experiences, where there is an over-reliance on data regarding academic attainment, employment and independent living status. Carroll (2015) suggests that research should incorporate broader outcome measures that explore friendships, relationships, recreational activities and social adjustment. The concept of positive youth development (PYD) might contribute to developing more nuanced research studies.

An ecosystemic approach (Bronfenbrenner and Evans, 2000) has been applied to conceptualize transition (Knox, 2011; Carroll, 2015). From this perspective, systems around the young person influence their development, including family, friends, education, health, care professionals and the wider community. Arguably, such a perspective is useful to consider multi-agency collaboration that aims to facilitate transition. McCrone *et al.* (2009) identified that collaboration between FE colleges and the LA can contribute to improved progression and engagement of young people in education and training. The types of collaboration between LAs and FE colleges included comprehensive post-16 provision; transition support; and information, advice and guidance. A range of factors was found to be beneficial. These included equality of standing between partners; trust, respect and transparency; regular and robust formal and informal communication; a joined-up structure; and a shared vision.

Support for transitions requires planning over months and years to ensure that provision is put in place in a proactive manner. As such, the process and planning should commence when the young person is in Year 9, since a good transition can improve health-related quality of life for young people (Morris and Atkinson, 2018). The Code of Practice (DfE and DoH, 2015) states that transition planning must be built into the revised Education, Health and Care Plan (EHCP), following the Year 9 review, and offer outcomes that prepare the young person for adulthood. A range of different agencies is vital to ensure effective planning and the implementation of support, which will be determined by the individual needs of the young person. It requires the collaboration of agencies and provides an excellent opportunity for multi-agency work. Many LAs have adopted a multi-agency approach to transition planning and published Multi-agency Transition Protocols.

Sloper *et al.* (2010) explored models of multi-agency services for transition into adult services. The process of transition is described as problematic due to a lack of information for young people and parents; insufficient attention to the concerns and priorities of young people and parents; and a lack of appropriate services into which young people can transfer. The authors employed a mixed methods approach to explore five differing models of multi-agency services, which included a parent survey and interviews with a sub-sample of parents and young people, who had received the transition service. Better outcomes were found when there was a designated transition worker who supported the young people and parents; the family had a written transition plan where person-centred planning was used; and where there was clarity regarding the role of the professionals involved in the multi-agency work. High levels of unmet need were found in many areas of young people's lives, for example, leisure and social life, housing, career and employment opportunities.

Overall, the research showed that dedicated, multi-agency transition services provided a valuable service for disabled young people and their parents. This was most likely the case when transition workers engaged directly with young people and families. Both the survey and case studies indicated that multi-agency transition services were largely focused on young people with SLD. There is a need to extend such services so that young people with complex health needs and those with high-functioning autism spectrum disorder (ASD) can receive co-ordinated multi-agency support (Sloper *et al.*, 2010).

Richardson *et al.* (2017) explored the perspectives of the professionals involved in multi-agency transition meetings for those with learning difficulties and disabilities, including teachers, careers advisers, EPs, speech and language therapists, occupational therapists, physiotherapists and social workers. This was conducted longitudinally, to explore changes to multi-agency work. Over time, collaborative practice was found to have an increased emphasis on including the young person in the planning process. It is suggested that this study provides a framework for future policy development. For effective multi-agency transition work, the following areas were deemed necessary:

- a transitional protocol, coupled with meaningful person-centred planning
- a trusted individual, who might be a member of the young person's family, to manage transition support
- a feedback process, so the young person can provide information back to professionals involved in planning and preparation
- earlier involvement of key adult services
- awareness of models of good collaborative practice among professionals.

While many other factors determine transition outcomes for young people with intellectual disabilities (ID), Kaehne (2010) argues that protocols shape partnership work and are a first step towards effective multi-agency collaboration. Yet little is known about transition protocols, whether they comply with government policy or how they address the issue of partnership work. Kaehne (2010) employed documentary analysis to 21 protocols from Welsh LAs. This revealed wide variations in the content. There was a lack of clarity in many of the protocols regarding the involvement of young people and carers in the planning process. Positively, most of the protocols were explicit about the individual tasks of professionals and clearly outlined duties of those involved. Protocols often gave the strong impression that the main pathway was the FE placements or residential facilities for those with ID. Kaehne (2010) concludes that 'only when casting the net wider will it allow professionals involved in planning transition to create genuine choices for young people with intellectual disabilities leaving school' (p. 186).

Where formal multi-agency transition arrangements are not in place, there can be long-term health and social care costs (Richards and Vostanis, 2004). They explored the views of practitioners, managers and policymakers from mental health, social, education and non-statutory agencies regarding transitional mental health services for young adults. Views were sought from a range of professionals including social workers, psychiatrists, nurses, mental health workers, clinical and educational psychologists. A key finding was that there was little variation in opinion across social care, education and health services. This would indicate that similar problems are faced by different agencies and can be addressed through inter-professional partnerships. Richards and Vostanis (2004) posit that good transition requires a dovetailing approach, with joint sessions between child and adult services, in a graduated manner. There was consensus across professionals that services need to adopt a holistic and flexible approach, since young adults often have multi-faceted needs. It was suggested that there is a need to formalize communication protocols and provide forums for discussion. Participants requested inter-professional service agreements, consistent age cut-offs, and clarity regarding roles and expectations.

Multi-agency partnerships have been neglected in the research regarding ID (Kaehne, 2011). Consequently, it is not clear what the requirements are of multi-agency services for successful transition from child to adult mental health services for those with ID (Kaehne, 2011). The author examined the views of mental health professionals regarding partnership work and service gaps in transition for young people with ID across three LAs. All professionals criticized the lack of co-ordination between services for planning transitions. In line with the research of Sloper *et al.* (2010), respondents highlighted that the lack of joint working may have a particularly negative impact on some potential risk groups, such as young people with mild ID and high-functioning ASD. The mental health professionals articulated a feeling of marginalization from the wider transition context in social care and education. A lack of multi-agency collaboration was posited as leading to fragmented services and abrupt cessation of services during critical times of transition for young people with ID.

The majority of studies discussed above were conducted prior to the Children and Families Act 2014. Richardson *et al.* (2017) completed their research in Scotland and the studies published by Kaehne (2010, 2011) were carried out exclusively in Wales. In the light of the legislative reform, studies are now required to explore models of multi-agency services for those transitioning into adulthood, across diverse populations (including those with IDs and mental health needs) in England.

Psychological approaches and techniques

Educational psychologists are frequently referenced in policy, protocols and research regarding multi-agency collaboration to support those aged 16–25 years (Richards and Vostanis, 2004; Sloper *et al.*, 2010; Richardson *et al.*, 2017). Morris and Atkinson (2018) suggest that support can be offered by the EP first by building links and relationships with post-16 settings, and second through multi-agency working. It is, therefore, necessary to consider some examples of the psychological approaches and techniques that can be employed by the EP engaged in work of this kind.

Person-centred planning

Person-centred planning (PCP) is often central to multi-agency work, where professionals collaborate to plan and review *with*, rather than *for*, the young person (Kaehne and Beyer, 2014). Person-centred approaches, such as the one-page profile, have been developed to gather the views of the young person, to facilitate meetings, reviews, action planning and implementation (White and Rae, 2016). PCP is an approach that was developed in the United States and gained importance in the United Kingdom, as it formed a key component of the 2001 White Paper 'Valuing People' (Mansell and Beadle-Brown, 2004). It is an approach that values aspirations expressed by the service user, as opposed to an emphasis on needs and deficits. The approach also attempts to include and empower the individual's family and wider social network, in the belief that this will broaden and deepen the range of resources available to the young person (Mansell and Beadle-Brown, 2004). The Code of Practice (DfE and DoH, 2015) advocates the use of PCP for supporting young people with SEND. Kaehne (2010) and Kaehne and Beyer (2014) suggest that person-centred approaches constitute an important aspect of discharging transition planning services to young people.

There is some criticism of PCP, however, namely that the 'supportive community', in which the plan is embedded, may not be typical of the social environments experienced by many with learning difficulties and disabilities (Mansell and Beadle-Brown, 2004). There is a paucity of evidence regarding the effectiveness of PCP, in comparison with other approaches. Further, there has been scepticism as to the authenticity of the participation of young people involved in PCP (White and Rae, 2016). Consequently, research has attempted to explore the experiences of young people and their parents involved in a PCP transition review. White and Rae (2016) attempted to clarify whether young people and their parents felt listened to, and whether PCP led to any changes to student knowledge about their learning, motivation, positivity towards school and locus of control (LOC). While there was no meaningful change to LOC or levels of understanding, motivation and positivity, a key finding was that the PCP transition review was a collaborative and empowering process for parents and young people. The process enabled family members to gain a shared understanding, and to reach agreement regarding next steps, with schools and support services (White and Rae, 2016). White and Rae also argue that the experience and training of EPs mean that they have the skills needed to facilitate PCP transition review meetings. EPs can draw on their knowledge of solution-focused techniques to support an understanding of a process focused on strengths as opposed to deficiencies. EPs can act as an advocate for the child, ensuring that his or her voice is incorporated into assessment and planning procedures.

Solution-focused techniques

A solution-focused approach prompts individuals and groups to consider different solutions, which creates the expectation of change (Morgan, 2016). Multi-agency working is successful when there is shared vision, respect and communication, which is in line with solution-focused principles (Alexander and Sked, 2010). A solution-focused framework, to underpin multi-agency meetings, has been developed in Scotland. The Psychology Service at the Highland Council wanted to facilitate meaningful inclusion of parents, children and multi-agency colleagues. Consequently, key elements underpinned by solution-focused principles were agreed by members of a group ('The Liaison Group'). This included a focus on solutions where goals are central; parent and pupil are to be equally included in the group and have an equal voice; and clear boundaries are presented. For example, the end time of the meeting is stated at the start. Alexander and Sked (2010) conducted two evaluations as to the success of the approach, which included gathering the views of core group members across education, health and social care. Results suggested that the solution-focused framework stopped the rehearsing of difficulties and allowed the group members to focus on the child's positive attributes. Moreover, the feelings of generating solutions helped to promote self-efficacy. Areas to be developed included ensuring the genuine involvement of the pupil, adequately preparing the parent for the meeting, and the need to ensure that action plans are consistently followed through.

Similarly, Morgan (2016) explored perceptions of a solution-focused approach, Planning Alternative Tomorrows with Hope (PATH), used with groups of professionals aimed at promoting systemic change. PATH is a team approach that makes use of a graphic recorder and a process facilitator who asks solution-focused questions to help to generate an action plan. Participants reported that the use of solution-focused language was particularly helpful. Morgan (2016) suggests that by allowing a group to perceive small steps to success, rather than focusing on issues beyond their control, participants remain 'within their own sphere of influence' (p. 143), helping to reduce feelings of helplessness. Future research could attempt to explore whether other problem-solving models and executive frameworks are supportive of multi-agency collaboration, particularly in the context of supporting 16–25s.

The Mosaic approach

There has been growing acknowledgement of young people's right to be consulted and included in any decision-making that affects them. Newman *et al.* (2009), as part of a multi-agency forum, conducted a consultation with young people regarding their experiences of planning for adulthood. In this consultation, 49 young people participated, aged between 14 and 25 years. The sample had a range of support needs including those with learning difficulties and disabilities, young people experiencing mental health difficulties, and those not in employment, education or training. The Mosaic approach (Clark and Moss, 2001) was utilized, which makes use of multiple methods of data gathering. It is intended that young people become actively engaged through a range of different methods, including observation, interview, photographs and videos taken by participants, etc (Pearson and Howe, 2017).

Newman and her colleagues offered their participants a range of different media to tell their stories, such as via video, photographs, PowerPoint presentations, interviews, etc. Consultation topics were agreed by the multi-agency forum and included outcomes; understanding transition; transition planning; and ownership of the planning process. The stories provided by the young people were transformed into a narrative and taken back to the young people for their approval. Newman *et al.* (2009: 50) state that 'to get transition right we need to listen to young people, whatever their communication needs, and ensure that they are central to the planning process'. The stories also revealed that transition planning needs to begin as early as possible to help to prepare the young person. Information needs to be widely available and offered in different formats. Newman *et al.* (2009) conclude that offering young people the opportunity to contribute using a range of methods meant that they had freedom and autonomy to choose the method with which they were most comfortable. The Mosaic approach can be a very time-consuming one in gaining the voice of the young person, but it can facilitate full participation. The authors state the need for, and the successful use of, the Mosaic approach to multi-agency consultation.

The Mosaic approach has been used in EP practice and research, for example, where children were active participants in a redesign of their school playground (Pearson and Howe, 2017). Mercieca and Mercieca (2014: 29) promote the use of the approach and state 'it is the attitude which the Mosaic approach highlights and which is helpful for educational psychology practice, if listening which does not silence is to take place'. The study conducted by Newman *et al.* (2009) and the theorizing of Mercieca and Mercieca point to the value of employing the Mosaic approach with those aged 16–25. Through this approach, EPs could meaningfully gather views and incorporate them into their multi-agency work, where they can act as advocates for the young person.

Facilitators of and barriers to multi-agency collaboration

In the literature, multi-agency working is generally viewed as positive and its benefits are reported to be numerous. Although the rationale for multi-agency working is varied, it is based on the idea that social problems should be addressed in a holistic fashion because social issues such as crime, poverty and low school attainment are connected, an idea proposed by Payne (2002) nearly 20 years ago, as an argument for multi-agency working within LAs. Further rationales for multi-agency working include promoting children's well-being and safeguarding, creative problem-solving and more 'pragmatic' justifications, such as increased efficiency in the context of diminishing resources and reduction of client frustration (Atkinson *et al.*, 2002). Crucially, it is also argued that a *lack* of multi-agency teamwork not only causes increased stress for families (Barnes, 2008), but also *creates* vulnerability in society (Lenehan, 2004). Table 15.1 outlines the factors that facilitate or impede successful multi-agency working, as identified in the literature. It is acknowledged that several of the factors identified can be interpreted as either facilitators or barriers.

Table 15.1: Influential factors on successful multi-agency working

Factor	Author(s)	Facilitator/ Barrier	Comments
Information sharing	Maychell and Bradley (1991); Normington and Kyriacou (1994)	Barrier	Record keeping by different agencies means that a holistic view is not captured by any single agency. In addition, it has been suggested that some agencies withhold information, citing matters of confidentiality when in fact this is to maintain authority in a multi-agency context.
Diverse opinions and ideas of different professionals	Machell (1999); Robinson and Cottrell (2005)	Facilitator	The differing perspectives of a range of professionals can lead to creative problem solving ('complexity theory', Fullan, 1999).
Power relationships and role responsibilities	Cline (1989); Scriven (1995); Milbourne *et al.* (2003); Suter *et al.* (2009), Spivack *et al.* (2014)	Barrier	An imbalance of power between the various professionals may mean that not all voices are heard or considered. Scriven (1995) recognizes that health professionals tend to play a more active role than educational professionals in initiating and managing collaborative partnerships. Clarity of role boundaries and responsibilities within the partnership is important in ensuring equal participation.

Factor	Author(s)	Facilitator/ Barrier	Comments
Organizational systems and structures	Maychell and Bradley (1991); Pearce and Hillman (1998); Atkinson *et al.* (2002); Robinson and Cottrell (2005); Barnes (2008)	Barrier	Engagement in multi-agency collaboration is affected by the way in which services are organized and their level of flexibility and efficiency. Furthermore, differences in organizational culture between different agencies can result in entrenched ways of working and rivalries among professionals.
Staff and time management	Maychell and Bradley (1991), Milbourne *et al.* (2003)	Barrier	Lack of time is identified as a reason often given for not engaging in collaborative working. Therefore, it is important to protect time to meet at mutually agreeable opportunities, while also managing demanding workloads.
Perceptions and expectations of the roles in the collaborative partnership	Hoyle (1982); Normington and Kyriacou (1994); Birchall and Hallett (1995); West (1999); Hymans (2008)	Barrier	Issues may occur when professionals misconstrue the roles, responsibilities and expectations of other agencies, as well as their own. Tensions may arise from perceived ideas regarding qualifications, status and expertise of other professionals. In addition, it is important to acknowledge the differing identities of individuals within the group (e.g. class, race, gender) to foster interpersonal relationships. It is recognized that an individual's construct of their own professional identity can alter as a result of their role in a multi-disciplinary team and time is needed to adjust to this change.

Factor	Author(s)	Facilitator/ Barrier	Comments
Shared goals and priorities	Maychell and Bradley (1991); Milbourne *et al.* (2003); Sloper (2004); Robinson and Cottrell (2005)	Facilitator	Strategic planning and a joint policy/protocols for multi-agency working enable agencies to have a shared vision and shared accountability. A shared understanding of what the joint work will look like in practice and what form it will take is critical to its success. Levels of commitment are also to be agreed.
Funding and resources	Scriven (1995); Capey (1997); Pearce and Hillman (1998); Milbourne *et al.* (2003)	Barrier	Financial constraints and austerity measures inevitably have an impact on inter-agency collaboration. Additionally, agencies are increasingly required to bid competitively for funding. Negotiating meeting locations and access to resources can lead to group tensions.
Finding a 'common language'	Hallet and Stevenson (1980); Bloxham (1996); Atkinson *et al.* (2002); Milbourne *et al.* (2003)	Facilitator	Shared training enables development of a common language between different agencies. It is considered a conduit by which agencies can clarify objectives and values.
Ongoing communication and co-ordination	Atkinson *et al.* (2002); Milbourne *et al.* (2003), Sloper (2004); Barnes (2008); Suter *et al.* (2009)	Facilitator	Good systems of communication underpin successful inter-agency collaboration. A named co-ordinator can be beneficial for providing clarity and consistency when working collaboratively.

Factor	Author(s)	Facilitator/ Barrier	Comments
Personal qualities and interpersonal skills	Barnes (2008)	Facilitator	Personal qualities – such as: commitment, good social skills, good communication skills, flexibility, co-operation, open-mindedness, respectfulness, enthusiasm, determination, persistence, approachability – are all considered important for effective multi-agency practice. However, professional challenges may arise as a result of incompatible personalities working together.
Relationship building	Hackman (1990); Bank (1992)	Facilitator	It is important for professionals to build trusting and reciprocal working relationships, which take time and effort. These positive inter-agency relationships are imperative to building a shared vision. Hackman (1990) highlights the possible detrimental impact that high staff turnover can have on relationship building.
Organization and planning	Milbourne *et al.* (2003)	Barrier	The early decisions made at the outset of multi-agency work are critical to the outcomes of the joint work and should not be done in haste.
Ongoing reflection	Guzzo *et al.* (1995); Barr *et al.* (2005); Robinson and Cottrell (2005)	Facilitator	Professionals need to allocate time to ensure ongoing evaluation and reflection of collaborative working. Robinson and Cottrell (2005) propose that the use of theoretical models can be useful in resolving difficulties at a systemic level.

Multi-agency work represents one option for EPs working to support those aged 16–25. This approach is not without its limitations. For example, Arnold and Baker (2013: 12–13), in their work regarding young people not in education, employment or training (NEET), suggest that 'Building robust plans for individuals living unstable lives is not easy. A common tendency is to widen their range of support – and thus increase the level of instability.' This can undermine multi-agency work, where an unwieldy range of professionals can become involved. Arnold and Baker caution, 'Among such professionals there might be different expectations and conflicting ideas about promoting the young person's best interests. Young people are asked to form a relationship with these adults, whose different agendas can inadvertently lead to greater instability and its associated consequences.' Therefore, work with some individuals may require a more restricted group of key professionals, where one key adult works directly with the young person, to provide greater consistency and stability (Arnold and Baker, 2013). A sensible and pragmatic approach is required in the setting up and functioning of multi-agency work, to ensure the right professionals are involved at the right time. Further, for the professionals involved, when multi-agency collaboration is not successful, it can lead to anxiety regarding professional identity, in response to the challenge presented by working with a range of different agencies (Morgan, 2016).

Nonetheless, such activity can provide the EP with opportunities for creative and fulfilling work (Gaskell and Leadbetter, 2009). It can provide the opportunity to build and strengthen relationships with others, including settings and services previously not closely affiliated with EP practice, such as FE institutions (Morris and Atkinson, 2018), as well as the chance to promote the role and services offered by the EP (Knox, 2011). It is apparent the EP can contribute to the multi-agency support offered to those aged 16–25, which may include PCP, solution-focused techniques and/or the Mosaic approach. Multi-agency collaboration can provide young people with a more comprehensive and co-ordinated service (Kaehne, 2011). Irrespective of the work undertaken by the EP (assessment; therapeutic intervention; multi-agency; or research and evaluation), ensuring that the young person remains at the centre and is an active participant is the first step towards achieving success (White and Rae, 2016).

Case study
Background
This piece of work was focused on a 16-year-old girl, Anna, who has severe learning difficulties. She was displaying extremely challenging behaviour at

school. There was some concern that the medication she was taking had been altered so regularly that medical professionals did not know what was helping and what might be contributing to her challenging behaviour. She was admitted to hospital to undergo a mental health assessment and to address her drug regime in a safe environment. Anna was supported by a network of professionals including social services, carers from her residential facility, clinical psychologists from the child and adolescent mental health services (CAMHS) learning disability team, key adults from her special school and her parents. This network was co-ordinated by the principal clinical psychologist.

Educational psychologist's contribution

The EP was asked to become involved by the principal clinical psychologist to support Anna's reintegration back into school from hospital, as well as support for her transition at 19 years, when she would leave her current school. This EP involvement would also include contributing to the updating of Anna's EHCP. Network meetings were arranged for staff from the hospital (including speech and language therapist, occupational therapist and a clinical psychologist) to feed back to the EP, clinical psychologist, parents and members of school staff. This led to the development of a reintegration plan, including a risk assessment and modifications made to her existing positive behaviour support plan. The EP gathered information from key professionals and from Anna, through visual media, photographs and pictures, to write an updated psychological advice, which contributed to her EHCP.

Outcomes and next steps

Anna's reintegration back into school was successful. After a two-week transition period she was attending school full-time. Network meetings continued where professionals from the adult mental health service and adult social care were invited to attend to plan her transition into those services. The EP liaised with the LA SEND officer and school staff to generate a plan regarding her transition into FE, which was then fed back into a network meeting with dates planned for visits to colleges over the next 12 months.

References

Alexander, S. and Sked, H. (2010) 'The development of solution focused multi-agency meetings in a psychological service'. *Educational Psychology in Practice*, 26 (3), 239–49.

Arnold, C. and Baker, T. (2013) *Becoming NEET: Risks, rewards, and realities*. London: Trentham Books.

Atkinson, C., Dunsmuir, S., Lang, J. and Wright, S. (2015) 'Developing a competency framework for the initial training of educational psychologists working with young people aged 16–25'. *Educational Psychology in Practice*, 31 (2), 159–73.

Atkinson, M., Wilkin, A., Stott, A., Doherty, P. and Kinder, K. (2002) *Multi-Agency Working: A detailed study*. Slough: National Foundation for Educational Research.

Bank, J. (1992) *The Essence of Total Quality Management*. Hemel Hempstead: Prentice Hall.

Barnes, P. (2008) 'Multi-agency working: What are the perspectives of SENCos and parents regarding its development and implementation?'. *British Journal of Special Education*, 35 (4), 230–40.

Barr, H., Koppel, I., Reeves, S., Hammick, M. and Freeth, D. (2005) *Effective Interprofessional Education: Argument, assumption and evidence*. Oxford: Blackwell Publishing.

Birchall, E. and Hallett, C. (1995) *Working Together in Child Protection: Report of phase two, a survey of the experience and perceptions of the six key professions*. London: HMSO.

Bloxham, S. (1996) 'A case study of inter-agency collaboration in the education and promotion of young people's sexual health'. *Health Education Journal*, 55 (4), 389–403.

Bronfenbrenner, U. and Evans, G.W. (2000) 'Developmental science in the 21st century: Emerging questions, theoretical models, research designs and empirical findings'. *Social Development*, 9 (1), 115–25.

Capey, M. (1997) *Pupils with Emotional and Behavioural Difficulties: Multi-agency working*. Slough: Education Management Information Exchange.

Carroll, C. (2015) 'A review of the approaches investigating the post-16 transition of young adults with learning difficulties'. *International Journal of Inclusive Education*, 19 (4), 347–64.

Cheminais, R. (2009) *Effective Multi-Agency Partnerships: Putting Every Child Matters into practice*. London: SAGE Publications.

Clark, A. and Moss, P. (2001) *Listening to Young Children: The mosaic approach*. London: National Children's Bureau.

Cline, R. (1989) 'Making case conferences more effective: A checklist for monitoring and training'. *Children and Society*, 3 (2), 99–106. Cited in: Normington, J. and Kyriacou, C. (1994) 'Exclusion from high schools and the work of the outside agencies involved'. Pastoral Care in Education, 12 (4), 12–15.

DfE (Department for Education) and DoH (Department of Health) (2015) *Special Educational Needs and Disability Code of Practice: 0 to 25 years: Statutory guidance for organisations which work with and support children and young people who have special educational needs or disabilities*. London: Department for Education. Online. https://assets.publishing.service.gov.uk/government/uploads/system/uploads/attachment_data/file/398815/SEND_Code_of_Practice_January_2015.pdf (accessed 23 August 2018).

Fullan, M. (1999) *Change Forces: The sequel*. London: Falmer Press.

Gaskell, S. and Leadbetter, J. (2009) 'Educational psychologists and multi-agency working: Exploring professional identity'. *Educational Psychology in Practice*, 25 (2), 97–111.

Guzzo, R.A., Salas, E. and Associates (1995) *Team Effectiveness and Decision Making in Organizations*. San Francisco: Jossey-Bass.

Hackman, J.R. (ed.) (1990) *Groups that Work (and Those that Don't): Creating conditions for effective teamwork*. San Francisco: Jossey-Bass.

Hallett, C. and Stevenson, O. (1980) *Child Abuse: Aspects of interprofessional cooperation*. London: George Allen and Unwin. Cited in: Scrine, J. (1989) 'Multi-professional education and the experience of social work students'. *Maladjustment and Therapeutic Education*, 7 (3), 158–62.

Hellier, C. (2009) 'Developing post-school psychological services in Scotland: Fit for purpose?'. *Educational and Child Psychology*, 26 (1), 22–32.

Hoyle, E. (1982) 'Micropolitics of educational organisations'. *Educational Management and Administration*, 10 (2), 87–98.

Hymans, M. (2008) 'How personal constructs about "professional identity" might act as a barrier to multi-agency working'. *Educational Psychology in Practice*, 24 (4), 279–88.

Kaehne, A. (2010) 'Multiagency protocols in intellectual disabilities transition partnerships: A survey of local authorities in Wales'. *Journal of Policy and Practice in Intellectual Disabilities*, 7 (3), 182–8.

Kaehne, A. (2011) 'Transition from children and adolescent to adult mental health services for young people with intellectual disabilities: A scoping study of service organisation problems'. *Advances in Mental Health and Intellectual Disabilities*, 5 (1), 9–16.

Kaehne, A. and Beyer, S. (2014) 'Person-centred reviews as a mechanism for planning the post-school transition of young people with intellectual disability'. *Journal of Intellectual Disability Research*, 58 (7), 603–13.

Knox, L.O. (2011) 'Special Educational Needs: From education to employment – exploring perceptions of "successful transition"'. Unpublished doctoral thesis, University of East London.

Lenehan, C. (2004) 'The National Service Framework and Every Child Matters – Key links'. Paper presented at the Removing Barriers to Achievement Special Educational Needs Strategy Conference, Queen Elizabeth II Conference Centre, London, 11 February 2004.

Machell, J. (1999) 'The lost boys or the great unwashed? Collaborative strategies to address disaffection'. Paper presented at the British Educational Research Association (BERA) Annual Conference, University of Sussex, Brighton, 2–5 September 1999.

Mansell, J. and Beadle-Brown, J. (2004) 'Person-centred planning or person-centred action? Policy and practice in intellectual disability services'. *Journal of Applied Research in Intellectual Disabilities*, 17 (1), 1–9.

Maychell, K. and Bradley, J. (1991) *Preparing for Partnership: Multi-agency support for special needs*. Slough: National Foundation for Educational Research.

McCrone, T., Southcott, C. and Evans, K. (2009) *Collaborative Good Practice between Local Authorities and the Further Education Sector* (LGA Research Report). Slough: National Foundation for Educational Research.

Mercieca, D. and Mercieca, D.P. (2014) 'EPs becoming ignorant: Questioning the assumption of listening and empowerment in young children'. *Educational and Child Psychology*, 31 (1), 22–30.

Milbourne, L., Macrae, S. and Maguire, M. (2003) 'Collaborative solutions or new policy problems: Exploring multi-agency partnerships in education and health work'. *Journal of Education Policy*, 18 (1), 19–35.

Morgan, G. (2016) 'Organisational change: A solution-focused approach'. *Educational Psychology in Practice*, 32 (2), 133–44.

Morris, R. and Atkinson, C. (2018) 'The role of educational psychologists in supporting post-16 transition: Findings from the literature'. *Educational Psychology in Practice*, 34 (2), 131–49.

Newman, G., Collyer, S., Foulis, M. and Webster, S. (2009) 'A multi-agency consultation project with young people with support needs at the transition between children's and adult's services'. *International Journal of Transitions in Childhood*, 3, 45–55.

Normington, J. and Kyriacou, C. (1994) 'Exclusion from high schools and the work of the outside agencies involved'. *Pastoral Care in Education*, 12 (4), 12–15.

Payne, C. (2002) 'An Exploration of Perceived Social Support for Children and Adolescents who Reside in Neighborhoods that Lack Social Cohesion and Trust'. Unpublished thesis. Loyola University of Chicago.

Pearce, N. and Hillman, J. (1998) *Wasted Youth: Raising achievement and tackling social exclusion*. London: Institute for Public Policy Research.

Pearson, R. and Howe, J. (2017) 'Pupil participation and playground design: Listening and responding to children's views'. *Educational Psychology in Practice*, 33 (4), 356–70.

Preparing for Adulthood (2013) *Delivering Support and Aspiration for Disabled Young People*. Bath: Preparing for Adulthood.

Richards, M. and Vostanis, P. (2004) 'Interprofessional perspectives on transitional mental health services for young people aged 16–19 years'. *Journal of Interprofessional Care*, 18 (2), 115–28.

Richardson, T.D., Jindal-Snape, D. and Hannah, E.F.S. (2017) 'Impact of legislation on post-school transition practice for young people with additional support needs in Scotland'. *British Journal of Special Education*, 44 (3), 239–56.

Robinson, M. and Cottrell, D. (2005) 'Health professionals in multi-disciplinary and multi-agency teams: Changing professional practice'. *Journal of Interprofessional Care*, 19 (6), 547–60.

Scriven, A. (1995) 'Healthy alliances between health promotion and education: The results of a national audit'. *Health Education Journal*, 54 (2), 176–85.

Sloper, P. (2004) 'Facilitators and barriers for co-ordinated multi-agency services'. *Child: Care, Health and Development*, 30 (6), 571–80.

Sloper, P., Beecham, J., Clarke, S., Franklin, A., Moran, N. and Cusworth, L. (2010) *Models of Multi-Agency Services for Transition to Adult Services for Disabled Young People and Those with Complex Health Needs: Impact and costs*. York: Social Policy Research Unit.

Spivack, R., Craston, M., Thom, G. and Carr, C. (2014) *Special Educational Needs and Disability Pathfinder Programme Evaluation: Thematic report: The Education, Health and Care (EHC) Planning Pathway for families that are new to the SEN system*. London: Department for Education. Online. www.gov.uk/government/uploads/system/uploads/attachment_data/file/275104/RR326B_EHC_planning_pathway_-_FINAL.pdf (accessed 4 February 2018).

Suter, E., Arndt, J., Arthur, N., Parboosingh, J., Taylor, E. and Deutschlander, S. (2009) 'Role understanding and effective communication as core competencies for collaborative practice'. *Journal of Interprofessional Care*, 23 (1), 41–51.

UK Parliament (2014) 'Children and Families Act 2014'. Online. www.legislation.gov.uk/ukpga/2014/6/contents/enacted (accessed 25 August 2018).

West, M. (1999) 'Micropolitics, leadership and all that... The need to increase the micropolitical awareness and skills of school leaders'. *School Leadership and Management*, 19 (2), 189–95.

White, J. and Rae, T. (2016) 'Person-centred reviews and transition: An exploration of the views of students and their parents/carers'. *Educational Psychology in Practice*, 32 (1), 38–53.

Index